THEOLOGY AND NARRATIVE

THEOLOGY AND NARRATIVE
Selected Essays

Hans W. Frei

Edited by
George Hunsinger
William C. Placher

New York   Oxford
OXFORD UNIVERSITY PRESS
1993

Oxford University Press

Oxford   New York   Toronto
Delhi   Bombay   Calcutta   Madras   Karachi
Kuala Lumpur   Singapore   Hong Kong   Tokyo
Nairobi   Dar es Salaam   Cape Town
Melbourne   Auckland   Madrid

and associated companies in
Berlin   Ibadan

Copyright © 1993 by Oxford University Press, Inc.

Published by Oxford University Press, Inc.
200 Madison Avenue, New York, New York 10016

Library of Congress Cataloging-in-Publication Data
Frei, Hans W.
Theology and narrative : selected essays / Hans W. Frei ; edited
by George Hunsinger, William C. Placher.
p. cm. Includes index.
Contents: Remarks in connection with a theological proposal
Theological reflections on the accounts of Jesus' death and resurrection
Theology and the interpretation of narrative
The "literal reading" of Biblical narrative in the Christian tradition
Conflicts in interpretation
Karl Barth, theologian
Barth and Schleiermacher in divergence and convergence
Of the resurrection of Christ
Response to "Narrative theology"
H. Richard Niebuhr on history, church, and nation.
ISBN 0-19-507880-2
1. Theology.   2. Narration in the Bible.
I. Hunsinger, George
II. Placher, William C. (William Carl), 1948– .
III. Title.
BT80.F74 1993   230'.3—dc20
92-36161

1 3 5 7 9 8 6 4 2
Printed in the United States of America
on acid-free paper

Contents

THEOLOGY AND NARRATIVE

Introduction

William C. Placher

Hans Frei's death in 1988 ended a rich and productive life. He was perhaps the greatest historian of modern biblical hermeneutics of his generation. His own hermeneutical proposals, among other things, developed the category of "realistic narrative" that plays such a prominent role in current discussions of biblical interpretation. More than anyone else in the United States, he reintroduced Karl Barth into the conversations of contemporary theology, and his own work in Christology showed him to be a creative thinker, anything but the sort of "Barthian" that Barth himself always despised. In over thirty years of teaching at Yale, he had influenced generations of students. He was the chief exemplar and inspiration of the theological method his friend and colleague George Lindbeck has called postliberal theology.[1]

Yet those who knew him professionally could not avoid a sense that his life had been cut tragically short, a sense that went beyond the feeling always occasioned by a sudden death. Frei had been a late bloomer. In 1957, a year after he completed his doctoral dissertation, he published two chapters in *Faith and Ethics*, the festschrift for his teacher H. Richard Niebuhr. But then he published virtually nothing for ten years, working along his own lines in isolation from the fashions of the times.

Only in the last decade or so of his life did things begin to fall into place. *The Eclipse of Biblical Narrative*, published in 1974, was quickly acknowledged as a masterpiece of sensitive historical scholarship. *The Identity of Jesus Christ*, which had originally appeared in 1967

3

as a series of articles in a Presbyterian adult education magazine, was published in book form in 1975, and, particularly now that it could be read in the light of *The Eclipse*, drew much wider attention. In the early 1980s, Frei was at work on a typology of contemporary theology, which he saw as an introduction to a major history of modern Christology, and he presented rough drafts of the typology in a number of prestigious lectures. It all felt, at least to others, more like the beginning of a career than the end.

With the generous encouragement of Frei's widow Geraldine and his colleagues, George Hunsinger and I edited some of his lectures on the typology into a book, *Types of Christian Theology*. That volume, *The Eclipse, The Identity*, and the essays in *Faith and Ethics* make most of what he wrote fairly easily accessible, but there remained a number of essays, some unpublished, others published in a variety of places. It seemed worthwhile to bring most of them together in this volume. We have provided each selection with a brief introduction, and the volume concludes with George Hunsinger's reflections on Frei's theology. It remains for this introduction to offer a brief sketch of his life and some notes on the development of his theology and some of the influences that shaped it.

1

Hans Wilhelm Frei was born in Breslau, Germany, April 29, 1922. His family had long been a distinguished one; a distant ancestor led a charge of the Prussian cavalry against Napoleon at the battle of Jena in 1806. Both his parents were physicians, his father, Wilhelm Siegmund, a venereologist who invented what is known as the Frei test to discover certain venereal diseases; his mother, Magda (née Frankfurther), a pediatrician. The family was Jewish by ancestry but thoroughly secular in outlook. In accord with the common practice of the time and place, they had their children baptized in the Lutheran church. When the Nazis came to power, however, such baptisms proved little protection for those of Jewish background. When he was a teenager, Frei's parents sent him to a Quaker school in England in order to get him to safety outside the country. In 1938 the whole family fled to the United States.

His family may have been safe in America, but they had very little money, and their situation was made even more difficult by his father's long illness. It was not clear how young Hans would be able to go to college. Quaker connections seemed to have secured him a place at Haverford College, but someone else claimed it first. The only scholarship the family could find was one for the study of textile engineering at North Carolina State University. Frei took what he could get and graduated with his B.S. in 1942, a year before his father died.

In later years, Frei generally avoided discussions of his religious development. (Starting with Calvin, Reformed theology has a long tradition of reticence on the subject of conversions.) On a number of occasions, though, he did report a childhood experience of seeing a picture or statue of Jesus on the cross and suddenly "knowing that it was true." In any event, by his college years he was active in a Christian student group. When H. Richard Niebuhr was invited down from Yale to give a lecture at North Carolina State, Frei attended and was deeply impressed. He began a correspondence with Niebuhr that eventually led to his accepting Niebuhr's advice and enrolling as a B.D. student at Yale Divinity School. On completing that degree in 1945, he became minister of a Baptist church in the small town of North Stratford, New Hampshire. In his two years there, he wrestled with two issues that led to significant changes in his life. First, he began to admire the greater doctrinal freedom of the Episcopal church and to explore the possibility of becoming an Episcopalian himself.[2] Second, he decided to go back to graduate school and try to pursue an academic career rather than remain in the pastorate. Both decisions, however, came only after long internal struggle.

He returned to Yale in 1947 and married Geraldine Frost Nye in 1948 (they had three children). He was ordained an Episcopal priest in 1952 and wrote a very lengthy dissertation, "The Doctrine of Revelation in the Thought of Karl Barth, 1909–1922: The Nature of Barth's Break with Liberalism," under Niebuhr's direction.[3] He received his Ph.D. in 1956, but in the meantime he held teaching positions at Wabash College (1950–1953) and the Episcopal Seminary of the Southwest (1953–1956) before returning to the Yale faculty, where he remained until his death. In some ways his academic career progressed slowly. He early established himself, however, as a popular undergraduate teacher, and in the 1970s served a year as Master of Silliman College and then two terms, a total of seven years, as Master of Ezra Stiles. His influence around the university grew steadily, and he served an important term as chair of the religious studies department at Yale from 1981 to 1984. He had bypass surgery in 1987 and suffered a mild stroke in July 1988, but he seemed to be fully recovered. His death, on September 12, 1988, was sudden and unexpected.[4]

2

The earliest essays in this volume were written when Frei was in his midforties and had already arrived at his mature theological views, though he continued to develop and modify them. To an unusual degree he tended to think his ideas all the way through before he wrote anything down, so that it is difficult to trace the devel-

opment of his thinking through what he wrote. The best insights into
the early trajectory of his thought probably come from considering
some of its sources.

The preface to *The Eclipse* mentions three authors as particular
influences: Karl Barth, Erich Auerbach, and Gilbert Ryle.[5] The
list is not complete—for one thing, it does not include H. Richard
Niebuhr—but Barth certainly helped shape Frei's thinking from the
start, and Auerbach and Ryle gave Frei intriguing new categories for
appropriating Barth's hermeneutics and Christology.

He first got excited about Auerbach sometime in the late fifties
or early sixties. Auerbach's masterpiece, *Mimesis*, published in 1946,
surveys "the representation of reality in Western literature," beginning with Homer and Genesis and ending with Marcel Proust and
Virginia Woolf. The starting point of his work, Auerbach explains, was
the contrast between Plato's attack on the poets, whose work was only
an imitation (*mimesis*) of an imitation, at two removes from reality,
and Dante's "assertion that in the *Commedia* he presented true reality."[6] He notes that, in the realistic tradition that begins with Homer,
the vivid concreteness of the narrative constitutes a kind of "realism,"
independent of its reference or lack thereof, to any reality beyond itself:

> The oft-repeated reproach that Homer is a liar takes nothing from
> his effectiveness, he does not need to base his story on historical reality,
> his reality is powerful enough in itself; it ensnares us, weaving its
> web around us, and that suffices him. And this "real" world into which
> we are lured, exists for itself, contains nothing but itself; the Homeric
> poems conceal nothing, they contain no teaching and no secret sec-
> ond meaning. Homer can be analyzed . . . but he cannot be interpreted.
> Later allegorizing trends have tried their arts of interpretation upon
> him, but to no avail.[7]

The primary meaning of such a realistic narrative lies simply in
the story it tells, and its "realism" lies in the way it presents the
characters and incidents of its story.

The Bible, Auerbach continues, includes realistic narratives of this
kind, but they have a particular characteristic of their own.

> Far from seeking, like Homer, merely to make us forget our own reality
> for a few hours [the Bible] seeks to overcome our reality: we are to fit
> our own life into its world, feel ourselves to be elements in its struc-
> ture of universal history. . . . The Bible's claim to truth is not only far
> more urgent than Homer's, it is tyrannical—it excludes all other
> claims. The world of the Scripture stories is not satisfied with claim-
> ing to be a historically true reality—it insists that it is the only real
> world, is destined for autocracy. All other scenes, issues, and ordinances
> have no right to appear independently of it, and it is promised that all
> of them, the history of all mankind, will be given their due place within
> its frame, will be subordinated to it.[8]

Some realistic narratives, like modern novels or other works of fiction, narrate what J.R.R. Tolkien called a "secondary world,"[9] without any claim of reference to our primary world. Others, works of history from Herodotus to Barbara Tuchman, claim that the events they narrate fit into the framework of the primary world of our experience. But the biblical texts, although functioning as realistic narratives, claim themselves to narrate the primary world, into whose framework all other events must be placed.[10]

Auerbach is here making an argument about the *meaning* of these texts. He is not insisting that they *do* render "the only real world," only that that is the *claim* they make, there to be noted by any careful reader, whether one then judges the claim to be true or false. Barth, of course, had also wanted to affirm the truth of the texts, but his analysis of the texts' meaning, Frei concluded, paralleled that of Auerbach: These narratives purport to define, in a way that any non-narrative translation loses, "the one common world in which we all live and move and have our being."[11]

Such a realistic narrative reading was, Frei maintained, not only the way Barth read the Bible, but the dominant way of reading Scripture throughout the first seventeen hundred years or so of the Christian tradition. To be sure, the Bible contains all sorts of texts, not just narratives. Even with the Gospels, Frei conceded (a point some of his critics have overlooked) "that it is difficult and even undesirable to reduce the Gospel story by formal analysis to any one type of literature."[12] Indeed, "one cannot even cover Luke and Mark by the same story analysis, to say nothing of non-narrative texts." But starting with the Gospel narratives, thinking of them as a kind of unity, and then seeing other biblical material as introduction or commentary on those narratives seemed to Frei "at least a good hypothesis," a "better . . . organizing principle" with "a wider range of applicability within the New Testament canon, than many another,"[13] more faithful both to the character of the texts themselves and to the way they have been read in the Christian tradition.

In that tradition, allegorical or moral or anagogical readings of Scripture were often permitted or encouraged, but only if they acknowledged that important stretches of the Bible have first of all a literal meaning. "'Jerusalem' might indeed designate the eternal city in the heavens toward which all creation hastens, as well as the church that is the bride of Christ, and the soul that longs for him— but not at the cost of dissolving the reference to the specific town in the Middle East."[14] And Christian interpreters "envisioned the real world as formed by the sequence told by the biblical stories."[15]

Somewhere around the eighteenth century, however, many people started reading the Bible differently. Their own daily experience seemed to define for them what was "real," and so they consciously tried to understand the meaning of the Bible by locating *it* in *their* world. They did that, to overgeneralize, in two ways. They saw the meaning of the biblical narratives either in the eternal truths about God and human nature that the stories conveyed or in what we could learn from them about historical events through the methods of critical history—a dichotomy of interpretations Frei traced from the eighteenth century down to Bultmann and David Tracy on one side and Pannenberg, the "new quest," and many evangelicals on the other.

Both approaches, Frei argued, distort the meaning of the texts; they lose the way these texts were read through most of the Christian tradition and the way a sensitive reader like Auerbach understands them. The meaning of a Dickens novel is never simply some general moral such as that the poor were ill-treated in nineteenth-century England; and in the Bible too the particular characters and episodes of a realistic narrative are not dispensable illustrations of a general lesson. On the other hand, no doubt the biblical texts provide historical information. But the stories themselves, in their relative indifference to chronology and their occasional inconsistencies, are only loosely related to questions of historical accuracy. Moreover, any residue including only the fragments that a modern historian will glean as historically reliable loses the narrative flow of the texts (particularly evident in the Gospels in the passion narratives) and the full development of the characters the story portrays—and thus loses part of the meaning of the story as story.

So why have most Christian theologians been misreading the Bible in such obvious ways for two hundred years? Frei said the mistake follows from beginning theology with apologetics. If one starts with contemporary human experience and tries to connect the biblical narratives with it so as to establish their truth, they fit in either as moral lessons or else as part of critically established history. Otherwise one has this story that has to be taken seriously as story but that is neither fiction nor critical history and one doesn't know what to do with it. So a theology that begins with our world and tries to fit the biblical narratives into it inevitably distorts their meaning in the effort to make sense of them. Theology should stick instead to its descriptive task of laying out the internal logic of Christian faith; as Frei put it, "What I am proposing . . . is that we raise the question in a drastically non-apologetic, non-perspectivalist fashion: 'What does this narrative say or mean, never mind whether it can become a meaningful possibility of life perspective for us or not.' Its meaning on the one hand, and its possible as well as actual truth for us on the other, are two totally different questions."[16]

Christians, to be sure, having understood meaning, do want to make claims about truth, claims Frei clarified when he turned to questions about Jesus' identity. Moreover, Christians reading these texts want to connect the world narrated there with other aspects of their world. After all, part of the logic of Christian faith is that it claims to be in some sense about every aspect of reality—the textual world of the biblical narratives, George Lindbeck's phrase, "absorbs the world."[17] And therefore the Christian theologian

> will do ethics to indicate that this narrated, narratable world is at the same time the ordinary world in which we are responsible for our actions; and he will do ad hoc apologetics, in order to throw into relief particular features of this world by distancing them from or approximating them to other descriptions of the same or other linguistic worlds. . . . But none of these other descriptions or, for that matter, argument with them can serve as a 'pre-description' for the world of Christian discourse which is also this common world, for to claim that would mean stepping outside that encompassing world; and that by definition is impossible.[18]

Frei was describing Barth's theological method in that passage, but the description fits his own theology as well. Such theologies describe the way the world looks to Christian faith and resist general theories from outside their own perspective about what counts as rational or how to read a text or how to define "religion"—resisting, even, general theories that forbid Christian theologians any contact whatsoever with general theories. In a relaxed and ad hoc way, these theologies feel free to draw all sorts of connections with philosophy or literary theory or anthropology in understanding the one encompassing world that Christians believe the biblically narrated world to be.[19] In *Types of Christian Theology* Frei explored the implications of such an account of theological method in greater detail, laying out a typology in which Schleiermacher and Barth turn out to lie near each other in the middle of the spectrum of types and to be the heroes of the story (though Frei finally argues for Barth over Schleiermacher). Both acknowledge the need for theology to make connections with the wider culture; neither lets that wider culture define the theological tasks. Both their approaches have problems, but a problem is "disastrous only if it means *either* a complete elimination of philosophy as an issue and a means for reflection in Christian theology *or* a pathetic obeisance to philosophy as the master key to certainty about all reason and certainty and therefore to the shape or possibility of Christian theology."[20] And Frei's argument for the superiority of these middle types in his typology—and finally for Barth—is finally that they best preserve the meaning of the biblical texts as realistic narratives.

3

If Auerbach provided Frei with categories for understanding the meaning of the biblical narratives, it was Gilbert Ryle who gave him a

way of thinking about personal identity that proved of great importance in Christology. In the preface to *The Identity*, Frei explained
his change of title from that of the earlier published version, "The
Mystery of the Presence of Jesus Christ," by acknowledging his
nervousness about that word *presence*, which had earlier seemed to
him "the distillate of the philosophical conceptuality under which such
otherwise very different people as Hegel, Schleiermacher, Kierkegaard,
and the dialectical theologians of the 1920s set forth their religious
and theological proposals."[21] Frei himself had been trained in that
"philosophical conceptuality," but, looking back in 1975 as he wrote
the preface to *The Identity*, he realized that the book had already moved
away from it. He no longer thought of persons as having an essential
self somehow indirectly manifested or present in their words and
deeds.

In the mid-1960s, a number of graduate students at Yale were
reading the discussions of personal identity by British analytic
philosophers like Gilbert Ryle and Peter Strawson. Frei directed a
dissertation by Robert H. King that drew on this work for thinking
about what it means to talk about God as acting.[22] Frei always took
his teaching seriously and was often influenced by issues he was
discussing with students; something of the sort happened in this
case as he began to think further about the British philosophical
discussions of personal agency and identity and particularly about
Ryle.

In *The Concept of Mind*, first published in 1949, Ryle had attacked
what he called "Descartes' myth" or "the myth of the ghost in the
machine," which seemed to him to have become the "official theory"
of the nature and place of minds. According to this view, he said:

> With the doubtful exceptions of idiots and infants in arms every
> human being has both a body and a mind. . . . A person therefore
> lives through two collateral histories, one consisting of what happens
> in and to his body, the other consisting of what happens in and to his
> mind. The first is public, the second private. . . . What has physical
> existence is composed of matter, or else is a function of matter; what
> has mental existence consists of consciousness, or else is a function
> of consciousness. . . . Material objects are situated in a common field,
> known as 'space,' and what happens to one body in one part of space
> is mechanically connected with what happens to other bodies in other
> parts of space. But mental happenings occur in insulated fields, known
> as 'minds,' and there is, apart maybe from telepathy, no direct causal
> connexion between what happens in one mind and what happens in
> another. Only through the medium of the public physical world can
> the mind of one person make a difference to the mind of another. The
> mind is its own place, and in his inner life each of us lives the life of
> a ghostly Robinson Crusoe.[23]

Those who accept the myth face in theory the problem of how to connect mind and body, ghost and machine, and in practice the worry of whether one can ever really know about the inner self of another person.

Ryle urged his readers to reject the myth. On the mythical picture, if I straighten my knee as a matter of pure reflex when the doctor taps it, I am doing one thing, a physical movement. But when I straighten it as a willed action, I am doing two things: an inner, mental act of will, and an external, bodily act of moving my leg—with a relation between the two that has proven notoriously difficult to explain. Ryle says that I am doing just one thing: I am deliberately straightening my knee. What makes the action deliberate is that it is done in a particular way, under particular circumstances, perhaps as part of a particular pattern of action, not that it is accompanied by some second act, invisible but independent. Similarly, to do or say something intelligently is not to do two things—a physical act of speech or movement and a mental act of thought—but to perform one action in a particular way and context. It follows that the human self is not some unknowable inner entity, whose nature may or may not be revealed by the words and bodily actions so mysteriously related to it. Rather, my words and actions constitute my identity.

In the 1960s the widely discussed "new quest for the historical Jesus" seemed to take for granted the "myth" Ryle was attacking. Günther Bornkamm, Gerhard Ebeling, and Ernst Fuchs in Germany and James M. Robinson in the United States conceded that the efforts of the "old quest" to write something like a biography of Jesus were doomed to failure. But we could, they said, by a new, existential method of history, come to know "not only the teaching of Jesus but certainly also the man Jesus as such."[24] Faith, Ebeling said, is "the one absolutely decisive and all-determining characteristic in the life and message of the historical Jesus."[25] That faith led to an inner certainty that was "the very nature of his person" and that took the concrete forms of freedom, authority, and love. "Jesus' life was an existence based on this kind of certainty."[26] For Fuchs, "the central theme of the sayings of Jesus is the decision which they demand. But this demand is simply the echo of Jesus' own decision. We have to understand his conduct as likewise determined by a decision, and we can infer what he did from what he demanded."[27] "To have faith in Jesus now means essentially to repeat Jesus' decision."[28]

Bultmann had set the dominant theological agenda of the time, but Bultmann's own position, as Schubert Ogden pointed out, seemed inherently unstable, for Bultmann claimed that only the Christ event made authentic existence a possibility in fact, but he was not

willing to give any content to that Christ event. To most who read
him, it seemed odd to have an event make such a difference when
one could not specify anything about it. Ogden offered one solution:
Authentic existence was possible in fact always and everywhere;
Jesus simply provided the decisive re-presentation of something
which had always been available.[29] To those who wanted to make
Jesus more crucial than that to Christian faith, the alternative
seemed to be to give some content to the Christ event after all—
and Fuchs and Ebeling and other new questers offered one strategy. We cannot trace Jesus' biography, but we can find the core of
his identity in his faith, his decision, his certainty. They insisted that
this wasn't a "psychological" claim, but to Frei and many others it
certainly sounded like one, and a dubious one at that. The inner
attitudes of Jesus seemed, if anything, harder to know than the
external course of his life.[30] But for Christian theology the problem went far beyond the new quest. From Schleiermacher's claims
about Jesus' God-consciousness to Tillich's account of Christ as the
expression of the New Being, a whole grand trajectory of modern
theology seemed caught up in these quasi-psychological claims about
Jesus' inner self.

Ryle's account of identity seemed to offer an alternative way of
thinking about such issues. A person's identity is not some possibly
unknowable inner essence but is constituted by the pattern of the
particular person's speech and action. As Frei wrote, "For descriptive
purposes, a person's uniqueness is not attributable to a super-added
factor, an invisible agent residing inside and from there directing
the body."[31] He was aware of the attacks on Ryle as a cryptobehav-
iorist who denied the reality of any human interiority, and Frei did
not want to go that far, or indeed to tie himself to the details of
any particular theory of human personhood. Human beings have
intentions as well as actions, he conceded, and when we try to trace
the way in which an intention turns into an action, "There is a real
or hypothetical 'inside' description of that transition, of which all
of us are aware but of which it is not easy to give an account."[32]
Frei's point was simply that it is the development of intention into
action that constitutes the self. The true self does not remain within,
manifested with greater or lesser authenticity; one is the person
one has come to be through one's enacted intentions.[33]

Therefore the Gospels could narrate Jesus' identity: "Jesus was
what he did and underwent, and not simply his understanding or
self-understanding."[34] As David Kelsey puts it,

> A skillful storyteller can make a character "come alive" simply by his
> narration of events, "come alive" in a way that no number of straight-
> forward propositional descriptions of the same personality could
> accomplish. He can bring one to know the peculiar identity of this

one unique person. Moreover, what one knows about the story's central agent is not known by "inference" from the story. On the contrary, he is known quite directly in and with the story, and recedes from cognitive grasp the more he is abstracted from the story. So too, biblical narrative can be taken as rendering an agent whose identity and actions theology is then to discuss.[35]

Such narratives help us know a person in the way that a great novelist or narrative historian can, and they provide insights we lose if we try to summarize the narrative in nonnarrative form.[36] Such was the christological approach found in the later volumes of Barth's *Church Dogmatics*—particularly in such sections of volume 4 as "The Way of the Son of God into the Far Country" and "The Royal Man"[37]—and in H. Richard Niebuhr's brief section in *Christ and Culture* entitled "Toward a Definition of Christ," which Frei found, from the beginning to the end of his career, Niebuhr's most suggestive remarks on christology.[38]

Stories that narrate a person's identity are of two kinds. Some simply illustrate the sort of person this was, functioning as illustrative anecdotes. If a story about Abe Lincoln's sense of humor or Simone Weil's single-mindedness captures the sort of people they were, perhaps with a vividness that any nonnarrative translation of the story would lose, then the story offers a true insight into their identity, even if the particular incident described never happened. On the other hand, some events can seem so crucial to the shape of a person's identity that the occurrence of that particular event really does matter. If Socrates spent his final day plotting escape and had to be forced to drink the hemlock, weeping all the while, then, even if the *Phaedo* portrays how Socrates often spoke and acted, we would judge differently the person Socrates was. The death scene itself really matters to our understanding of his identity.

Frei thought that many of the episodes in the Gospels function as illustrative anecdotes: They show us the sort of person Jesus was, whether or not this particular incident took place. The story of the crucifixion and the resurrection, however, is the place "(1) where the bond between intention and action in his story is more clearly evident; and (2) where the direct bond between himself as individual subject and his outward self-manifestation is strongest and most clearly unitary in character."[39] Therefore, at this point, we are bound to ask, "Did this actually take place?"[40]

The question is a good one, but Frei thought the means of answering it necessarily complex. First, if the resurrection was, say, a psychological illusion or a deliberate fraud, then it is an ordinary historical event like other illusions or frauds to be investigated as such. On the other hand, if God really raised Jesus from the dead, then this is an event without analogy. The usual historical questions about the relative probability of different explanations of the data break down.[41]

Second, the place of this episode in the biblical narratives and the particular nature of those narratives make a difference. As the Gospels tell the story, Frei says, Jesus is who he is above all in his resurrection. Further, if we read the Old and New Testaments as in some sense a unity, the identity of Jesus as the Resurrected One seems central not only to his own identity but to the storied world the text presents. If Jesus was not raised from the dead, then he was not who this story claims he is, and the narrative coherence of the story considered as a unity radically collapses. For Christians this story does not merely have a unity of its own; it sets the frame within which they understand the whole of their existence, so that, if this narrative falls into incoherence, so does the sense they make of "the one common world in which we all live and move and have our being."[42]

Frei saw here an analogy to Anselm's ontological argument for the existence of God as Barth had interpreted it. For Anselm, the logic of talk about God implies that God exists; God cannot be conceived as not existing. The alternative to belief in God is the outsider's sense that this odd talk about God simply makes no sense at all. For Frei, the Bible, as Auerbach had said, "seeks to overcome our reality: we are to fit our own life into its world,"[43] and its world is one in which Jesus has been resurrected. The logic of Christian faith implies that a Christian cannot, as a Christian, imagine a coherent world in which Jesus is not the Resurrected One.

The appropriate theological account of why a Christian believes in the resurrection would therefore take the form of describing how the world makes sense as seen from a Christian perspective; how the biblical narratives, seen as a coherent whole, shape such a perspective; and how Christ's resurrection forms a central and necessary element of such an understanding of those narratives. Such meditation on the structure of Christian faith may have its own kind of persuasive power—Barth used to say that a good dogmatics was the best apologetics—but does not in any usual sense constitute an argument to persuade the unbeliever, and Frei thought it best not to speculate too much on the processes by which unbelievers become believers. Such lines of thought lead to apologetic strategies that distort both the logic of faith and the meaning of the biblical texts, and they risk seeking to define and regulate the mysterious grace of God.[44]

4

The approaches to hermeneutics and Christology that appear in the earliest of these essays continued throughout Frei's career, but different contexts led to different emphases and further development of his position. At the beginning of his career, the dominant approach to the biblical texts, influenced by Bultmann, had been to analyze individual pericopes. Frei had had to make the case for attending to the narrative shape of the gospel texts as a whole. With the influence of redaction critics, literary approaches to the Bible, and Frei's own work, that argument no longer needed so much to be made by the 1980s. But Frei was convinced that too many theological interpreters still failed to take the narratives as narratives with sufficient seriousness.

In "The 'Literal Reading' of Biblical Narrative in the Christian Tradition: Does It Stretch or Will It Break?" (originally read at a conference in 1983 and then published in 1986) he criticizes the hermeneutical theory represented by Paul Ricoeur and David Tracy, a topic he had first addressed in "Theology and the Interpretation of Narrative: Some Hermeneutical Considerations" (a lecture delivered at Haverford College in 1982). For Ricoeur and David Tracy, he argues, the Bible is a particular instance of the class "religious text" that lays out a particular "mode-of-being-in-the-world." It is an approach, Frei claimed, that distorts the reading of the gospel in at least three ways. First, it assumes that a person's identity, contra Ryle, is an inner selfhood, known if at all by a hermeneutical process called understanding. On this account, "Like anyone else, Jesus is . . . not in the first place the agent of his actions, not the enacted project(s) that constitute(s) him, nor the person to whom the actions of others happen; he is, rather the verbal expressor of a certain preconceptual consciousness which he then, in a logically derivative or secondary sense, exhibits in action."[45] What matters, for instance, is not that he was crucified but "only that he was so consistent in his 'mode-of-being-in-the-world' as to take the risk willingly."[46]

Second, and even worse, on this view, "What narratives present (whether or not 'literally') is not in the first place ascriptive selves that are the subjects of their predicates, not even really the self-expressive, centered consciousness or transcendental ego, but the 'mode-of-being-in-the-world' which these selves exemplify and which is 're-presented' by being 'disclosed' to 'understanding.'"[47] The text isn't ultimately about Jesus, but about a human possibility Jesus instantiates. But such an interpretation contradicts both the general claim Frei had set out about the irreducibly narrative quality of the biblical narratives and the particular claim that "The story of Jesus is about him—not about someone else, or about nobody in particular, or about all of us."[48]

Third and finally, Frei claimed that on this hermeneutical theory, "the very possibility of reading those narratives under its auspices has to stand or fall with the theory's own viability in the first place."[49] Only if we can understand—in a particular defined sense of "understanding"—the mode-of-being-in-the-world presented by the text, only if we are at least to some extent caught up by the vision of human possibility it offers us, can we understand what it means. But that, Frei says, rules out as impossible what a non-Christian careful reader like Auerbach seems able to do so well: to recognize correctly the odd claims this particular text makes while still remaining outside the world it narrates.

Whether these claims are fair to Tracy and Ricoeur is a complex question.[50] What is clear from the determination with which Frei pressed them is his opposition to anything that even looked as if it might be the application of a general hermeneutical theory to these particular texts. Respect the local, mistrust the universal, he would have said. Let the character of these particular texts shape the way we understand them rather than letting a general theory limit our way of interpreting them in advance. Such suspicion of general theory was basic to Frei's position. When he found himself cited as one of the founders of a new form of general theory called narrative interpretation, he began to think he needed to restate his own position.

By the 1980s, as a range of hermeneutical approaches began to take narrative more seriously in biblical interpretation, many people started talking about something called "narrative theology," and Frei became very nervous about being classified as an instance of this species.[51] Some narrative theologians wanted to start with the narratives of the lives of contemporary Christians, and Frei's project was very nearly the opposite of that sort of theology as biography. Others interested in narrative and theology wanted to begin with some theory about the narrative quality of human experience from which one could derive conclusions about the appropriateness of a narrative religious text.[52]

Here too Frei resisted beginning with a general hermeneutical theory—even one about narrative—and making the biblical texts fit the theory. These texts, he wanted to say, are quite odd. They make particular kinds of claims one can recognize through a careful reading of them: "There may or may not be a class called 'realistic narrative,' but to take it as a general category of which the synoptic Gospel narratives and their partial second-order redescription in the doctrine of the Incarnation are a dependent instance is first to put the cart before the horse and then cut the lines and claim that the vehicle is self-propelled."[53]

Was Frei's own work, with its dependence on Auerbach and Ryle, guilty of such a prioritizing of general theory? Evidently, it had at least been open to misunderstanding. To try to correct the problem Frei went back to an ambiguity present in what he had said from the start. What is wrong with readings of the biblical narratives that find their meaning in the moral lessons they illustrate or the history we can pull out of them? Frei had given two answers: They distort the meaning a sensitive reader like Auerbach can recognize in the texts; they abandon the way a consensus within the Christian community had read these texts for nearly eighteen hundred years. Both answers appeared, but Frei's early emphasis was on the first of them.[54] But perhaps the second better preserved the particularity of these texts. Why take the roundabout road of finding these texts to be a particular instance of what Auerbach says about realistic narratives with the attendant dangers of cutting them to fit the Procrustean bed of even the most cautious of general theories? Why not simply attend to the way these texts have generally been read in the community with the longest history of reading them, the Christian church?

In that long history, a literal reading of the text has with some consistency had a kind of informal priority. If we try to define it in terms of some particular literary theory, the literal reading may "break" in the face of changes in literary fashion or discrepancy between practice and theory; as the modest set of rules characterizing the practice of Christian reading of biblical texts, it will "stretch" to fit any number of theories of human personhood, historical reality, and textual reference: "The less entangled in theory and the more firmly rooted not in a narrative (literary) tradition but in its primary and original context, a religious community's 'rule' for faithful reading, the more clearly it is likely to come into view, and the stronger as well as more flexible and supple it is likely to look."[55]

Frei's thinking turned in this direction in the context of the work of a number of his friends and colleagues. "To call a set of texts 'scripture,'" David Kelsey had written, "is, in part, to say that they ought so to be used in the common life of the church as to nurture and preserve her self-identity,"[56] and Kelsey developed an account of the authority of Scripture in terms of its functions in the life of Christian communities. George Lindbeck's *The Nature of Doctrine* proposed a "cultural-linguistic" way of interpreting religious doctrines, one in which their meaning was their use as rules in the life of a religious community. The biblical narratives "absorb the world" by providing and illustrating the language within which it is possible to live as a Christian. The way the Christian community uses them in that way, then, is their normative meaning. "Culture," Frei quoted Clifford Geertz as saying, "consists of socially established structures of meaning," and then Frei adds, "I'm suggesting that the Church is like that—a culture, not only of course for the observer but also for the agent, the adherent, who would understand it. There is a sacred text—a typical element in a religious system—and there are informal rules and conventions governing how the sign system works in regard to sacred scripture. The kind of theology that I like best is the kind that is closer to this outlook rather than to philosophy, or to historiography."[57] Or, one might add, to literary criticism.[58]

To be sure, one could to some extent map changes in Frei's account alongside changes of fashion in literary theory—from the New Critics and Auerbach at the time of his early work—with their careful attention to the formal structure of texts—to deconstructionists and Stanley Fish in the 1980s—with their interests in the social context in which interpretations take place.[59] But Frei was also remaining true to some basic themes in his own thought. A person's identity, he had said under Ryle's influence, lies not in some inner essence but in the shape of the person's life. So, similarly, a religion is not some inner essence but the pattern of what people say and do (as a descriptive anthropologist might observe them), and the meaning of the scriptural texts of the religion lies in the way the texts are used in the life of their community. Such ways of thinking do seem all of a piece.

Even more, first to last Frei championed the particular. Don't come with a general theory in hand, determined to apply it. Look at the way these particular texts work. In the face of those who wanted to ignore their narrative character, that meant emphasizing that they were realistic narratives of a particular kind. In the face of theories about narrative in general, it meant emphasizing the particular ways these texts function in the communities where they have their most traditional home.

5

That very emphasis on the particular shapes some of the promise and the problematic of Frei's theology. In his famous essay on *The Postmodern Condition*, Jean-François Lyotard defined the postmodern as "incredulity toward metanarratives."[60] That is, it is characteristic of our postmodern age to reject those overarching stories—whether the Enlightenment account of the advance of Reason or the Marxist chronicle of the class struggles that culminate in the proletarian revolution—that allow meaning to the pieces only as parts of a universal whole. Lyotard contrasts such metanarratives with a modest and particular "narrative knowledge" content to pursue its own forms of insight within its own context, which "does not give priority to the question of its own legitimation."[61] Narratives function within particular cultures and "define what has the right to be said and done in the culture in question, and since they are themselves a part of that culture, they are legitimated by the simple fact that they do what they do."[62]

However much talk of postmodernism has become a cliché, one can recognize the phenomena Lyotard is describing. Women, ethnic minorities, and a variety of oppressed people refuse to accept a dominant group's rules of discourse and rationality as universal. From very different points on the political spectrum, Hans-Georg Gadamer celebrates tradition and prejudice, whereas Michel Foucault warns against the dangers of totalizing discourse. Every scholarly convention seems to claim to celebrate the virtues of pluralism. One could make a case, in this context, for Karl Barth and Hans Frei as good postmodern theologians who reject universal rules of hermeneutics and scholarly method and attend to the particularities of the texts and communities before them.

On the other hand, many of those same pluralistic voices raise questions about whether one can claim any significant unity for that varied collection of texts that makes up the Bible, whether talk of consensus within the Christian community always represses minority voices, and whether it even makes sense to seek narrative coherence or talk about *the* meaning of a text. Frei's theology, for all its insistence on the singularity of Christian faith, community, and Scripture, does seem to make claims about the coherence of that faith and the unity of that community and scriptural text. And, after all, one might make a case for Christianity as one of the oldest continuing metanarratives still in business. A fundamental question for a theology like Frei's, then, is whether one can foster particularity so as to make space for the distinctive voice of such a theology without moving to a stage of deconstruction that undercuts the unities such a theology needs to presuppose. I am not sure of the answer; it is, I think, a tribute to the importance of Frei's thought that it so clearly focuses the question.

Such concerns arise primarily when Frei's work is read in an academic context; a different sort of question arises in the context of the church. Frei would have insisted that Christian theologians should speak primarily from and to the church, addressing the Christian community and inviting that community to let the biblical narratives shape its vision of the world. To what extent that community will respond to such invitations remains to be seen. "The most fateful issue for Christian self-description," Frei wrote in "The 'Literal Reading,'" "is that of regaining its autonomous vocation as a religion, after its defeat in its secondary vocation of providing ideological coherence, foundation, and stability to Western culture."[63] With the passing of what Kierkegaard called Christendom, Christians no longer define the shape of Western culture and need to learn to cultivate their own distinctive voice, their "autonomous vocation as a religion." But it remains uncertain whether the leaders or the ordinary members of Christian churches have much interest in learning such lessons from theologians. More specifically, can the idea of reading the Gospels as realistic narratives that render Jesus' identity have an impact on preaching and living in Christian congregations? Can Christians today understand a nonfundamentalist theology that invites them to let the world of the Bible define the shape of the world in which they live? Once again, the answers remain unclear, but these do seem the right sort of questions for theology to be asking.

Frei would have argued that the theologian's vocation remains in any event. In the last essay in this volume, Frei wrote about H. Richard Niebuhr, the teacher whose influence had brought him to theology and whose work had been the topic of his first published work. Like the earliest essay included herein, it was a lecture written for presentation at Harvard (read there, as it happened, after Frei's fatal stroke). Frei reflects in this lecture how Niebuhr might have responded to worries about theology's influence:

> Why be a poet, Holderlin asked, in these non-lyrical times? Why, we might ask of H. Richard Niebuhr, be a theologian in our utterly untheological times? I think he would have made short shrift of that question. He would have asserted, I believe, that our responsibility to affirm the glory of the Lord, and his glory alone, has not been altered one whit, and that this remains our duty in propitious or unpropitious times. We theologians could have expected from Niebuhr an unsentimental call to do our duty, no matter whether we were finally of weighty cultural influence or not.[64]

Like Richard Niebuhr himself, Frei never found being a theologian an easy task. His own views implied that the church community ought to be a theologian's primary intellectual context, and he knew that his own primary social and institutional context was the university, not the church. That made him unusually sensitive in describing the cultural ambiguities of modern theology, but it created for him personally a real element of pathos. Still, he felt in himself the vocation of a Christian theologian, and he sought to respond faithfully to that unsentimental call to duty.

Notes

An earlier version of this essay appeared as "Hans Frei and the Meaning of Biblical Narrative" in *The Christian Century*, vol. 106, no. 18 (May 24–31, 1989), pp. 556–59.

1. George A. Lindbeck, *The Nature of Doctrine: Religion and Theology in a Postliberal Age* (Philadelphia: Westminster Press, 1984), p. 119. As the foreword to this book suggests, Frei was a much more important

influence in its development than the relatively sparse references to him might suggest.

2. Professor Lansing Hicks, himself an Episcopalian, remembers hearing from his Baptist brother in North Carolina in 1939 or 1940 of a remarkable young student named Hans Frei who was active in a Baptist student group but was interested in Episcopalianism. They never made contact at that time, though Hicks came to know Frei many years later at Yale; I cannot find out any more about this story. This does suggest an earlier date than is otherwise attested for the beginnings of at least a curiosity on Frei's part about the Episcopal church.

3. In addition to its discussion of Barth, the dissertation contained a long review of nineteenth-century theology. Frei used to tell the story on himself that Niebuhr, having read the large dissertation, said, "Either one of them would have been acceptable."

4. I am grateful to Geraldine Frei, John Woolverton, Charles Campbell, David Kelsey, and Vincent McCarthy for help in writing the biographical section of this introduction. Professor Campbell also shared with me drafts of some chapters of his dissertation, which will be, when completed, a most important contribution to the study of Frei's work.

5. Hans W. Frei, *The Eclipse of Biblical Narrative: A Study of Eighteenth and Nineteenth Century Hermeneutics* (New Haven: Yale University Press, 1974), p. vii.

6. Erich Auerbach, *Mimesis: The Representation of Reality in Western Literature*, trans. Willard R. Trask (Princeton: Princeton University Press, 1953), p. 554.

7. Ibid., p. 13.

8. Ibid., p. 15.

9. J.R.R. Tolkien, "On Fairy Stories," in *Tree and Leaf* (Boston: Houghton Mifflin, 1965), p. 37.

10. Frei drew other insights from Auerbach as well, among them the importance of typological interpretation (see, in addition to *Mimesis*, Erich Auerbach, "Figura," in *Scenes from the Drama of European Literature* [New York: Noonday Press, Meridian Books, 1959], pp. 11–76), the originality of serious narratives of the lives of ordinary people in the biblical texts, and the relation of doctrine and story in these texts so that, as Frei liked to put it, the story is the meaning of the doctrine, not the doctrine the meaning of the story.

11. Hans W. Frei, "Eberhard Busch's Biography of Karl Barth," in *Types of Christian Theology*, ed. George Hunsinger and William C. Placher (New Haven: Yale University Press, 1992), p. 161.

12. See chap. 2, p. 57.

13. See chap. 1, p. 43.

14. Frei, *Types of Christian Theology*, p. 138.

15. Frei, *The Eclipse*, p. 1.

16. See chap. 1, p. 40.

17. Lindbeck, *The Nature of Doctrine*, p. 118.

18. Frei, "Eberhard Busch's Biography of Karl Barth," in *Types of Christian Theology*, p. 161.

19. The typology of theologies Frei developed in *Types of Christian Theology* distinguishes theologians who think of theology primarily as an academic discipline, a kind of *Wissenschaft* subordinated to philosophical principles, and those who think of it primarily as an exercise in Christian self-description, with its first home in the Christian community. Types I and II give a priority to philosophical accounts under which theology is somehow subsumed. Type III, represented by Schleiermacher, tries to preserve a delicate balance between the two understandings of theology. Type IV, of which Barth is Frei's principal example, thinks of theology as first of all Christian self-description, but, unlike the Wittgensteinian fideists of Type V, allows for an element of ad hoc apologetics. Chapters 5 and 6 of *Types of Christian Theology* make in detail the argument Frei derived in part from his reflections on Auerbach: It is just this kind of primarily, though not exclusively, descriptive theology written within the Christian community that provides the context for the least distorted reading of the biblical texts.

20. Hans W. Frei, "Barth and Schleiermacher, chap. 7, p. 197.

21. Hans W. Frei, *The Identity of Jesus Christ: The Hermeneutical Basis of Dogmatic Theology* (Philadelphia: Fortress Press, 1975), pp. viii–ix.

22. Robert H. King, "The Concept of Personal Agency as a Theological Model," Ph.D. diss., Yale University, 1965. King developed the dissertation into his book, *The Meaning of God* (Philadelphia: Fortress Press, 1973). Frei cites the dissertation in "Theological Reflections," see chap. 2, p. 91.

23. Gilbert Ryle, *The Concept of Mind* (New York: Barnes & Noble, 1962, pp. 11, 13.

24. Gerhard Ebeling, *Word and Faith*, trans. James W. Leitch (Philadelphia: Fortress Press 1963), p. 297.

25. Ibid., p. 296.

26. Gerhard Ebeling, *Theology and Proclamation*, trans. John Riches (London: Collins, 1966), p. 89.

27. Ernst Fuchs, *Studies of the Historical Jesus*, trans. Andrew Scobie (London: S.C.M. Press, 1964), p. 23.

28. Ibid., pp. 28–29.

29. Schubert M. Ogden, *Christ Without Myth* (New York: Harper & Row, 1963), p. 153.

30. The excursus on the new quest at the end of "Theological Reflections" (see chap. 2, pp. 87–91) indicates how much it was on Frei's mind at this point. See also "Remarks in Connection with a Theological Proposal," chap. 1, p. 37. Schubert Ogden and Van Harvey were the bestknown critics of the conclusions of the new quest, but Frei accused them of sharing some of its assumptions. Ogden and Harvey, he thought, rightly insisted that we couldn't get "inside" Jesus' self, but, like the new questers, they believed that inner self constituted identity, and they therefore concluded that we

couldn't know Jesus' identity. See "Remarks in Connection with a Theological Proposal," chap. 1, p. 38.

31. Frei, *The Identity*, p. 42.

32. Ibid., p. 43. "One can, I think, describe the passage of intention into action (and the categories for it) and the unity and mutual dependence of intention and action, without appealing to the ontological ground of that unity, of which we have no direct or descriptive knowledge such as we have of the unity and passage from intention to action itself" (see "Remarks in Connection with a Theological Proposal," chap. 1, p. 37).

33. Ibid. See also "Theological Reflections," chap. 2, p. 73.

34. See "Barth and Schleiermacher," chap. 7, p. 184.

35. David H. Kelsey, *The Uses of Scripture in Recent Theology* (Philadelphia: Fortress Press, 1975), p. 39.

36. Frei's argument focused on the Gospels as an identity description of Jesus Christ, but he thought of the Bible as a whole as providing an identity description of God. This obviously raises at least two sorts of questions: 1. Particularly in dialogue with Judaism, what is the relation of the narration of God's identity in the Gospels with the narration of God's identity in the Hebrew Scriptures? 2. In what sense can one think of God as a person who acts in a way that could begin to constitute God's identity? On the first question, see Michael Goldberg, "God, Action, and Narrative: *Which* God? *Which* Action? *Which* Narrative?" *Journal of Religion* 68 (January 1988), 39–56. On the second question, see Thomas F. Tracy, *God, Action, and Embodiment* (Grand Rapids, Mich.: Eerdmans, 1984) and Kathryn Tanner, *God and Creation in Christian Theology* (Oxford: Basil Blackwell, 1988).

37. Karl Barth, *Church Dogmatics*, vol. 4, part 1, trans. G. W. Bromiley (Edinburgh, Scot.: T. & T Clark, 1956, 1958), pp. 157–210; vol. 4, pt. 1, pt. 2, pp. 154–263.

38. For Niebuhr, "The being of the person Jesus Christ is not—as it is for the psychologizing school—an ineffable state of awareness behind act and teachings, nor is the full personal being inaccessible to us—as it is for theologians influenced by form criticism. The unity of the person of Jesus Christ is embedded in and immediately present to his teaching and practice" (Hans W. Frei, "The Theology of H. Richard Niebuhr," in *Faith and Ethics*, ed. Paul Ramsey [New York: Harper & Row, 1957], p. 115). See also Frei, *Types of Christian Theology*, pp. 143–46.

39. See "Theological Reflections," chap. 2, p. 46.

40. Ibid., p. 82. Gary Comstock, in a widely cited article, sets out a crucial thesis of his interpretation of Frei: "Is it enough to say that the biblical narratives are *meaningful*? Or are Christians also committed to saying that they are *true*? Frei thinks that the answer to the first question is yes, so he does not pursue the second," ("Truth or Meaning: Ricoeur versus Frei on Biblical Narrative," *Journal of Religion* 66 (April 1986), 118. Frei so often acknowledges the appropriateness of the truth question that I am puzzled by this interpretation.

41. See "Theological Reflections," chap. 2, p. 87. David Hume made the

same point in his essay on miracles. Is Jesus' resurrection then a "historical fact"? If those are the categories you want to use, Frei responded to Carl Henry, then certainly one should say yes rather than no. "But they weren't always the categories employed by the church. . . . I do not believe, as Dr. Henry apparently does, that they are as theory-free, as neutral as he seems to think they are. I do not think that the concept 'fact' is theory-neutral." And Christians ought to resist imposing one set of philosophical categories as the only set within which one can correctly understand faith in the resurrection. See Frei, "Response to 'Narrative Theology: An Evangelical Appraisal," chap. 9, pp. 211.

42. Frei, "Eberhard Busch's Biography of Karl Barth," *Types of Christian Theology*, p. 161.

43. Auerbach, *Mimesis*, p. 15.

44. In any event, Frei wrote, pilgrimages from unbelief to belief may have "very little to do with any kind of talk and much more to do with the eloquence of a consistent pattern of life that has seemingly suffered an inexplicably wounding and healing invasion, rare though that sort of thing is" (*The Identity* p. 8).

45. See Frei, "Literal Reading," chap. 4, p. 126.

46. Ibid.

47. Ibid., p. 127.

48. See Frei, *Types of Christian Theology*, p. 140.

49. Ibid., p. 51.

50. I made a case for Frei's side of the argument in "Paul Ricoeur and Postliberal Theology: A Conflict of Interpretations?" *Modern Theology* 4 (October 1987), 35–52.

51. See, for instance, Michael Goldberg, *Theology and Narrative: A Critical Introduction* (Nashville: Abingdon: 1982); George W. Stroup, *The Promise of Narrative Theology* (Atlanta: John Knox Press, 1982).

52. The classic source is Stephen Crites, "The Narrative Quality of Experience," *Journal of the American Academy of Religion* 39 (September 1971), 291–311.

53. See Frei, "Literal Reading," chap. 4, pp. 142–43.

54. In one of his earliest essays, Frei wrote, "My proposal . . . is that in regard to aesthetic or quasi-aesthetic texts, particularly narratives—and the Gospels are such in part—'normative' interpretations may be possible. That is to say, the meaning of the text remains the same, no matter what the perspectives of succeeding generations of interpreters may be. In other words, the constancy of the meaning of the text is the text and not the similarity of its *effect* on the life-perspective of succeeding generations" (Frei, "Remarks in Connection with a Theological Proposal," chap. 1, p. 32). In his later essays, at minimum the emphasis changed, and likely he would not have said that at all. I am trying here to give an account of Frei's development; I suppose I should in passing note that my own sympathies are more with his earlier position.

55. Ibid., p. 139. Frei was influenced by Raphael Loewe's work on early Jewish exegesis, in which, Loewe said, "What is understood as *peshat* [plain sense] was not necessarily the natural meaning of the biblical text [i.e., the grammatical meaning] but rather the meaning traditionally accepted as authoritative or at any rate familiar, however far from the primary sense of the words it might be" (Raphael Loewe, "The 'Plain' Meaning of Scripture in Early Jewish Exegesis," *Papers of the Institute of Jewish Studies in London* (Jerusalem, 1964), vol. 7, p. 167).

56. Kelsey, *The Uses of Scripture in Recent Theology*, p. 150.

57. See Frei, *Types of Christian Theology*, p. 13, quoting Clifford Geertz, *The Interpretation of Cultures* (New York: Basic Books, 1973), pp. 12–13.

58. See also Wayne A. Meeks, "A Hermeneutics of Social Embodiment," *Harvard Theological Review* 79 (January–July 1986), 176–86.

59. The relation of textual meaning and community of interpreters in Fish's more recent work offers a closer analogy to what Frei was doing. (See Stanley Fish, *Is There a Text in This Class?* [Cambridge: Harvard University Press, 1980]).

60. Jean-François Lyotard, *The Postmodern Condition: A Report on Knowledge*, trans. Geoff Bennington and Brian Massumi (Minneapolis: University of Minnesota Press, 1984), p. xxiii.

61. Ibid., p. 27.

62. Ibid., p. 23.

63. See Frei, "Literal Reading," chap. 4, p. 149. It is, I think, worth noting that Frei seems to concede a larger cultural task, at least under some circumstances, as a legitimate "secondary vocation" for Christianity.

64. See Hans W. Frei, "H. Richard Niebuhr on History, Church and Nation," chap. 10, p. 231.

1

Remarks in Connection with a Theological Proposal

In this previously unpublished lecture, which was delivered at the Harvard Divinity School in December 1967, Frei reflects directly on the theological proposal he had offered in the essay that is now chapter 2 of this book. The lecture not only clarifies what he saw at stake in that essay but also establishes his larger theological program as a whole. Indeed, it is virtually a tour de force. *The lecture's evident mastery of the history of modern theology from the seventeenth to the twentieth centuries, its erudite assessments and employments of both Continental and analytic traditions in philosophy, its provocative orientation toward contemporary hermeneutical discussion and literary criticism—all are placed in the perhaps unlikely service of an essentially Barthian project (note, among other things, the remarks about a "high Christology") in Christian dogmatic theology. Despite all this, the argument remains engagingly tentative and open-ended. Though one may sense somewhat poignantly in retrospect that more promissory notes were issued than the author, in his later writings, ever quite managed to redeem, the range and scope of his thought are nonetheless evident and impressive.*

The lecture exhibits themes that run throughout Frei's career as a historian, a theologian, and a hermeneutician: the distinction between explanation and description, with a decided preference for the latter, across a number of academic disciplines; the plea for modest, non-

speculative interpretive devices in expounding scripture; the nontheo-
logical modes of conceptual analysis used to elucidate the logic and con-
tent of dogmatic theology; the distrust of apologetic strategies that
dissolve into the worst forms of relativism; the insistence on the par-
ticularity of the synoptic gospel narratives and the figure of Jesus
as they depict him. The dissenting tradition of modern thought that
had Kierkegaard urging "existence is not a system" and that found Barth
echoing that if so, then all the more is God's self-revelation not a system,
is perhaps continued by Frei on the hermeneutical plane. For in a kin-
dred way he insists that biblical narrative, itself not a system, finally
eludes all attempts to capture its singularity through resort to the closure
of grand interpretive schemes. Like Kierkegaard, Barth, and others, Frei's
theological imagination was governed, it seems, by a sense and taste for
the singular.

* * *

The conviction underlying these pages is that the story of modern
Christian theology (beginning with the end of the seventeenth century) is increasingly, indeed, almost exclusively that of anthropological and Christological apologetics, that the new interest in
hermeneutics by and large serves the same aim, that this development has now just about run its course, and that whether it has
or not, it is time to search for alternatives. Finally, I am convinced
that the alternative is *not* a substitution of eschatology for Christology
as the central Christian affirmation because the two are invariably
interlocking doctrines, and it would be hard to assign priority to
one over the other. I am convinced that the alternatives are either
a nonapologetic and dogmatic, rather than systematic, theological
procedure in which Christology continues to be the crucial ingredient or else a metaphysic or ontology in which Christology would play
a peripheral role.

　　To repeat part of the first assertion: Theology has been almost
exclusively apologetical, and the main focus for the apology has been
anthropology. I should, in another context, defend the thesis that the
theological procedure and arguments of eighteenth-century theology
are much the same as those of the nineteenth and twentieth centuries.
What has changed has been the sensibility, the image men have of
their humanity, that constitutes the raw data on which theological
analysis of an anthropological kind goes to work. In this respect only
has there been a shift since the eighteenth century, and here the early
nineteenth century is still today our main source of supply of raw
material. It is perhaps possible but not certain that a new image is
now emerging—who knows, certainly the advocates of "futuristic
man" are zestful enough—but the apologetic, anthropological procedure remains the same. *Plus ça change, plus c'est a même chose.*

Bultmann's famous dictum that all theological assertions are anthropological assertions is a summary of the largest part of the theological household's convictions—Barth aside. It is, more than anything else, the conviction of those who do systematic theology. Some aspect of the doctrine of man has usually served them as the integrating, organizing, or enabling principle around which to gather at least the meaning and often to evaluate the truth of theological assertions.

If the *aim* of the theological enterprise has been almost wholly apologetic, its organizing or *systematic principle* largely anthropological, its *doctrinal content* has been well-nigh exclusively Christological, or Christocentric if you will. I do not wish to specify this content with precision, but let me mention two all-but-universal preoccupations in modern Christological theology: (1) What stake does the theological enterprise have in "positivity" (i.e., in the fact claims about an historical, salvific occurrence)? And how is such a fact claim related to the content or shape of this putative fact? (2) What is the connection between the occurrence and its shape, and the human condition in general (i.e., What is the meaning of history?), as well as the contemporary individual's faith and life in particular?

In other words, preoccupation with the historical Jesus and with the *work* of the kerygmatic Christ—rather than the metaphysical definition of his *person*—have been the hallmarks of Christology in the modern age. This befits a Christology closely related to anthropology. Yet this has gone hand in hand with another, almost contrary tendency in Christology. Theology, like philosophy, has been agitated by epistemological and ontological rather than metaphysical questions. (I suggest—it is admittedly an arbitrary suggestion—that ontology, in contrast to metaphysics, raises the question of being as a question systematically related to human beings as the indispensable focus for the apprehension of being.) Under their impact, Christology has tended, especially since the early nineteenth century, toward a convergence of the doctrines of the person and work of Christ. This has happened by way of a doctrine of revelation, in which the *content* of unveiling is the whole self-giving subject in his self-communicating presence. This self-revelation or self-giving of God in Jesus Christ has at the same time been regarded as the unique *act* of God, apprehended in past, present, and future. Revelation theology and act-of-God theology have been virtually synonymous. The person is *in* his self-giving act or work: He *is* his work.

Though not itself influential, Kant's procedure in *Religion Within the Limits of Reason Alone* was symptomatic of the future. He substituted a Christology of action for the doctrines of Christ's person and work. In the unity of the original event with the contemporary appropriation of it, two different acts, each in its own integrity, join in one action, divine and human. More than anything else, it is an action in back of the outward, visible scene—be it that of nature, history, or the moral life. This action is also revelation because it takes place toward and in man's subjectivity. Now this action-revelation—we might as well call the contemporary (in contrast to the originating) end of it "conversion"—has been taken in most post-Kantian theologies to have two poles. There is, first of all, the original, historic unity of two actions in the self-consciousness of Jesus, and then the same interaction-unity in the disposition of the believer. But the two, the original and the contemporary, must be seen as oriented toward each other. Christus *extra nos* must be seen as Christus *pro et in nobis.* Systematic theology is precisely the enterprise of indicating that history and faith hold together. Notions of progressive revelation, tradition and tradition history, the Church, all may help in the task, as do more nearly methodological devices such as resort to paradox or, in the early nineteenth century as again today, ontologies, to span the hiatus between temporal positivity of the past and moral or self-conscious presence (i.e., contemporary faith). To use more traditional language, systematic theology has largely been an endeavor to unite the doctrines of Christ and the Spirit at the level of immanence rather than transcendence. But the same kind of transition between history and faith may also be provided by an appeal to future instead of present verification, that is, through a reliance on a historical dialectic of events to provide the bond between the past with its promise and the future's fulfillment when the promise will be verified. (One may note parenthetically that on most of these issues Kant himself, unlike the more ambiguous Hegel, returned negative findings. The notion of an original revelation-action he regarded as archetypal rather than historical—if one were to be able to relate it to conversion at a given present time. And even in present conversion he could find only one action at the crucial initiatory stage rather than the unity of two. That action, to the extent that one can apprehend it, is human rather than divine, even though it has to be *represented* as a dialectic of two: divine-human and human. Kant's *Religion Within the Limits* contains *in nuce* almost all the problems systematic theologians have worried to and fro since his day.)

I am saying that we have lived for almost three hundred years in an era in which an anthropologically oriented theological apologetic has tried to demonstrate that the notion of a unique divine revelation in Jesus Christ is one whose meaning and possibility are reflected in general human experience. The business of theology has therefore

been that of pointing to the potentiality of human existence for
Christocentric faith and for Christocentric interpretation, no matter
whether the chief instrument for allowing this faith and interpretation has been the immanently insuperable self-alienation of man in
the present, the present's hope and promise of the future, or some
other device. To say it another way: Theology has to validate the
possibility and, hence, the meaning of Christian claims concerning
the shape of human existence and the divine relation to it, even
though the *actual occurrence*—and thus the *verification* of the claim
—is a matter of divine, self-authenticating action and revelation.
And it doesn't matter if human existence was conceived in rational-
moral fashion, as in the Enlightenment; in aesthetic fashion, as by
Schleiermacher; in phenomenological-ontological fashion, as by the
contemporary hermeneutical school and its nineteenth-century forerunners; in existentialist-phenomenological fashion, as by Bultmann,
Ogden, and Buri; in universal historical terms, as by Pannenberg;
in dialectical-historical fashion, as by Moltmann; in various personalistic mixtures of these categories, as by Brunner and Althaus; or in
a mixed historical, ontological, and evolutionary vision, as by Karl
Rahner. Here I agree with Karl Barth. Although I may have my
own preferences in analyzing the shape of human existence—and
I happen to prefer Moltmann among theologians, mixed in unsystematically (perhaps contradictorily) with a liberal dash of British
Empiricism, such as that of Sir Peter Medawar or Sir Karl Popper
who suggest that neither nature nor history has a "shape," as though
they were holistic, unitary, dialectical, or evolutionary processes—
I believe that it is not the business of Christian theology to argue
the *possibility* of Christian truth any more than the instantiation
or *actuality* of that truth. The possibility follows logically as well
as existentially from its actuality. Hence, I should want to draw a
sharp distinction between the logical structure as well as the content of Christian belief, which it is the business of theologians to
describe but not to explain or argue, and the totally different logic
of *how one comes* to believe, or the possibility of believing immanent in human existence, on which the theologian has relatively
little to say and on which he should in any case not base the structure of his theology. Yet doing so has been the preoccupation of theologians for nearly three hundred years.

Now we are all aware that there has been an insistent, nagging,
indeed, growing hermeneutical question going along with this apologetic enterprise. It was at stake, for example, in the reflections of
F. C. Baur concerning Christian history and *Tendenzkritik* and in
the break of Ritschl with him. Except for Schleiermacher and
Dilthey, the term *hermeneutics* wasn't much used from the early
nineteenth century until recently; but the problem was there con-

cerning the meaning and, hence, the understanding of texts, the continuity between generations of interpretations, and the relation of interpreted meaning to the historical events and/or institutions to which some of the texts at least have reference. At the beginning of the twentieth century we had a debate about the essence of Christianity, and we are ripe for it again. For before we disagree about how to validate Christian truth claims, we should at least debate what the thing is or how to understand it. But in fact, the same problems and attitudes I referred to will arise again over the notion of what it is to understand Christianity. For, some will say, understanding does not take place apart from decision. All issues of the meaning and of the truth of Christianity arise together because they are located in the decision-making process. Hence, the analysis of how a "faith" understanding of texts is possible and how historical understanding is related to it becomes the hermeneutical preoccupation.

My plea here is—the more formal, the less loaded one can make the notion of understanding, the better. And that, in turn, involves a search, in deliberate opposition to most of what I find in contemporary theology, for categories of understanding detached from the perspectives we bring to our understanding, including our commitments of faith. Whether such a thing can be successful remains to be seen. In any case, it involves a search for a notion of understanding that is as little as possible moved by considerations of man's understanding as moved by his being—existential, historical, or ontological. In some ways I see my aim for "understanding" as diametrically opposite to the perspectivism of a theologian like the late Carl Michalson, for whom the present interpreter's life stance is just about all there lis to be the hermeneutical and historical understanding, and most sympathetic to the notion of the judgment of historical events put forth by Van Harvey. But my plea is that his detachment from perspectivism be extended beyond the judgment and estimate of factual data to the understanding of the meaning of texts. And this Professor Harvey does not do convincingly, probably because he is not clear on the nature of the problem.

My aim is to take a first step toward getting at the question: What is the essence of Christianity? My plea is that this be done in a nonperspectivist way if possible. I acknowledge the difficulty of the matter because there is considerable puzzlement not only over the hermeneutical principles but also over the proper data to be examined: All of Christian history in order to find some strand of continuity, e.g., tradition—if we can discover what *its* essence is? The Bible? But where is its unity? Or do we appeal to a canon within a canon? How much of the Bible in that case and on what grounds of selection and with what arguments that we have understood that portion aright? My simple answer is that for a beginning let's start with the synoptic Gospels, or at least one of them, because their peculiar nature as narratives, or at least partial narratives, makes some hermeneutical moves possible that we don't have available elsewhere in the New Testament. And having started there, I would propose to go on to say, let's see how much more of the New Testament can be coordinated by means of this series of hermeneutical moves.

My proposal, which I can really test only in application and not in abstraction (i.e., by a hypothetical evaluation of its internal consistency) is that in regard to aesthetic or quasi-aesthetic texts, particularly narratives—and the Gospels are such in part—"normative" interpretations may be possible. That is to say, the meaning of the text remains the same no matter what the perspectives of succeeding generations of interpreters may be. In other words, the constancy of the meaning of the text is the text and not the similarity of its *effect* on the life-perspectives of succeeding generations. No reference to the situation of the interpreter is necessary in understanding the text. I propose, then, an aesthetic understanding of a text—provided the text itself is at least partly aesthetic. My suggestion is that when we apply this proposal to the exegesis of the Gospels, what we find to be the meaning of the Gospels is what one might term a "high Christology," and I would propose *that* as the basic datum for a start toward an answer to the question, "What is the essence of Christianity?"

My proposal involves more yet: If there is an actual exegesis of a text, which is not governed by our perspectives, so that not only the *actual* meaning but also the *possibility* of our understanding the text has no reference to a theory of our preunderstanding—then the text may force a scramble of our categories of understanding, even though we must always keep these categories clean and distinct in the abstract, and therefore can never know (in the abstract) how on earth they may be scrambled. More about that in a moment.

In trying to work out the hermeneutical principles of this program of interpretation, I found that a certain kind of understanding is involved, which is perhaps best exemplified by what goes on in the nineteenth-century realistic novel and in the attempt to understand it. (George Eliot's *Adam Bede* and *Middlemarch* come to mind, those great English artifacts which, according to F. R. Leavis, rank right below the accomplishments of Tolstoy himself.) And then I found that it is not only understanding of literature or literary theory but also understanding of understanding that is involved in my aesthetic approach. (Is "hermeneutics" the first or second of these activities, or is it both?) And then, to my alarm, I found that historical understanding and anthropology also became hermeneutical issues. But in the essay itself I restricted myself to a cursory examination of the principles of anthropology involved in this aesthetic reading of the Gospel story.

In regard to understanding, (remember: for this particular exegetical task!) I find myself influenced increasingly by Wittgenstein and J. L. Austin rather than by the Idealistic tradition that has dominated the field for so long, whether in its pure form (e.g., in Dilthey), in existentialist form, in a more historical form like that of Pannenberg, or in a more ontological form like that of Heidegger, Gadamer, and among theologians Fuchs and Ebeling. There is, it seems to me, a variety of descriptions for any given linguistic phenomenon, and hence, above all, no ontological superdescription or explanation for it. Furthermore, the "grammar" (use according to rules of such a construct) is more readily exhibited or set forth than stated in the abstract.

In the theory of literary criticism (where I am really a babe in the woods) I find myself more in agreement with the old-fashioned "newer critics," (like William Empson, William Wimsatt, and Cleaneth Brooks) as well as the more moderate representatives of the same outlook (like René Wellek and Austin Warren) and with the historians of literary style like Erich Auerbach, than I do with outright intentionalists like E. Donald Hirsch. And yet I agree with both "newer critics" and "intentionalists" more than I do with psychological or historical critics or with mythopoeic critics like Northrop Frye or Joseph Campbell. I am interested less in archetypal experiences reflected in literature and in literary genres than I am in normative or valid interpretation (to use Hirsch's terms) of single texts. But at least at times—and I would say this is true of the Gospels to the extent that they are narrative literature—valid interpretation (Hirsch to the contrary) does not depend on the difficult assumption of a necessary and traceable connection between the text and the author's intention or will. On the contrary, precisely this hypothesis and the endeavor to demonstrate its validity leads, in the case of the Gospels, away from normative interpretation into speculative historical inference. Normative interpretation is a matter of the structure of the narrative itself and seeing if the text *as given* has a genuine structure. I agree with Hirsch as well as the "new critics" that this detachment from the author must *not* mean that in order to achieve normative understanding and interpretation one goes ahead and ontologizes meaning and language (as something distinct from their referents) in order thereby to provide a common "horizon" between text and later interpretation, after the fashion of the "new hermeneuticians." No: That way lies the worst of relativism, for then the only thing in common between any text

and later interpreters becomes the common linguistic effect produced in every generation. And because linguistic effect or "linguistic
event" here seems to be the same, or nearly the same, as personal
life-meaning, it looks to the outsider as if the new hermeneutic's
ontology of language reduces to the claim that the meaning of a text
is its perennially similar affective impact. No, once again. The formal
structure of the narrative itself is the meaning, not the author's
intention nor an ontology of language nor yet the text's impact.

My proposal involves a similar slant on what is involved in
understanding *historical* narrative that, apart from questions about
fact estimate, I would regard as having many features in common
with fictional, novelistic narrative. (Note: *historical narrative*. If
there are ways of writing history that do not involve a significant
recourse to narrative structure, I have no claim to make about them
in the present context.) What they have in common is their insistence that the direct interaction of character and circumstance not
be abstracted from each other. And whatever theme there is—and
there is bound to be a unifying theme in a historical as in a fictional narrative—emerges from this interaction rather than as an
independent, *a priori* moral. A novel written simply to illustrate a
preconceived moral is almost by definition a bad novel, and one sus-
pects the same about history writing of a similar sort. The explanatory theme or life-pattern has no reality, not even an abstract status apart from its emergence in the narrative description. To
paraphrase it by abstracting it from the interplay of character and
circumstance is like paraphrasing a poem in didactic language.
What is gone is the novel or the poem or the history. In this respect
I follow analysts of historical explanation like William Dray, W. B.
Gallie, and Arthur Danto rather than, say, Wilhelm Dilthey or
R. G. Collingwood, for whom (protests notwithstanding) there is an
entry into the being or mind-set of the historical agent that is sufficiently separate from his action and his interaction with circumstances to make the interior knowledge, which we share with him
in our common humanity, the clue, and the outer expression of
action a secondary element in historical understanding. Hence,
understanding history is for them essentially understanding ideas
(Collingwood) or the expression of life attitudes (Dilthey).

I must stress again that this understanding (1) of understanding,
(2) of literature, and (3) of history finds its paradigm in a certain kind
of narrative: That in which character, circumstance, and theme are
nothing without each other and become themselves only in their
mutual interaction. I have cursorily tackled the kind of understanding that seems to me called for by this kind of narrative only at the
level (4) of anthropology. And here I have been influenced by philosophical psychologists such as Gilbert Ryle, Stuart Hampshire, Peter

Strawson, and Elizabeth Anscombe—and theologians like Austin Farrer and Karl Barth. One has to assert not only the coexistence and mutual dependence of person and circumstance in the literary description but also by virtue of that interaction the cohesion of "inner" and "outer" human being. And the point here is not to start with one rather than the other side of human being, but with their unity—especially the unity of intention and action and that unity of subject and its objective instantiation (i.e., the body in its external context). That outer instantiation is neither an objectified alienation of the true subject, nor is it a privileged human or transcendent status of the coordinating point where subject and world flow together. One hears a great deal today about man's body and—more than that—about the whole natural context becoming hominized, nature not having any independent status or power apart from its appropriation or conversion by Man (Moltmann, Metz). That is *not* what I'm talking about. There is a perfectly ordinary (nonhistorical, if you will) interaction, a mutual fitness between man as body and the natural environment, so that in my description of this and other modes of human life and interaction, the ordinary public, natural, and impersonal use of language and a private, or privileged, and highly personal use flow together. It is my conviction that the interaction of character and circumstance, subject and object, inner and outer human being cannot be *explained* (except hypothetically under formal metaphysical schemes—and these are fine, except that I am not very skillful at them).

But it *can* be *described,* and that is the point. One can, up to a point—and only up to a point—render a description, but not a metaphysics, of such interactive unity. It is done by the rendering of certain formal categories; but finally, the categories themselves are outstripped, and then all one can and must do is *narrate* the unity. How I would go about this description of human being in interaction with circumstance and how I see the categories for it outstripped, so that finally one can only have recourse to the story of the interaction itself for supplying the understanding of it, I have tried to show in part—but only in part—in this essay. I should want to sketch it in greater detail and with some hierarchical structuring of the descriptive tools. I think I shall want to argue that the intention-action category of the philosophical psychologists is more crucial, hence more basic in a descriptive anthropology shaped toward narrative, than is the subject–self-manifestation–in–word description of the Idealist tradition. However, I would not want to discard the latter because without it I do not think I can say anything significant about personal *continuity* over a period of time and a range of actions. Nor would I want simply to discard the analysis of the self as manifest or instantiated in cultural objectification, which is an expansion of this Idealist claim, according to which words, speech, or language are not only the self in manifestation but provide the common structure of selves and societies. But the reason for my basic preference for the other category for analyzing narrative is that narratives quite obviously present the connection of intention and action, and also that of persons and circumstances in interaction. They do so in a nexus in which inwardness and the subject at the moment just prior to and moving into event are not a privileged perspective— either in what is described or in the device used for description. The novelist knows his subject from the inside in a more intimate way than the historian, because he knows (and by way of his knowing) the unity of private and public life, of character and circumstance, in the whole web of the novel's transactions and in the case of each character. Historical narrative—especially of the biographical kind, but also of the life in sequence of a cultural unit—is built on the same paradigm, except that the historian does not know the intention-action links of his agents in as close and integrated fashion as the novelist.

A man is known precisely to the extent that he is what he does and what is done to him. A character in the realistic novel may not be simply his public role or *persona;* but his role is that of describable action and to that extent our *slant* on him is public. He is neither envisaged nor formed nor read as a private, inferred, hidden self for which action is merely symbolic. The novelist also knows, in a way the historian does not, the direct connection between his characters and their words, but I should want to claim that he knows these only to the extent that a character is firmly ingredient in his public life, in the interaction of what he does and what is done to him, by which—rather than through his words—he becomes himself. (In short, I should want to claim that the most characteristic instance of action is that of bodied, external action rather than that in which the speaking itself is the doing—without wishing to deny for a moment the usefulness or integrity of the category of "performative utterance.") Intentional action is causal knowledge internally connected with bodily movement in an external context. These two descriptions, intentional action and self-body descriptions, interweave. Self-word or self-culture description comes last in the order of importance of identity description. Except on the basis of the other two, I doubt that it makes sense. I think that in connection with the Gospels this fact is well illustrated by the difficulties that "new questers" and hermeneuticians have in trying to glean the identity of Jesus from his message rather than, first of all, from the description of what he did and underwent.

But I want to say that intentional action description *categories* finally break down, though the description itself does not. One can,

I think, describe the passage of intention into action (and the categories for it) and the unity and mutual dependence of intention and action without appealing to the ontological ground of that unity, of which we have no direct or descriptive knowledge such as we have of the unity and passage from intention to action itself. One can also describe how an external occurrence or somebody else's action can become ingredient in a person's intentional action. In other words, I can describe my response to my interpretation of and reaction to something done to me. But the interaction of character and circumstance is more than this. I become what I am also by what is done to me and becomes a determinative part of me—and that not only by my interpretation of, or reaction to, it. Events and character interact in such a way that the events themselves become part of our identities and are not merely fielded by an already existent, finished identity structure. And for this interaction there is no categoreal description scheme. Here the intentional action description scheme is outstripped. To show that this situation is really so, that there is such a direct mutual determination of character and circumstance, all one can do is to tell the particular story of it. But I want to claim that in certain narrative or aesthetic contexts, these two things—character and circumstance—belong so closely together that for descriptive purposes we know the person or persons portrayed through his or their story. This is the case in the last stage of the gospel story, and on this basis I would say that the person of Jesus, and not only his message, is both indispensable to, and known in, the story. Who is Jesus in the gospel story, and under what identification or description do we know him? He is who he is by what he does and undergoes, and chiefly we must say that he is Jesus crucified and raised. That is the simple fruit of identity analysis of the New Testament narrative, both in the mode of intention-action description (with its categories finally transcended) and in the mode of subject–self-manifestation description. Hence my claim that we have in these narratives a high Christology —not before, but after any "demythologization" or transfer of the "meaning" of the story to "our day" that may be necessary.

It is an instructive contrast to see James M. Robinson at work in *A New Quest of the Historical Jesus*. In the full flush of excitement over the discovery of the "new" category of *existentiell* self-understanding that gives us access to the "historical" Jesus in a way in which an "objectifying" historical method supposedly did not, we find Robinson constantly making reference to that subject who is, in his *existentiell* self-understanding *immediately* and not remotely in back of his decisions and their outward enactment. But whether remotely or immediately, the point is that he remains in back, at least, of the enactment and circumstances *(New Quest,* pp. 67–68).

What in fact we see here is one more failing endeavor to account
for a unity between decision and outward happening after they have
been irremediably pulled apart. And hence we have a final appeal
to an undemonstrated unity of Jesus' message and person in order
to guarantee the unwarranted unity of his person and deeds (cf.
New Quest, pp. 69–70) Robinson's is a particularly drastic or simplistic case of this procedure, but we see it on all sides: Bornkamm,
Funk, Conzelmann, Ebeling, Fuchs—name them! The move of the
new hermeneutic to unite past and present meaning through an
ontology of language so that "language" itself speaks and thereby
bridges the gap between a past and present "linguistic event" and
meaning, advances the situation not one whit; it makes it merely
more obscure. Language still remains private and at best instantiated in inner attitudes: The outer world and the embodied self
remain detached from that inner "world" even if, or especially if, it
is claimed that the world is constituted by language. Despite ambiguous moves in a contrary direction, Pannenberg finally also grounds
his Christology in the dubious linkage between message and person in the Gospels. What lies in back of this procedure, so deeply
embedded in the contemporary exegetical and theological tradition
that its presence is hardly noticed any longer, is the twofold Idealistic assumption that the basic phenomenology of human being is
that of the subject-self revealed in, or present through, words; and
that the thread of continuity in history finally lies in ideas inside
people's minds, to which we have access—even if these ideas take
the shape not of speculative concepts but of hopes or expectations
to be fulfilled, decisions constitutive of the self that makes them,
or words that constitute events.

All the strictures by Schubert Ogden and Van Harvey against
Robinson's procedure, especially that of finding the clue to the person in the message, are quite right. But this (contrary to Ogden
and Harvey) does not mean that there is no way of finding out if
Christology is the meaning of the gospel story and if the person of
Jesus in known to us as a character in that story. Harvey and
Ogden—the latter more than the former—are much too beholden
to their opponents' Idealist analysis in anthropology and biblical
hermeneutics—in which the "true" self is hidden in back of its action
and word, so that the meaning of texts is invariably in part the fruit
of the life-perspective with which we approach them—to be able to
adjudicate that question properly. My plea then is that formaliza-
tion of the categories of understanding, their application is an aesthetic context, and a procedure of aesthetic analysis in which even
the formal categories must finally be left behind (at least in part)
can help us solve the hermeneutical problem of the synoptic Gospels. We can, at least in part, overcome the perspectivist position

and the *existentiell* self-understanding assumption of interpretation that underlies the analyses both of the new questers and their opponents.

Now it is perfectly patent that this claim has some radical apologetic drawbacks. Left-wing and right-wing Bultmannians and some others all agree—from Michalson through Robinson and Bornkamm to Harvey, Ogden, Braun, and Buri—that "meaning" (in connection with the Gospel narratives) is more than aesthetic; it is, at least potentially, life-meaning and, therefore, always a potentially common perspective between past and present, text and interpreter. Concerning the meaning of the historic Christian texts, Michalson has this to say:

> The faith, being history, carries its own power to convince. There is nothing magic in this liaison. History occurs when an event which was meaningful for others becomes meaningful for me. There is no way of establishing a meaningful connection with an event from outside the event. Yet, when the event does become meaningful *through one's inner connection with it* it does so with a suddenness and illumination which dispels resistance and thus dispenses with apologetics. (*Worldly Theology: The Hermeneutical Focus of an Historical Faith* [New York: Scribner, 1967], pp. 101 f.; italics mine. Cf. *The Hinge of History* [New York: Scribner, 1959], p. 184)

Michalson rightly characterizes the view that confines what we understand by the meaning of a past event to its "inner connection" with "me" as "omnicompetent exegetical procedure." There is nothing that left-wing Bultmannians cannot agree with here, provided that "event" is understood as the kerygma or *message* in its impact (or "inner connection" with "me"), and not as the kerygmatic *person* known in his impact. (Van Harvey will want to opt out of Michalson's game on other grounds, namely, Michalson's well-nigh incredible tendency to identify our knowledge about the *occurrence* of a past event with our perspective on its meaning.) The point to be made is that his omnicompetent procedure of inner connection with "me" (i.e., with the perspective I bring to it and find illumined, accepted, or defeated there) is precisely what Michalson says it is not. It *is* apologetic. Meaning is personal or life-meaning. It is to this general genre, and to the question it raises, or rather to the question I am in raising it that the meaning of the text belongs. The text cannot help it. The omnicompetent procedure makes sure of it.

In other words, perspectivism raises the hermeneutical question inexorably as a material rather than formal question of meaning (i.e., as a question of life-meaning uniting the texts) and a present (or "pre-") understanding of life, either in harmony or in significant conflict. This is once again, but now at the hermeneutical level, the same apologetic question raised by the dominant systematic and anthropological tradition in theology. In this context it is the question: How can we so read the text that a life-perspective we find in it can become a significant or genuine possibility for us? What I am proposing instead is that we raise the question in a drastically nonapologetic, nonperspectivist fashion: "What does this narrative say or mean, never mind whether it can become a meaningful possibility of life perspective for us or not?" Its meaning, on the one hand, and its possible as well as actual truth for us, on the other hand, are two totally different questions. If we do that, it seems to me that we come up with a result that the meaning of the narrative is, indeed, Christological in a very strong sense, and Christological in a sense that is focused on Jesus, and either not at all or only from him on the story focused on our relation to him. If that is the case, if the Christology focused by Jesus' death and resurrection is the real meaning rather than a mythological or time-conditioned form of the real meaning of the narrative, it may well mean to the left-wing Bultmannian that the meaning of the gospel story and the possibility of accepting it or having it render life-sense are mutually exclusive. The logic of that narrative, as well as the kind of "hermeneutical morality" appropriate to it, may be antipathetic to the logic and "morality of historical knowledge" as he has defined it. Well, why not? Isn't there something to be said in favor of this clean cut, instead of an apologetic, dying a death of a thousand qualifications by postulating an infinite and perhaps wholly unnecessary regress of the meaning of the gospel story, the tacit assumption of which is really that there are no criteria for estimating what it is, except its effect? It means what you feel like having it mean. The only way to claim more than that on grounds other than those I am suggesting would be to have an acknowledged authority telling us what it means. In the absence of that authority—and there is no way in which tradition can establish its authority except by authoritarian means—the story seems to mean whatever you want, depending on what "perspective" or "modern view of man" you happen to come from as you read the story and want to find substantiated there.

Now it is perfectly obvious that there are certain implications to my proposals. First of all, I want to plead that the aesthetic model or approach, by virtue of which I claim the story has a definite meaning, be allowed its own integrity. I said earlier that the predominance of the text over the categories or methods of understanding it may force us to scramble our methods. I want to reiterate that claim now. It may well turn out that the text, precisely when approached aesthetically and, hence, quite formally and nonexistentially, may force, for example, existential considerations of the most serious kind on us. It wouldn't be the first text to do so!

But the main point I want to make is that we may be in the position of understanding stories in a way far better than the account we can render of the methods or categories by which we understand them. Our understanding of a text is often far greater than our understanding of how we can understand it. It is my claim that the aesthetic and formal approach I have proposed does greater justice to that possibility than the restrictive and exclusive methodological devices of the existentialist and hermeneutical schools. It does so in various ways, but finally by pointing radically beyond its own categories and simply to the story itself. Hence, my plea that this aesthetic procedure, precisely because it may allow a jumble of methods in which the text itself is dominant over the methods, be allowed its own integrity as one distinct approach. We must finally get out of the eternal round of chasing to and fro (or concluding uneasy compromises) between "historical" and "faith" or "kerygmatic" or "existential" approaches.

Obviously, my next plea would be for a *priority* of this distinct approach over others, equally distinct—with which it must not be confused—that have their own rights and freedom. But this is obviously in one way an arbitrary priority choice. One can equally well go about it in another way and make a historical or kerygmatic preference choice. I am only saying that to the extent that the gospel stories are, indeed, in the form of narratives, let us treat them that way when we ask about their meaning. This does not deny the validity of source, form, and redaction criticism—in other words, of a variety of historical approaches both to the fact estimation and the meaning of these stories. Nor does it deny—on the contrary, it affirms— the active, though unsystematic, interplay of historical, aesthetic, and religious understanding in comprehending a text. Who knows what may result when we scramble methods? The only plea I make is for distinction and priority choice. Let us keep our methodological principles sharply distinct, but let us by all means acknowledge that in the actual reading of the texts they enter into each other in ways for which there is usually no general, abstractable superprinciple. It is impossible to state a general theory covering the interaction of historical and aesthetic criticism: They interact in practice! But depending on what we do, one kind of reading will have priority. And if we try to understand the text *internally* (to itself), we must try for a reading in which the text itself is the meaning, the narrative form indispensable to the narrative's meaning.

The Gospels, historians generally agree, are late products in the formation of the early tradition. Very well, what does it matter? Our

knowledge of what is earlier—and its relation to what comes later—
is bound to stay inferential, speculative, or proximate as Kierkegaard
called it. If we wish, we can make our priority choice historical and
then try to cull out the central meaning of the New Testament from
the presumed shape of the earlier strata and their reconstructed meaning. I should prefer to do it the other way (i.e., order the aesthetic
above the historical analysis) precisely because of the built-in inference and ambiguity factor between the factual-historical estimate
and the meaning consequently allowable, if one proceeds historically (to say nothing of the possible influence a life-perspective of
mine with regard to the New Testament might have on my estimate of what is earlier and what is later in order to show forth one
meaning of the earliest tradition rather than another—for example,
that the earliest tradition was more nearly eschatological rather
than Christological, or the other way around).

It seems to me that the crucial point about the authority of the
New Testament—and the beginning, at least, of an answer to the
question, What is Christianity?—is precisely that we must start at some
point where meaning is firmly grounded in the text and nowhere else.
This identity or unity of text and meaning does not of itself bestow
authority, but without it there can be no authority.

If we take seriously the fact that in a story character and circumstance are nothing without each other, at least one puzzle over the
text's meaning will become easier—that concerning the priority of
Christology or eschatology. Jesus *is* his story. (Karl Barth makes the
same point when he says that Jesus *is* reconciliation and not simply
the Reconciler who would then, in a separable action or sequence,
enact reconciliation.) Now that story is only in one sense finished; in
another sense it is part of a larger story, an aspect of which came before
this part of the story, another aspect of which succeeds it and is not
yet finished. What is important is not simply Jesus, but the circumstance interwoven with him: The triumphant coming of God's reign.
This is one way we can say that we have a series of stories (Old
Testament, the Gospels, history since then and to the end) among
which it is possible to work out one or a variety of literary rela-
tionships (e.g., "typology", "anticipation-fulfillment"). In another way
we have to say that what we have is stages in one cumulative story
or even a smaller story (the gospel story) set within a larger one.
The point is that since Jesus' story is only in one sense finished
and since character and circumstance are always united, there can
be *no* priority choice between Christology and eschatology in understanding the meaning of the smaller story—the Gospels themselves—or the larger story, that of human history. The choice we
face is really on another matter: Shall we, as it were, radiate out
from the Gospels with their firm meaning (in the interaction of

character and circumstance) to the earlier and later story (that of the Old Testament and that of human history since Jesus Christ)? Or shall we reverse the procedure and move from the wider or narrower context of history and experience (do they actually of themselves constitute even incipiently a unified story or a narrative pattern? I doubt it—*pace* Moltmann, Pannenberg, and Sauter) to the Gospels for deeper insight on that wider context and the pre-understanding of it that we bring with us? I doubt that the latter procedure will yield much significance from the gospel story. Why not proceed the way the Church has traditionally done, even if the Gospels are bound to be an *incomplete* clue to the rest of Scripture, and a necessarily *ambiguous* clue to the experience of history, both as narrated in the Old Testament and as we, simply as members of the human race, experience it. Incomplete, even ambiguous—yes, but not without meaning, as long as we understand that in the gospels Jesus *is* nothing other than his story, and that this both is the story of God with him and all mankind, and is *included* in that story—that the Gospels are not simply the story of a being who is to be served by this story for purposes of the metaphysical definition of his being.

Obviously, an aesthetic model such as I have advocated is highly nominalistic or pluralistic with regard to texts. Only one narrative at a time can be interpreted—one cannot even cover Luke and Mark by the same story analysis, to say nothing of non-narrative texts. Yet I would claim that even though the New Testament cannot be covered by any one hermeneutical principle or set of devices, this one will have a larger range of concrete application than others. To mention only John and Paul: Are we not better off if we regard what they have to say centrally, as commentary on this story (or sequence of narratable events from passion to resurrection because Paul, at any rate, presumably did not have the story before him in the same form as we do) rather than on the basis of some other organizing principle (e.g., justification by faith)? We are obviously at liberty to do otherwise, but I should think it is at least a good hypothesis that this organizing principle is better, i.e., has a wider range of applicability within the New Testament canon, than many another.

That leaves the question of the transition from the aesthetic, nonapologetic understanding to the truth claim—historical, metaphysical, and existential. I'm not a bit sure what I can say here that Anselm or Calvin or Barth have not already said. All I can add is that to the Christian the truth of the story can present no problem, and, therefore, its meaning in formal aesthetic description *is* its truth. To the unbeliever, on the other hand, its meaning and its possible as well as actual truth are two totally different things. To the pilgrim—and who isn't?—the possibility of its truth is not often a matter of the evidence for it, but of the surprising scramble in our understanding and life that this story unaccountably produces: Understanding it aesthetically often entails the factual affirmation and existential commitment that it appears to demand as part of its own storied pattern.

2

Theological Reflections
on the Accounts
of Jesus' Death
and Resurrection

This important essay sets forth Frei's provocative proposal about the Gospel narratives. When approached with literary or aesthetic sensitivity, yet with a real appreciation for the results of critical biblical scholarship, the depictions of Jesus' death and resurrection in the Gospels cannot be made to square, Frei argues, with the kind of Christology that has dominated modern theology. What they offer by their peculiar literary structure, indeed, what they urge so insistently, is not a universal "religious symbol," however conceived, but rather the singularity of Jesus in his exclusive identity as the savior.

Frei's argument gains much of its power from specifically literary and philosophical modes of thought. The argument is not so much a theological appeal to faith as an analytical appeal to reason. The literary analysis is inspired by Eric Auerbach and the philosophical analysis by Gilbert Ryle. The former pits "realistic narrative" against "myth" as the genre that more nearly illuminates the Gospel accounts; the latter rejects Cartesian dualism, with its lingering "ghost in the machine," in favor of more holistic approaches to depicting personal identity. On these grounds Frei protests against any conceptual devices—whether they be ambitious philosophical "systems" or Kierkegaardian resorts to "paradox"—that threaten to overwhelm the narratives. When the literary structures are taken on their own terms, it is finally Jesus who holds his own predicates together in the story, not they him; just as it is finally he who bestows meaning on the titles the story uses to describe him, rather

45

than the reverse. Although later presented in a more elaborate form by Frei's book The Identity Of Jesus Christ *(Philadelphia: Fortress Press, 1975), the proposal in this earlier version has often been judged by Frei's readers to be superior for its relative straightforwardness and clarity.*

* * *

The story told in the Gospels, which became the cornerstone of the Christian tradition of belief, is distinguished from other, parallel accounts by its urgent insistence that the story of salvation is completely and exclusively that of the savior Jesus from Nazareth in Galilee. This exclusiveness distinguishes the story both from ancient dying and rising savior myths and from a kind of story to which it is formally much closer: that of the Christ figures of some modern novels. The form of the Gospel story is sufficiently novel-like that we have to say that the pattern of redemptive action exhibited in Jesus is so identical with his personal story that he preempts the pattern. It is *his* story and cannot be reiterated in full by the story of anybody else—just as any particular person's story, whether fictional or real, is exclusively his own and not also that of somebody else.

The inextricable, mutual involvement of specific, unsubstitutable chains of events with equally specific individuals is a common feature of historical description and the narrative of the classical novel. (Beyond it there are of course great differences between the two.) However, in both instances, history as well as fiction, we meet with a problem of interpretation. Without some perspective of our own the story has no discernibly significant shape for us; but on the other hand we must not imprint either our own life problems or our own ideological analyses on it. The proper approach is to keep the tools of interpretive analysis as minimal and formal as possible, so that the character(s) and the narrative of events may emerge in their own right.

The significantly unique identity of an individual, in this instance Jesus of Nazareth, is to be discerned by asking (1) where the bond between intention and action in his story is most clearly evident; and (2) where the direct bond between himself as individual subject and his outward self-manifestation is strongest and most clearly unitary in character. The answer to both questions is in the crucifixion-resurrection sequence. Here he is most of all himself in his unique and specific human identity as Jesus from Nazareth in Galilee. In this sense the story, whether fictional or historical, is quite clearly nonmythological. (Myths are stories in which character and action are not irreducibly themselves. Instead they are representative of broader and not directly representable psychic or cosmic states,

states in some sense "transcending" the scene of finite, particular occurrences.)

The obvious implication of this claim is that if one is to make the mysterious and always problematical transition from literary description to judgments both of historical fact and of faith concerning this particular story and its significance, it is at this climactic point of Jesus' resurrection that one must do so. Similarly, the point of transition and connection between the person and teaching of Jesus in the Gospels and the "kerygma" concerning Jesus Christ and true life through him in the early church's faith, mirrored in the New Testament writings, can be none other than the story of the resurrection. A further implication—which I do not develop in this argument—is that the resurrection must, in the eyes of those who believe, be a factual occurrence of a wholly unique kind, the conceptual content of which is the climactic establishment of Jesus' identity. This means that the resurrection events are not, in the first place, reducible to an ontological status allowing us to call them peculiarly "verbal" in contrast to "objective" or "factual" events (the position of Gerhard Ebeling).

Secondly, it goes almost without saying that the conceptual content of the resurrection, whether fictional or real, cannot be reduced to the faith of the disciples (the position of Rudolf Bultmann). Finally the resurrection cannot be reduced to a kind of occurrence, for the credibility of which historical evidence from the New Testament and from the experience of historical life in general would be pertinent. And, therefore, the character of the resurrection appearances cannot be compared and contrasted speculatively to that of other occurrences: e.g., we cannot say that they are more like visions than like experiences of a physical miracle, or vice versa (the position of Wolfhart Pannenberg).

The Distinctive Patterns of the Story of Jesus

Gods were raised from the dead in liberal numbers in the ancient world, especially at the time of the birth of the Christian community. We ought to make clear to ourselves at the outset that the claim of the early Christians was in one sense, therefore, not all unique. Historians of religion often point out this fact, and its implication is obvious. If you have a very large number of candidates for the same unproved miraculous occurrence, the likelihood is that the claim of one is as good as that of the others, that it is none too good for any of them, and that for the *real* explanation of resurrection you had best look elsewhere—to the mythforming, poetic, and religious yearning and imagination of ancient peoples.

Against this sort of argument Christian believers, searching their Bibles, find that they have no ace up their sleeve. Even the form of the particular resurrection story which lies at the heart of the New Testament Gospel may have certain parallels outside the Scripture, reducing its uniqueness even as a literary account, to say nothing of its unique factual claim. Yet we would be remiss if we did not also recognize that there are tenacious and often haunting qualities about the New Testament death and resurrection story concerning Jesus Christ which do not easily fit the patterns of other ancient accounts of dying and rising gods. The precise literary parallels would have to be demonstrated by those looking for them.

Caution in generalizing on this matter becomes the layman. However, it appears that there are at least two types of the "redeemed redeemer" motif in the religious syncretism of the era of late antiquity. There is the ritualistic, ecstatic participation in the dying and rising god of mystery religion. There is also the Gnostics' reflective, depth-introspective insight into the identity of the mythical, fallen archetypal man with the ascending mythical divine savior figure. I take it that the debate about the extent to which the Gnostic version of the redeemed redeemer motif is either typical of or original with the Gnostics is so far inconclusive. I assume further that there is some real question concerning the parallel between the phenomenon in both forms and the thoroughgoing, on the surface at least much more radical, application of the same or a similar motif to Jesus in the Gospels. I should want to raise the question at least if, for example, in the case of both Gnostic and mystery savior the relation between his fallen (dying) and his redeemed (rising) states is not much more natural and organic than it is when the motif is applied to Jesus Christ in the Gospels.

The Unique Descriptive Identity of Jesus

One thing is sure. The early Christians identified the mysterious, to most minds no more than half-way personal savior figure *exclusively* with Jesus of Nazareth, allowing no other name to be substituted. In two ways this claim was quite uncanny in their religious surroundings. First, as we have said, in this association of cosmic redeemer and human person they would allow no *human* substitute for Jesus. Secondly, they tended strongly to have the human person, Jesus, bestow identity upon the savior figure rather than the other way round (although we have to note that while the testimony of the New Testament is unanimous on the first point, it is not nearly so unambiguous on the second). The emphasis was on the confession that *Jesus* is the mysterious Lord of the cosmos. They emphasized this rather than the reverse, i.e., that everyone believes in the hope and reality of a cosmic redeemer and Jesus happens somehow to fit him or remind us of him.

People have often been converted against their own wills and most strenuous inclinations. Many of the New Testament writers had been either pagans or paganized, Hellenized Jews in origin. At times—I am thinking of Mark as well as the Pauline and Johannine writings—it seems almost as if the pagan cosmic savior figure or the Jewish Son of man figure is still very vivid and real to the New Testament writers, and that they are still astounded by the fact that to think of him at all they now have to think of him as Jesus of Nazareth; yet so think of him they must. It was this exclusive identification that made Christianity more clearly than most others the religion of the "redeemed redeemer." In other religions the savior's having to be redeemed (he undergoes death) and himself doing the redeeming (we rise with him) easily merged into one process. Likewise it seems that the line which separated his bestowal of immortal divine salvation upon men from their achievement of it by their own insight—knowing him through a kind of mystical inward penetration rather than by meeting him in the occurrences of the world —was often very thin and blurred. A good many paths to salvation seem to have depended on first making and then overcoming such distinctions as these.

But in the case of the Gospels the figure of the cosmic redeemer was indeed so completely identified with the human being Jesus of Nazareth, and he in turn was so completely at one with his human brethren, that *he* the *savior* became just as helpless as they (a statement that must, however, be modified drastically in the case of the Gospel of John). There is no natural, organic transition from his need for redemption to his being redeemed. The divine figure suddenly stands before us without his divine power, especially as that power would affect himself. Indeed, there was truth in the sarcastic remark that he could bring salvation to others but not to himself.

The theme on which we are touching now is dangerous and has sometimes been driven to the point of a literalistic, simple-minded, speculative, and rather incredible heresy (i.e., that in the incarnation the Word of God divested himself deliberately and self-consciously of omnipotence over the world). But a heresy is often the sign that orthodoxy has sacrificed the elements of mystery, and along with it tentativeness or open-endedness, to an oversimplified consistency. Jesus' followers in the early church did not doubt that the work of saving men was the work of omnipotence. But it is equally true and far more easily forgotten that they believed this power to be mysteriously congruent with Jesus' all too human helplessness and lack of power in the face of the terrible chain of events leading to his death, once that chain had begun to be wound around him. We find these two apparently contradictory tendencies converging in the

gospel narrative. To make them harmonious by means of an explanation or theory of Jesus' passion would be very difficult indeed;
but in the story—the descriptive and interpretative retelling of the
events—they fit together naturally and easily. We are given hints
of his abiding power, of the abiding initiative that remains in his
hands even at the moments when he is most evidently helpless,
when acted upon rather than agent. But his helplessness is at least
equally manifest and genuine. The two are never merged; one may
say both that they coexist as well as that there is a transition
through circumstances from one to the other.

However, it is easy to exaggerate the contrast between Jesus'
power and his powerlessness, so that before long he appears to be
nothing more than the human point of coordination where these two
contrasting qualities (and any two others for that matter, e.g., love
and wrath) come together. He is then seen as the embodiment of
paradox—an affirmation which has often been made by theologians
and in a different way by modern novelists who have been preoccupied with this figure. But that way lie lifelessness and the dehydra-
tion of any man's humanity. For a man's being is not the juxtaposition of characteristics or sets of qualities, contrasted or otherwise, that
become embodied in him. A man's being is the unique and peculiar
way in which he himself holds together the qualities which he embodies—or rather, the qualities which he *is*.

Modern scholars have told us rather convincingly that we do not
know much about the "historical Jesus" who stands behind the gospel portraits of him. Nevertheless, the descriptions themselves as
descriptions, whatever we may or may not be able to conclude about
the "real" man in back of them, surely portray something profoundly
human in at least one respect. They are the portrait of a person and
not of a series of characteristics or changing circumstances, paradoxically or otherwise related and held together in one (of necessity) by a person-figure. If there is the paradoxical embodiment of
contrasted qualities about him and his experience in the portrait,
they are held together because they are *his*. As he is sketched out in
the gospel accounts, he holds these contrasts together, not they him.
That is why the word "paradox" ought at least to be used with caution in reference to the personal being of Jesus of Nazareth, and why
this warning was necessary even with regard to our own description,
seeing that we had drawn intention to one such basic "paradoxical"
contrast between power and powerlessness.

When we speak of the contrast of power and powerlessness in
Jesus as he is depicted in the Gospels, we have in mind then no mere
paradox, tension or transition between two states, qualities, or elements in a cosmic, spiritual power struggle. Rather, we have in mind
the mystery and the changing situation of a human being whose

consistent intention is also portrayed as that of his and the universe's God: the accomplishment of men's salvation. For that reason the contrast and its holding together are best expressed in terms of the quality of love in his relation to his fellow men. But we must stress that the quality is not simply and directly predominant over all other characteristics that we may see together with it.

The unity of his personal being depicted in the Gospels, we are saying, is not to be seen directly, by adumbrating the personal excellences discernible in him and then choosing that most noticeable in comparison to the others as the first. That unity is seen more nearly indirectly as the shaping of all his personal qualities in conformation to his mission or aspiration in obedience to God. In this sense love to men governed his life. In this respect his intention was, as far as the portraits show him to us, wholly assimilated to the intention of his heavenly Father who, in the words of the fourth Gospel's commentary on the story of Jesus, "so loved the world that he gave his only son" (John 3:16). It may not be too bold to say, though we have no warrant for it by direct instance from the gospel stories, that in the service of this love Jesus was willing to govern and exercise the power appropriate to it, just as he was willing for its sake to be governed and suffer helplessly when the occasion demanded.

In other words, the coexistence as well as the transition between power and powerlessness, of which we have spoken, are ordered by the single-minded intention of Jesus to enact the good of men on their behalf in obedience to God. It is he who holds and orders all his qualities, and he, insofar as his single-minded intention is his being or his identity, who orders the situation about him as it affects him. In short, he makes his power and his powerlessness congruent to each other.

The Failure of the "Christ Figure"

There has been one particularly interesting result of the modern and direct (in contrast to the Gospels' more nearly indirect) identification of the mission or intention with the personal character of Jesus as love, an identification that has resulted in the elevation of love over every other personal virtue in him as the single excellence of his character The result has been a simplistic overdrawing, frequently pressing all too close upon the mysteriousness of the figure of Jesus who after all, does not, in the portraiture of the Gospels, come provided with a single clue to unlock his character, not even with a clear-cut predominance of love deportment.

The resultant direct characterization distorts and exaggerates the modern writer's refracted picture. It is often quite right—yet it is simplistic and doctrinaire. Modern writers, especially novelists, have often discerned the well-nigh modern personal and historical vividness of the original man in his portrait (in contrast to so much unhistorical, not genuinely personal ancient writing).[1] Hence, writers of this century have taken Jesus to be the paradigm of humanity more than other ancient fictional figures except perhaps Odysseus or Oedipus and more than other ancient historical personages.

But they tend to forget that love as mission and as sole personal deportment or virtue is not identically and without differentiation the same thing. They forget furthermore (or wish they could forget), that there are stylized elements in the original accounts that cannot be ignored. The conceptions of the savior figure, eternal life, sacrifice, God, miracle, and salvation are intrinsic to the original accounts. Modern writers by contrast (and perfectly correctly) take only the historical, personal, and not the stylized elements of the story. That is, after all, what the character of a novel demands. They see the intention and the personal character of a wholly personal love, and they make these the clue to a character-in-action description. The result is often ironic. For now we get, in the name of flesh-and-blood life and in protest against conceptual stylization, a stylized and stereotyped figure whom critics can then label with the rather awful and by now tired term, "Christ figure." It is sufficiently stereotyped and artificial that it often comes to life only if, in addition to its obvious mirroring of Jesus, there are some important details in which the figure comes into its own, either in contrast to or at least in deviation from the portrait of Jesus.

Many times, however, there is something artificial and predictable about the prefashioned qualities or states of potential conflict in character and historical circumstances, both within the savior figure and between him and his environment, which are put together in order compositely to produce a saving man—in the literature from Victor Hugo's *Les Misérables* and Dostoievsky's *The Idiot* to the defeated yet conquering, shameful yet pure heroes of Graham Greene's and François Mauriac's novels. The savior figure here becomes unwittingly and ironically stylized, even though the intention is evidently just the opposite—to rescue him as far as possible from ancient stylization and to invest him with a fully personal dimension. In the wake of this stylization of a human, personal figure (rather than an ancient savior figure) there seems often to be an empty place—a purely passive, *vague lacuna* exactly at the point where (in a genuine human being) one expects to find the focus, centeredness, and capacity both for initiative and receptivity which breathe life into the virtues and qualities of his humanity.

While theologians were engaged in trying to restate the uniqueness of the New Testament savior in terms other than the "mythological" ones of the original sources, novelists were doing the same.

Writers of fiction have attempted to find a modern and personal equivalent to ancient stylization and miracle about Jesus. They have done this by trying to show that utterly contrasted qualities, situations, and perspectives come to focus on this figure, whether in conflict or in harmony. *Here*, they have suggested, such conflicts and contrasts (e.g., murder and innocence or purity) which usually remain unresolved, can be shown to cohere in poignantly, indeed exemplarily lifelike fashion. This coherence of clashing elements in or about the personal being and/or fate of the savior figure has been the modern substitute for the ancient concept of miracle and for that contrast between the ordinary and the unique which miracle implies.

Thus modern novelists indicate the veiled coherence of his authority with his helplessness as these are manifest especially in his stance in the presence of religious (and other) viciousness, power, and hypocrisy. The savior figure mysteriously combines rebellion against constituted authority (showing it up for a brutal fraud, and along with it a good many ordinarily decent standards) with great and selfless goodness, the prime quality of all self-sacrificing, absolute love.

The combination of rebellion with pure selflessness usually means some route of opposition to prevalent authority and evil other than that of violence, even though there are times when the latter is involved. But even then there is about this violence often a kind of primordial innocence, so that the basic purity of the figure remains untouched by it. (Yet even this must be modified. At times he combines utter goodness with full guilt—an especially appealing way of portraying miracle or the paradox which the savior unites.) Ordinarily, however, he combines innocence, even ignorance, with wisdom and sensitivity. He manifests and embodies sheer purity in such a way that, paradoxically, it is of greater comfort to those who are themselves soiled than to those who are or at any rate seek to be too much like him. (Thus he is, as the church's Lord, taken to be among those outside rather than with those inside the fold.) So he is invariably more nearly at home in soiled, broken, and vitiated rather than conventional communities; he is almost invariably anti-bourgeois; he is in the demi-monde rather than in the family (which, together with constituted authority, is one of the savior's most persistent, evil, and hypocritical opponents—most often in the form of marriage partner or parent). Additionally, however, one often finds that he is present in all communities, good or evil, ordinary or extraordinary, as a visitor and stranger from elsewhere.

The refracted portrait usually draws attention to his hidden intention to manifest and embody love, utterly without obsessive possessiveness and therefore usually willing to suffer painfully and passively in the face of rejection. It is an intention that is never self-

advertised and yet steadily seeks the good of the other person; but—
and the point is important—the intention is content to remain consistently veiled, or at least half veiled, ambiguous, and defeated in the
man's lifetime, never quite discernible though always nearly so. Hints
of the mystery break through, but they are clearly apprehended (with
pain and sometimes with healing, sorrowing relief) only after his
apparently futile death. Indeed all that he is and does come to focus
in this final denouement and in our retrospective glance from and
toward it.

After that climactic event, which he must risk totally without
comfort not only in its terror but also in its possible futility, the
waters of the tide of events close once again over the whole episode, as they do over all things historical—leaving the situation at
one and the same time just as it was before, ambiguous and with
evil to the fore, and yet wholly different, with a moment of truth
a now unveiled and with meaning newly enhanced in the consciousness of some participant character(s) and/or the reader. It is always
too late and yet not too late in the world of time, so that futility and
victory now join together in this transition from the figure's denouement to the new consciousness within and beyond the confines of
the fictional world. He conquers, yet he does not conquer because he
is defeated. But if he conquers it is by virtue of the fact that his victory is veiledly identical with his defeat. It is the victory and defeat of
love.

It is not only the heroes of modern fiction, in their veiled, unadvertised, and unadvertising intention to seek the good of others
(often looking like its very opposite), who correspond to this refracted
portrait. In their very anonymity, serving Christ secretly or as outsiders because that is the only way to serve him with passionate disin-
terest in the distorted yet pitiable world, some recent historical figures have echoed and embodied that same portrait in the eyes of many
people: for example, Søren Kierkegaard (in at least one stage of his
life) in the last century; Simone Weil and Dag Hammarskjöld, in this.

Who would not be able to hear the echo of the original story in
these elements of its reiteration? To many a convinced Christian
this reiteration is indeed by far the most convincing argument for
Christianity—far greater than theoretical argument, sacrament, and
proclamation (granted that these various things may "convince"
concerning different matters). Yet the portrayal of this intention,
the mysterious and self-sacrificing enactment of men's good on their
behalf, is bound to depart from the New Testament story in various ways. The main clue to that fact lies in the reversal to which I
have already pointed. There are elements in the New Testament
which are cast into ancient, stylized thought patterns (Jesus as the
fulfillment of the figure of the cosmic savior, the redeemer of Israel,

miracles, etc.) and are therefore bound to look mythological to the modern reader. Jesus does indeed, in the New Testament, bestow in a most startling manner a human, personal identity upon the stylized savior notion. But the latter element does and must remain part of the original; otherwise we simply do not have the New Testament portrait of Jesus as the Christ (to borrow Paul Tillich's phrase).

To try to historicize these stylized concepts is obviously impossible for the modern fiction writer. But his own consequent reversal is equally unfortunate. He transfers the intent of the stylized element to the personal, historical description and tries to indicate by means of the mysterious coincidence of clashing elements in personal encounters (victory with defeat, purity vicariously present to impurity, guilt with goodness, etc.) the miraculous ingredient at the heart of the figure, corresponding to the stylized element in the original account. The result is the predictable pattern of a savior figure whose person and history are the embodiment of preestablished opposite human or personal qualities. The result in other words is a stylization of the humanity of Jesus through the juxtaposition of predictably contrasting predicates (contrasting either within himself, or between himself and his context). They have, at their juncture or point of coordination, a subject who is hardly a subject in his own right and therefore cannot hold the predicates as his own. In short we have a modern equivalent of the ancient denial of Jesus' humanity in the Christ-figure motif.

In the Gospels, on the other hand, the stylized elements are there, but they do not overcome the concreteness of the man portrayed. He is, as we have suggested, not simply the coincidence of those opposites that come together in and about him, nor is his saving activity a function of their coincidence. His saving activity, though nothing without his enactment of it in his and his people's circumstances, is in one sense prior to these circumstances and even to the qualities which he comes to embody. He *intends* the enactment of his saving love, and he consents to its defeat. And in harmony with his intention, his power as well as his helplessness take shape in appropriate response to varying circumstance. It is *he* who holds the pattern, including that of opposites, together, not they him—not even love as the most dominant quality, which would tie itself and its opposite into one.

The point is to be made, then, that if one identifies the savior figure with a fully human being, the story cannot be retold by substituting somebody else as its hero who is then made to be fully identical with that original person. No matter who the savior may be, if he is *a* person, once the identification is made he is *that* person and no one else.

This must be especially true for that type of fiction which owes so much to the gospel stories in the first place—the novel and the short story—for which a personal figure is unique, particular, and unsubstitutable within his equally unique and unsubstitutable circumstances. If such fiction is to remind us of Jesus and tell us his story over again, it must remind us by some other unique, particular person's or people's identity and story. And to do that means that in the very likeness of the mirrored story to the original, the concrete, specifying *difference* will have to stand out as clearly as the similarity, so that that other person will have his own individuality and not simply echo Jesus. But when I say "difference" I do not mean "absolute contrast"; for the story and its refractions being what they are in their mysterious combination of opposites, the absolute contrast to Jesus very often comes, in the hands of modern writers, to look suspiciously like total identity (e.g., in the recurrent modern celebration of the coincidence or paradoxical identity of total sinfulness and total loving goodness).

The particular story of Jesus, then, is pre-empted by him and him alone. Only those refractions of it will be credible and concrete that do not seek to reiterate it completely but only in part, not from too close by but at a distance, in the figure of a disciple rather than in the cosmic, miraculous, and abysmal destiny of the original. Such stories may be more ordinary and and less profound, but on the other hand they may have a credibility and authenticity of their own which may well be deeply convincing aesthetically as well as religiously. (One thinks of a book like Alan Paton's *Cry the Beloved Country*.)

The Central Enactment of Jesus' Identity

In the story of Jesus we recall his transition from initiative to increasing passivity in the face of circumstances, beginning with the scene in the Garden of Gethsemane. It may be fruitful to add to this an instance (recorded as taking place immediately afterwards) that not only points in a like direction but actually perfects the previous instance. In the Matthean version of the passion story Jesus reminds an ardent partisan, who would defend him, that he himself could pray to his Father, and more than twelve legions of angels would come to his aid: "But how then should the scriptures be fulfilled, that it must be so?" (Matt. 26:54). There was indeed the envisagement of a possibility of his own salvation. But it was envisaged only to be rejected decisively, in this transition from power to powerlessness. What we have in the story of Jesus' arrest is the external parallel, or more correctly the enactment of the same transition which had taken place, just before this, on the inner plane, in Jesus' prayers in the Garden of

Gethsemane. Both of these instances in their very unity point up the fact that there is an inner and outer, yet unitary, fine point of transition when an intention is being carried into action—a point where a free resolve initiates and at the same time meshes into a chain of circumstances which, once started, cannot then be reversed. Jesus is the unity of this intention-action pattern which is particularly and uniquely his own.

What is a man? What we learn from the New Testament about this question is in part gained from its portrayal of the man Jesus of Nazareth. A man—in this instance the fully human savior who, by his action peculiar to himself, bestows a particular human identity upon the mythological savior figure—is what he *does* uniquely, the way no one else does it. It may be that this is action over a lifetime, or at some climactic moment, or both. When we see something of that sort, especially if we see it at some climactic stage which recapitulates a long span in a man's life—when we see the loyalty of a lifetime consummated at one particular point, but even if we see several hitherto ambiguous strands in his character pruned and ordered in a clear and decisive way at that point—then we are apt to say: "Here he was most of all himself."

In that kind of passage from free intention into action, ordering the two (intention and act) into one harmony, a free man gains his being. He becomes what he is; he gains his identity. Something like this seems also to be the portrayal of Jesus in the Gospels. Jesus, in this portrayal, was most of all himself in the short and climactic sequence of his public ministry, rising to this resolve and this entry into the situation of helplessness. We must, above all, not abstract one from the other: as if, in the New Testament, the event of the crucifixion were anything without Jesus' resolve, or the resolve anything without the event in which it took concrete shape! In his general intention to enact, in obedience to God, the good of men on their behalf, and at the crucial juncture in his specific resolve to do so if necessary in this terrifying way—and in the event in which this intention and resolve were enacted—Jesus was most of all himself in the description of the Gospels. This was his identity. He was what he did and underwent: the crucified human savior.

We now enter into the most puzzling portion of the New Testament report concerning Jesus Christ. He was raised, it is said, from the dead. We have noted the theme of tension between the power and helplessness of Jesus in the testimony of the synoptic Gospels. Obviously the theme rises to a climax now. The redeemer himself, we have said, stands in need of redemption. Indeed it is by his fitting his intention to such radical participation in this our need that he is said to save us. But is he himself redeemed? If the answer has to be that he is not, then how is his failure of redemption to avail as salvation for us? The question has been raised, implicitly and explicitly, by modern writers, theological as well as fictional. The answer often seems to be that the sacrifice of the Messiah is in itself sufficient for us. In his very failure of redemption, voluntarily assumed, he saves us. The crucifixion in that case is the *event* of which the resurrection is the *meaning*.

Whatever may be the case in the independent or refracted modern stories of Christ figures, the story of Jesus is that of the redeemer both in need of redemption and yet also in fact redeemed from death and the power of evil. No matter, then, how much the ancient authors may share our own modern difficulty in making the transition from death to resurrection, they do trace it perfectly naturally under the conviction that this transition is not one from a personal account of a man's death to its stylized or mythical religious application (the naming of an immortal savior figure), but rather that the one who died is the same one who is risen. *The identity of the crucified Jesus and that of the risen Lord are one and the same in the accounts.* This is the important theme that we must now pursue.

Apart from our long inherited and incredibly yet so casually anthropocentric outlook, it is indeed an astonishing thing that the cosmic, immortal redeemer figure should be not mirrored by but identified completely with a human being of particular historical identity. Quite likely it was as astounding to the original authors and the little community from which they emerged as it is to any of us—if not more so.

Formal Elements of Identity Description

But what is the import of speaking of the "identity" of the crucified Jesus with the risen Lord? And what is it to have or to be an "unsubstitutable identity"? It is certainly not a self-evident notion. We face a dilemma as we now raise the question of its nature. On the one hand we ought not to apply a modern notion too precisely, for fear of pressing foreign thoughts on to what we find in the Gospels. On the other hand we must approach the Gospels with some conceptual tool in hand, otherwise we understand nothing at all. To say that this dilemma presents a "small" problem may seem to be a gross understatement. It has, in fact, become the topic of one of the most persistent discussions among biblical exegetes and theologians in our day. But in a certain sense theologians have to proceed in piecemeal fashion, confronting one problem or question at a time. In doing so they must be careful not to foreclose other issues which are not at that point up for consideration. This seems a better procedure than the endeavor to reduce all questions in theology to a basic systematic position which can then be applied ready-made to any and all problems that come along. For that reason the dilemma just mentioned, the necessity and yet the distortion of approaching the interpretation of the Bible with conceptual tools in hand, while it may in itself be an important one, does not loom large in our present context.[2] We are concerned with other matters. Let us simply try to leave our description of "identity" sufficiently loose and minimal, so that the conceptual device may not overwhelm the subject matter to which it is to be applied, understanding the account of the resurrected Jesus Christ.

My thesis, already touched upon, will be that the development of the gospel story is such that Jesus' identity as the singular, unsubstitutable human individual that he is comes to its sharpest focus in the death-and-resurrection sequence taken as one unbroken sequence. Therefore, no matter what one may believe about the possibility or impossibility, factuality or nonfactuality of his resurrection, the story of that resurrection is literarily not of the type of a mythological tale. For surely in such tales, unsubstitutable personal identity developed in interaction with equally unsubstitutable transpirings does not constitute a significant theme. Comparison of the Gospels with various types of literary forms, ancient and modern, is always a problematical business. But if one is to do it, it seems that this drastic focusing of Jesus' unsubstitutable identity in the crucifixion-resurrection sequence makes this part of the story not a mythological tale but something much more like the realistic novel (despite certain problems in this parallel which we have already discussed). For this type of literature depicts the plausibility of character and situation in their interaction precisely by means of the singularity or unsubstitutability of both. I do not mean to imply that the Gospels are throughout more nearly like the novel than any other form of ancient or modern literature. I am speaking only of an aspect of the passion-resurrection sequence. Obviously there are also other elements, e.g., tragic and epic motifs, about the Gospel story as a whole and the passion narrative in particular. I assume there is general agreement that it is difficult and even undesirable to reduce the gospel story by formal analysis to any one type of literature, even if it should be that of a divine comedy.

Obviously my analysis of identity will be shaped toward the claim that Jesus' identity is most sharply focused in the passion-resurrection narrative sequence. I may hope that the concept of identity can be significantly and appropriately applied to the contents of that claim, without being narrowly dictated by it. Respect for the integrity of the New Testament text and for the conceptual tools of interpretation as well as their mutual appropriateness is the obvious aim in such a conceptual analysis and its application to the text. The concept of identity will involve, both in general and in regard to the Gospels in particular, an affirmation that the singular and true identity of a person is mysteriously and yet significantly manifest and therefore accessible, rather than being a remote and ineffable, unknown quantity. I shall affirm that this significant, singular human identity is, in the case of the gospel narrative about Jesus, both most fully focused and therefore most fully accessible to the reader in the passion-resurrection sequence. As a character in a story we know him far better here than in the earlier parts of the story. Whatever judgments one may wish to make about the veracity and significance of this sequence in the accounts, beyond such strictly literary judgments concerning Jesus' place and accessibility within the narrative, constitute a wholly different problem on which I shall touch briefly in conclusion.

"Identity" is obviously a highly personal term, applied to non-personal beings, alive or unalive, only by transfer. Identity is essentially the action and testimony of a personal being by which he lays true claim to being himself and the same at an important point as well as over a length of time. It is personal in the sense that it involves, in order to be at its most typical, the recollection or memory of one's intercourse with others as well as oneself and the willingness to accept responsibility for actions in which one's own intentions have played a prime part.

There is something essentially circular about such terms as "identity." Whenever we try to describe them we find, as Augustine did about time, that they are elusive, known, and yet not easily describable, because their use seems to involve constant reference to themselves as already in use, rather than to something else in terms of which they may be described. Expressive of this situation is the habit from which we all find it so difficult to depart, even though most of us admit its wrong-headedness. The self, we say, is not a thing among other things, a second substantial but not physical existent together with the body and causally related to it. We have been taught this negative conclusion firmly by modern philosophers all the way from the post-Kantian Idealists to Gilbert Ryle. Still, the old doctrine, the "official doctrine" Ryle calls it, is tempting. For it refers the self to a larger class of knowables ("substances"), i.e., to a genus inclusive of specific differences. As a result it seems to avoid (whether it does so in fact is another matter) that hidden or open circularity which so often makes the upshot of modern philosophical reflection about the self look either banal or else esoteric to the point of unintelligibility.

In this awkward situation, and before we go on, I should like to offer four brief methodological comments.

1. It may well be that self-description necessarily involves the use of analogies, one analogy always qualifying another. The traditional dualism of body and soul, particularly the concept of a soul, probably involves such an analogical situation; so may a certain social view of the self, in terms of which the unity of the self is a complex one, at least articulated if not actually conceived after the fashion of an absolutely irreducible "other" who becomes my listener or judge standing over against me, but from within. But the usefulness at least of the first pair hinges on the meaning of the term "substance," the traditional common term applicable to both "soul" and "body." Whatever is meant by it, it cannot have a purely univocal meaning derived by inference from sense experience. (I should add that in what follows, analogy is once or twice drawn upon, but I shall not use it as a systematic instrument or particular type of self-description.)

2. The use of polar or dialectical description may be useful in self-description. That is to say, circularity may at least be postponed, though perhaps not at last avoided, by describing the central term, the self, by means of an unabstractable relation between two different terms, in fact by referring each term finally to the other. Thus, as we shall reiterate in a few moments, an action is an explicit intention, an intention an implicit action, and the self is to be described as each and yet one and the same in the unity of the two.

3. Most important in the present context is the fact that we shall confine ourselves to *self-description*. This is different from a metaphysical explanation. Confinement to description allows for possible alternative descriptions of the same data (rather than the claim that these are additional data not accounted for in the first description), without covering all of the *descriptions* under an inclusive superdescription. Metaphysical explanation, I take it, must account not only for all the data but must also include all the descriptions in one scheme. Without wishing to prejudice the latter possibility, I would want to say that the substitution of self-description for self-explanation, which really had its philosophical beginnings with Kant's distinction between the noumenal and phenomenal perspectives upon the self, is extremely helpful to the theologian who wants to use philosophical concepts for relatively modest, descriptive purposes, and for whom a certain degree of flexibility in regard to self-description is about all he asks of philosophers.

4. The enterprise of description instead of explanation does not, it seems to me, preclude the possibility of some weak, systematic connection or even a variety of possible connections, *between* descriptions. "Weak" means simply that the connective principle cannot serve as a central clue for the construction of the type of supertheory to

which reference was just made. Moreover, the presence or absence
of such a link is not sufficient either to establish or damage the possibility of the simultaneous or rather alternating use of the several
descriptions. I believe that a polar or dialectical relation between descriptive terms may obtain not only within one description but among
descriptions. However, I am not at all sure that the point is of great
importance. As long as two alternative descriptions do not conflict,
there is really no need that one maintain a connection between them.

Intention-Action Description

One characteristic of self-descriptions under the consensus that the
self is not a private mental thing inside the body, a "ghost in the
machine," that the "para-mechanical" like the "para-political" myth
of the self ought to be abandoned,[3] is the one just referred to—their
polarity. It is also a feature of the first of our descriptions, intention-action description of the self's identity. We referred to this earlier when we said that one way to know a person's identity is to know
his typical action. So when we say of him in a certain situation,
doing and undergoing certain specific things, "Here he was most of
all himself," we identify him by these occurrences. To know a person's
identity in this specific context involves the total coincidence, nay
unity, of abstract defining virtues or qualities with the specific way
they are being held together in and by an individual and enacted by
him. His style of action and expression is himself. To say of an individual that the relation between his *ousia* (the "what" of him) and
his *hypostasis* (*that* he is) is accidental for purposes of formal description, that one (at least the first) may be describable without the other,
and that the second adds nothing to the defining knowledge of the
first—to say all this is not only existentially but analytically
unenlightening in the context of this description. The strong link
between a person's continuing centeredness in himself on the one
hand and his personal qualities, changing bodily structure, and overt
activity in both physical and social contexts on the other is so tough
and organic that it is perfectly proper to describe what a person *is* by
what he *does*, and *who* he is by what he is and does.

A description of a human act may be exhaustive in each of two
ways, psychophysical and intentional. However, the intentional
description does not have either antiphysical or antisocial bias. Indeed,
the matter must be put more strongly. Such description must be bodily
and social description from an intentional perspective. As some of the
phenomenologists have reminded us, the body is at once—and
under different descriptions—the link *between* the self and the public
world and the intentional self in, or enacted in, the public world.
Knowledge of my own intention and its transition into action is im-

mediate rather than inferential, and the description I give of it seeks to be a description of that passage. Knowledge of another's action is less immediate. But even it cannot be said to be simply inferential or analogical (I don't want to linger long in the large arena of arguments about the knowledge of one's own and others' intentions), if the connection between intention and action is strong and direct rather than inferential and remote. The kind of knowledge we have of the intention of an agent with whose activity we actually have to deal is often as much like the knowledge one has of a character in a story as it is like the inferential and analogical understanding by which the historian reconstructs persons' intentions from their public actions and sayings.

The *desideratum* of self-description, certainly not always possible to reach, is the description of intention-with-action-in-public. But where it is incomplete we still describe it by this norm. And the relation between the two terms in such description is inescapably polar. To describe an occurrence as an action I must describe it as explicit intention; to describe an intention as just that and not as a putative mental "thing," I must describe it as an implicit action. In this description it is a distortion to treat the "act" of intending as having a separable, self-sufficient mental location ("to perform intelligently is to do one thing and not two things"),[4] but it is equally incorrect to eliminate intention by reducing it to a function (or even no function) of physical behavior.

In a limited sense the latter reduction is indeed more viable than the former. For it may well be possible to give an exhaustive behavioral description of any and all acts, including intentional ones, while it is impossible to describe all physical or social behavior exhaustively as intentional action. But this does not alter the fact that some occurrences may be given exhaustive description under either perspective, so that in such cases the claim that one kind of description is improper is simply inaccurate.

Who a person is, is first of all given in the development of a consistent set of intentions embodied in corporeal and social activity within the public world in which one functions. When a person's intentions and actions are most nearly conformed to each other—and further when an intention-action combination in which he plays a part is not merely peripheral to him but is of crucial importance, involving his full power in a task—than a person gains his identity. A person's identity is constituted (not simply illustrated) by that intention which he carries into action. If we look for the kind of description to do justice to this perspective, we must look to self-knowledge (perhaps simultaneously also to knowledge of others, but I am not at all certain of the degree to which this is true) and to the kind of illumination on the passage of intention into action and

the interrelation of character with circumstances that we get in a novel
or a short story. Henry James wrote, "What is character but the
determination of incident? What is incident but the illustration of character?"[5] As for the historian, he does many things. Whether and to
what extent, when he deals with the person of a given individual who
is known only from a given set of peculiarly slanted documents, he
deals with him in the same way as the self (and perhaps other-self)
describing agent and the novelist or dramatist, I want to leave as an
open question in this context.[6]

Description of the Ascriptive Subject

But now what of that "I," the "index word" Ryle calls it,[7] which serves
to indicate that *to which* both states of consciousness and physical characteristics are ascribed,[8] the *ascriptive* center or focus of intentional
activity? No doubt it was this, whatever it is or whatever we may hope
to say of it, which was the metaphysician's hoped for "subsistent substance" and the ontologist's hoped for "subject."

The fascination of it lies in its *ultimacy*, its *elusiveness*, and its
persistence.

1. It is ultimate, for states and qualities are predicated of it;
but it is itself unpredicable of anything else. But it is not ultimate
in the sense that reference to it involves a self-description more basic
and inclusive than intention-action description. To say that one is
engaged in describing the self under a subject-predicate scheme
obviously forces one to go on to say that the subject is "ultimate" in
relation to its predicate. But it does not of itself support the claim
that the subject-predicate scheme gets at something more "basic"
about the self than does a description of the self under an intention-action scheme.

2. The "I" is elusive and elusively "now," for—to put it with
Ryle—"a higher order action (i.e., concerning oneself about oneself
as one would with another, an action analogous to that of a reviewer
who reviews book reviews instead of books) cannot be the action
upon which it is performed. So my commentary on my performances
must always be silent about one performance, namely itself, and
this performance can be the target only of another commentary."[9] This
is obviously another way of stating Kant's distinction between
noumenal (subject) and phenomenal (object) self-description, except
that it does not involve Kant's judgment that the subject is the reality of which the object is the appearance.

3. It is persistent, though the way this persistence is rightly to
be claimed has always been a matter of great difficulty. It has often
seemed that one could elucidate it only by sacrificing the articula-

tion of the reality of change in the self, i.e., the reality of those specific qualities, states and actions of its own which modify the self itself and by means of which it is directly immanent in the public domain. Conversely, it was often assumed that insistence on such concrete and specific predicates and acts loosened our grasp on the subject's persistence to the point of its disappearance.

In respect of persistence (and probably of elusiveness also), self-description as the description of the unity of intention and action is notably weak. For if intention-action is one and the intention is the action-as-purposed and not an inferred, independent, mental action, it is hard to see how intending in a given case can be understood to be any more perduring than action, which, ideally speaking (if we take Aristotle's description of the drama as a model or heuristic ideal), has a beginning, a middle, and an end. Indeed, intention-action description is usually description of the self's enactment in a completed act. But the intender-actor knows perfectly well—whatever the conceptual difficulties—that he is anterior to that beginning and subsequent to that end, that the action is his qua enduring subject. If the description cannot take that persistence into account, we do not say, "so much the worse for the idea of persistence," but, "so much the worse for the description." Despite the obloquy positivists heap upon anything savoring of introspection, it seems safe to go further yet and say that the intender-actor knows himself to be anterior and subsequent to each intention-action in a way that he does not know that he is anterior and subsequent to himself. There is indeed such a thing, in part through self-ascription and in part through other-ascription (at least for some modern philosophers the two seem to go together without reducing either or both to behavior description),[10] as knowledge of the self as at least a limited persistent. Surely nobody would want to adopt a position that denies the possibility of biography or autobiography, or that makes accounting for them a strenuously complex business. I have argued in this paragraph that even though intention-action description may describe the identity of a person exhaustively, it is in a sense open-ended, for it points to the possibility or need of another (though perhaps more difficult) description of the same identity or the same basic data. It is this open-endedness which involves the possibility of a weak, systematic connection between them of which I spoke earlier. I stress, however, that neither description depends for its validity on this weak systematic connection with the other. Description of the ascriptive subject (if it can be undertaken) is not that of his completed action but of his ongoing, open-ended persistence in continuity with himself.

We have claimed that the self may be known as limited persistent but have said nothing so far about the description under which it is so known, if such is to be a knowing at all. "Knowledge" would be largely though perhaps not wholly empty if it did not involve describability. But is there in fact a description of the subject of ascription in its ultimacy, elusiveness, and persistence? Or does its elusiveness, its subjectivity, which defies "objectification" of itself, deny such an ambition? It is useful to stress again that description is a modest endeavor, involving no supertheory of what is "most real" about the self, or what description is most inclusive. For the temptation to do these things is obviously greatest when we speak of the self as subject of ascription. It must further be reaffirmed that (equally obviously) the description of the self as ascriptive subject must indeed be more elusive and indirect than that of intention-action description which holds firmly to the self as publicly enacted. The description of the ascriptive subject cannot do this in a simple, straightforward manner. But on the other hand ascriptive subject description is not merely description by inference from public to purely private data, nor ought we to suppose that there is a total lack of resemblance between the specific data of the two types of description.

Congruence between the two kinds of description means not only a parallel in descriptive method but a cross reference between their descriptive contents. But this cross reference is based on the unitariness of the self and is not simply descriptively locatable. We do not have the superdescription which would integrate the contents and descriptions. Some sort of analogical scheme of concepts seems inevitable here. There is then a certain justification for using expressions like "verbal occurrence," "performatory utterance," or "verbal action" and (conversely) "bodily speech." But such phrases get their meaning from that complex unity of data and descriptions which, in the absence of a metaphysical theory, I want to leave alone. That only would be the final justification (if one is needed) for the conditional use of such a transfer or *communicatio idiomatum.* But these expressions and others like them, precisely because they involve analogical predication, cannot serve as primary or exhaustive descriptions of the self's identity in being what it does and who it is. To make such expressions do the work of proper description results in a mixture of descriptions in which (frequently without one's knowing it) the contents of one kind of description are often reduced to illegitimate contents of the other. Thus (in present-day theology) "verbal event" may in fact mean the reduction of "event" to the verbal manifestation of a thought, and that surely is not the genuine meaning of "event."

The description of the ascriptive subject in its persistence is an indirect matter, but it is not impossible if the elusive subject is not ineffable. It is indeed elusive and its location is therefore correspondingly fugitive. How is one to answer properly such questions as "Who am I?" or "Who is he?" Ryle has pointed out that any higher order commentary cannot be commentary on itself; only the next comment can be that commentary on what is to it now a previous performance. Retrospectively—a point at which Ryle is perfectly content to leave the matter—no thought of the I is a mystery. But as to its present thinking, Ryle puts the matter very nicely: "Even if the person is, for speculative purposes, momentarily concentrating on the Problem of the Self, he has failed to catch more than the flying coat-tails of that which he was pursuing. His quarry was the hunter!"[11] (He then proceeds to take away most of what he has just given because he apparently does not understand the uniquely nonobservational and anticipatory nature of the knowledge which an agent has of his own intentional activities.) It is the hunter with whom indirect description of the ascriptive subject is concerned. As far as possible such description—in obvious contrast to Ryle's "higher order description"—must at least mirror the prospective direction of the self, its unending forward movement rather than its specific and completed act.

We have repeatedly emphasized that ascriptive subject description must be indirect. The instrument for this indirect portrayal is the scheme of polarity. Now there are two different polar schemes available for subject description.

Subject Manifest in Difference

The first is that of describing identity by means of self-differentiation in self-manifestation. A word, for example, is taken to be nothing other than the verbal self-manifestation of the speaker. One must be cautious not to reduce all meaning to personal, and in that sense nonpublic, meaning nor to cut the nerve of connection between the two. Nor must one reduce the speaker to a function or the sum total of his words. Nonetheless it makes sense to say in some contexts that a person is wholly present in the words with which he identifies himself. Performatory utterances and some kinds of rhetoric are of this sort. The person himself stands surety for his utterance. Verbal manifestation then is identity with oneself in a medium different from himself. Identification with one's name is undoubtedly the paradigmatic instance of identity-in-difference. The classical document of the modern theological use of this kind of ascriptive subject description is Karl Barth's phenomenology of revelation in *The Doctrine of the Word of God: Church Dogmatics* I/1. In patristic theology Augustine's *De Trinitate* bears resemblance to this method. The medium of differentiation from the ascriptive subject is, in this description, neither a basic distortion of it, nor an accidental accretion to it. In addition to the word, this sort of description uses the unique location or perspective of the body that is at once mine and myself as a paradigmatic instance of the identity-in-difference of the elusive subject. There is, by virtue of the polarity between identity and difference, between a subject that both *has* and yet also *is* a body, no fear of rending the unitary self into mental and physical components. In philosophy, Merleau-Ponty and some Dutch phenomenologists are proponents of this position; in theology, Austin Farrer and once again Karl Barth.

Subject-Alienation Description

The other form that ascriptive subject description has taken is the polarity of identity and *contrast* rather than *difference*. The self in the public world is understood to find its identity there, but as though in a distorting mirror violently caricatured. The subject qua subject is frozen or "objectified" in the public world. Because for both forms of subject description the medium of manifestation is not in any simple or univocal way "other" from the subject, neither the identity-difference nor the identity-alienation or contrast scheme presents the I as the ghost in the machine, though I believe there is an inescapable tendency in the latter to do so, unless checked by a counterdescription. In the subject alienation description the medium of manifestation hovers between absolute continuity with and total alienation from the subject. It is rare that the body plays a significant part in this scheme. The assumption of the dialectic of total opposition to and total identity with the subject is not designed to relate the body to it. In this scheme the world which is both the mirror and the distortion of the self is much more often the social and historical than the natural world. The significance of temporal, social events is then said to be their subject reference rather than their public character. They are, in objectified form, the crucial stages in the transition of the subject toward full self-penetration or reconciled selfhood. The subject here is usually, especially for existentialistic phenomenologists and theologians, the individual self. For some thinkers it is the social consciousness or spirit of an epoch which then passes over into the next. History thus becomes its own inward or subjective bond, the dialectical transition of the I toward itself through the stages of its own alienation, its journey into a far country and its return home to itself. Where the emphasis of a commentator is more nearly on the moral side of this transition than on the transition as insight or self-recognition, it is apt to be represented as one crucial transition rather than an indefinite series. Yet even then that one decision has to be reiterated constantly at the level of temporal existence. In either case, the crucial transitions take place not precisely privately but certainly subjectively rather than in their character as public transpirings.

In the subject-alienation form of ascriptive subject description, the identity question may be most troublingly raised. This is especially true of that form of the question involved in the process of naming. "Who is he?" or "Who am I?" (the latter is unfortunately an often rhetorical and overdramatized remark) is a question that may involve a number of issues. It may be a formal inquiry, trying to solve the difficult problem of locating the logical status of the ascriptive subject. It may involve inquiry concerning the specific self-referral of a unitary focus of personality characteristics, conscious and physical states. It may also point to the focus of individual coordination of a number of overlapping human communities, from a family to ethnic and professional groups. The highly diverse problems which concrete specifications of identity pose for individuals are often covered under the general name of "identity crisis." This large term covers a broad penumbra of issues, of which we may distinguish two. At the very least it may mean the individual's sense of isolation from any and all communities which alone could serve to identify him to himself as well as to others. Beyond this, it may also signify a disruption in the sense of temporal self-continuity which the subject ordinarily has in the process of integrating his own changes as well as those within the communities which should help him maintain that self-continuity. "Who am I?" may only symbolize such questions of identity, or it may be a direct and concrete expression of them. In either case, the process of naming, which is presumably the most concentrated answer to the "who" question, illustrates most acutely the issue of ascriptive subject description in such situations. It also illustrates in sharpest fashion the difference between the two forms of this description.

In the first form of subject description, that of the subject manifest in differentiation from himself, the naming question points to an illuminating mystery rather than a haunting problem. Who I am is answered by my presence in and to my verbal expression, most perfectly in my being named and naming myself that same name, thereby accepting and standing for the identity between myself and my name.

In the second form of subject description, on the contrary—that of the subject-alienation scheme—naming and being named constitute not an illuminating mystery but a haunting problem. Who am I? The name a community bestows upon me is precisely not identical with me, though I cannot say that I have an identity safely hidden somewhere else which escapes unscathed from this intrusion. My name now is not the perfect expression of the subject in the medium of self-differentiation; nor on the other hand is it a thing-in-itself isolated from that manifestation. On the contrary, the world is also a distorted mirror or even form of the self. My name in the world presents myself as subject, but in alienated, distorted, "objectified" form. In this world my identity is itself alienated; in this world I am without true identity. "*X*" is what I should be named or rather what I should name myself in the world of historical communities. My journey through that world is a journey in search of myself, constantly mirrored though not truly present to myself nor self-reconciled in the world. What would constitute such reconciliation, or the achievement of true subjecthood, is answered variously and does not here concern us.[12]

A Biblical Application of Identity Description

In the Old Testament, Exodus 3:13–15 is the classic example of naming as the first form of ascriptive subject description—description through identity in the medium of self-differentiation. (Cf. the cumulative impact of the "I am" passages in Deutero-Isaiah.) In the New Testament the fourth Gospel in particular illustrates the same sort of subject description in its repeated ἐγὼ εἴμι passages. These sayings are especially instructive, for they are obviously written by an author who is intimately and not only as it were externally acquainted with Gnostic wisdom and therefore with something like the other form of identity description, that of subject–in–self-alienation.

At least some of the ἐγὼ εἴμι passages in the fourth Gospel, as well as its prologue's proclamation that the Word was made flesh (1:14), clearly seem to express the immanence of the subject in a medium different from himself yet fit to receive him. As a result they express the accessibility of the mysterious ascriptive subject center for and to those who will believe. There are certain expanded ἐγὼ εἴμι passages (especially John 14:6, "I am the way, and the truth, and the life") in which the "I am" is analytically, not synthetically, related to—or as it were made transitive in—its own predicates. In all of these, who or what he is is *not* primarily a matter of certain acts or *transpirings*. In this respect such theological exegesis of these passages as Karl Barth's[13] seems to me mistaken. Rather the relation is that between the subject who is the same in himself and in his manifestation. Neither is he a static substance accidentally connected with what is externally manifested of him so that he does not himself appear in it, nor is he an identity distortedly manifest so that he does indeed appear in his manifestation but only in alienation or *Entäusserung*. Rather, once again, he is the same subject in the medium of external appearance that he is in himself (here Barth's exegesis[14] seems to me perfectly correct), truly manifested in his identity. Hence predicative description is a description of the subject himself in his transitivity.

I do not mean to imply that the ἐγώ εἰμι sayings are antagonistic to identification through action or eventfulness—not at all. I do, however, think that that scheme is simply not applicable to this approach to identity, captioned by so weighty a pronunciation of "I AM. . . ." There certainly is no bias in the Gospel against the cruciality of identification of a person with his significant events. Nonetheless, it is by and large true—especially in 14:6 which is not (as some other ἐγώ εἰμι sayings are) commentary on a preceding public act—that knowledge of Jesus as the truth and liberation by that knowledge are matters of crucial insight rather than results of crucial changes accomplished through public events within a temporally connected and significantly developing series.

But if the identity of Jesus is here described, in terms of our analysis, most nearly under an ascriptive subject manifestation scheme, it is important to remember once again that with regard to Jesus the manifestation is one of difference rather than alienation from his subject center. The point is that the identity-alienation scheme is, in the fourth Gospel, not even formally applicable to the knowledge of Jesus. That is to say, one cannot even contrast him with others by saying that like others he is also manifested in distorted "objectification," but that unlike them he does own a true subjecthood in himself beyond this distorted external manifestation. The identity-alienation scheme is not applicable to him even to this extent.

On the other hand, such a Gnostic scheme would be applicable, formally and materially, to the nonbeliever if he could come within the author's purview as a person having some sort of integrity of his own being. But one must hastily add that this is, of course, impossible, precisely because Jesus does have an identity, and we have our identities in him, so that the nonbeliever's very conception of himself and man's situation is sinful and unintelligible. The nonbeliever is alienated at the same time from Jesus and from his own true self, so that if *per impossibile* one were to adopt his own perspective, one would have to say that as long as he does not believe his only "truth" is to grasp his nonidentity in the world as being mysteriously one and the same as his identity in himself. That is to say, the "truth" for the nonbeliever would indeed be that in a hidden way his supposed insight that he has no final, true identity is one and the same with his true identity. For him, in the end, silence and negativity would be all. But this is, of course, his sinful error. For Jesus is he who is the way, the truth, and the life for men because he is these things in being the true Son of the Father, and thereby we also have identities.

All in all, one may say that Gnostic thought schemes (identity-alienation polarity) are very much within the horizon of the fourth Gospel's author; but it needs to be added that he is so keenly aware of their implications that he rejects them not only materially but formally. He claims not only that true man does have an unequivocal identity, but that even posing the question of identity in terms of the polarity of identity-alienation is already part of the very problem it would overcome.

To make a wholesale judgment regarding the sense of identity in Old and New Testaments and what description would be appropriate to them would at least lack proper caution. However, it is evident that the subject-alienation description of identity will at the very least have to be balanced by the other subject description scheme. In all likelihood both kinds of subject description have to be balanced by intention-action description.[15] All this becomes especially clear when we reflect on the fact that so much of the sense of divine agency in both Testaments is attached to public events that can be narrated in their important temporal transitions.

Ascriptive subject description is deeply concerned with the continuity or persistence of the subject, which intention-action description cannot well show forth. But the opposite difficulty plagues subject description, especially in the forms of the subject-alienation scheme. What is the link between stages of temporal, public human events? For subject description the answer has to be, in large part, the subject itself. This bid for the description of subject continuity can produce startling results. In the case of Hegel it led to the rejection of any and all links between subjectivity and the passage from event to event which were not amenable to description in terms of the development of communal subjectivity. Others (e.g., some existentialists) are not so radical, but even for them the extent to which events in their transition from stage to stage resist a description which links them through a subject's activity or awareness represents the threat of absurdity to a self's continuity and its continuity with the rest of the world. Every endeavor to articulate a way to transcend the awkward choice between the absurdity for the subject of nonsubjective events on the one hand and an all-devouring subjectivity on the other has proved to be most difficult and problematical (e.g., for the later Heidegger). The danger, certainly in subject-alienation description, is that the very success of its analysis of the subject may have to be measured by the loss of any and all significant external connectedness between the subject and the material and social world in which he is set. The danger obviously does not plague intention-action description, nor indeed indentity-difference description. In the alienation scheme that danger becomes obvious at two points. In the first place, the body obviously cannot mirror the self either in its persisting subjectivity or in the radical distortion of true subjectivity to nearly the same extent as can the social or historical world. In this view, the body and in fact the physical world tend to be foreign and disjunctive entities to the self. Secondly, as we have already discussed, even the social world is in one sense only the estranged manifestation of the self, and therefore, qua manifestation, absolutely continuous with the subject. But in its estrangement, in the "objectified" public transpirings of historical events, the world is alien; the "I" becomes posited at an infinite distance from its own public world. It is, in short, difficult for this view, at least in isolation from other identity descriptions, to escape the "ghost in the machine" position.

Here then we have two (or three, depending on the arrangements) descriptions of the self, each containing a polar relation within itself (intention-action, identity-manifestation in difference, and subject-alienation). In addition, however, there is the possibility of a polar relation between them, either by necessity because of the open-endedness of each, or more loosely because each is an exhaustive description of the self within one situation or schematism—but in that case the other situation remains outside as an awkward appendix. Ascriptive subject description is a significant description of the experience of the question "Who am I?" in the context of social-historical and personal, verbal experience; but in one form at least (not in the other) it tends to treat the body as an appendage or instrument simply of subject or intersubject relatedness. Intention-action description is more successful in describing the unity of thinking and acting, a bodied self not only being but doing directly in the public world. It can describe how a person is what he does and undergoes; but the elusive I with its mysterious search for self-identification through historical experience and naming escapes this description altogether.

What then do we mean by a man's identity? Until a supertheory comes along, we will be content to say that we know him when we can say of him over a period of time or in a crucial occurrence, "when he did and underwent this, he was most of all himself," and when we can say of him, "his self-manifestation was a rightful expression of who he was." A person's identity is known to us in the inseparability of who he was and what he did.

Identity Description and the Story of Jesus in the Gospels

We return to the synoptic Gospel accounts. We have already said that in the story itself, especially from the arrest to the crucifixion, the identity of Jesus is focused *in* the circumstances of the action and not in back of them. He is what he does and undergoes. It is an intention-action sequence. Indeed, in and by these transpirings he becomes

what he is. But in the synoptic Gospel accounts there is a profound
ambiguity about him up to this point in terms of subject description.
It is important to say that it is not that he stands mysteriously or
ineffably in back of his manifestation. Rather, in terms of the story
(though, undoubtedly, not in the authors' conviction) there is an
ambiguity about *who* Jesus is. It is this ambiguity that is resolved in
the resurrection account, especially that of Luke.

About this resolution, four things are to be said.

1. It is indeed a matter of ascriptive subject description.

2. Even though this description is to the fore in the resurrection account, it is not done in abstraction from action. The resurrection is not simply the manifestation of the meaning of that event
which is his death. But the action recedes into the background. It
becomes as ambiguous as its line had been clear before this. In the
description of Jesus in the gospel accounts, then, his identity is
describable (a) through intention-action description, clearly in the
passion narrative but ambiguously in the resurrection story; (b)
through ascriptive subject description, ambiguously in the passion
narrative but clearly in the resurrection story.

3. The subject description delineates the identity of the human
individual, Jesus, at once as the manifestation of the presence of God
acting and as the one who, having a true identity of his own, can
bestow it without distortion on the community of Israel in which he
is a member.

4. The shape of the story is such that in the resurrection Jesus
is declared to manifest himself as who he is, the one who as the
unsubstitutable human being, Jesus of Nazareth, is not a myth but
the presence of God and savior of men.

All this is right in the marrow of the story. As a literary account, the
gospel story makes Jesus accessible to us. The question is, does it
open up the possibility of a more than literary accessibility of Jesus to
us? If so, at what point? Where could one make the transition from
literary description to historical and faith judgments?

The implication of what I want to suggest is that those who
endeavor on old and new "quests for the historical Jesus" as well as
their opponents have looked for Jesus' identity with a faulty, one-
sided understanding of identity.[16] They end with abstractions of
their own making, in which the being of Jesus finally is not intrinsically connected with narratable occurrences, and such events
therefore have no genuine significance. Moreover, both have looked
for Jesus' identity with a faulty, one-sided view of the New Testament
narrative as *purely* historical and/or kerygmatic—never literary. In
contrast to both, I believe one may affirm (a) that in the narrative

the person of Jesus is available to us descriptively; (b) that there is
identity between Jesus so described and the savior's description; and
hence (c) there is continuity between Jesus and the proclamation of
his name in the early community. I believe further that this descriptive availability, identity, and continuity represent not a transformation of Jesus into a myth but the demythologization of the savior myth
in the person of Jesus. If this is true of the descriptive narrative, that
narrative has met one criterion for allowing us to say that at the crucial juncture (death-resurrection) it *may*—though it *need not*—be true
in fact.

According to the gospel accounts Jesus is not simply in need of
redemption; he is in fact redeemed, though the Story of the connection between his death and resurrection is not an organic but a
dramatic transition. Just as his power and powerlessness were not
merged but coexisted or were present still in and after the transition from one to the other, so the vindication of his intentional action
does not mean that there is a simple mergence or supersession of
his need of redemption by the fact that he was redeemed. The point
is that the accounts tell us that the one who is the risen Lord is
also the crucified savior, and that the abiding identity of each is
held in one by the unity of him who is both in the transition of the
circumstances. The resurrection is not the stylized ending to a
realistic tale, the naming of a mythical figure. Nor, on the other
hand, is the crucifixion the shadowy death stage of a rising savior.
The crucifixion remains an indelible part of Jesus' identity.

Manifestation and action are ultimately inseparable in the understanding of identity, and our careful methodological distinctions
are undoubtedly too refined and neat to do justice to the synoptic
narrative. Yet there are different stresses concerning identity in
differing personal situations. It would not do to say that the Gospels bespeak the identity of the resurrected Jesus simply as the
manifestation of who he is. No; they still portray him as embodied
in a range of events or actions. But whereas in the crucifixion the
stress is on identity in event or action, and the identity of manifestation, while present, is ambiguous and not sharply focused on him,
the reverse is true in the resurrection. The distribution of the formal elements of identification now is different. Action is indeed
present. It is the action of God who began to supersede Jesus' initiative beginning with the arrest and now is climactically the agent
here. But the divine action remains in the background, dark and
veiled. Something does indeed take place in the resurrection, but it
is not described and doubtless cannot be described. And even its
effects in further act and event (the resurrection appearances as
transpirings) are swathed in confusion and contradiction (the place
of the empty tomb in the chronology of the accounts; the order of

appearances in Galilee or Jerusalem). The foreground and the stress in the resurrection belong not to the action of God but to its confirmation of Jesus' identity. It is he who is present and none other when God is active. Jesus alone is manifested.

Indeed his identity as God's presence which is singularly he himself, Jesus of Nazareth as that one and unsubstitutable individual, is climactically manifested in the resurrection. In the story up to his death it was right and proper to say of Jesus that his identity was embodied in the activity of his passion, his own activity as well as its gradual supersession, as it were through identification, by that of God. Here he was most of all himself. He *was* this transpiring of circumstances in action. It is equally right to say of his resurrection that here his identity is most fully *manifest*. In the resurrection he is most sharply revealed and attested not as a mythological figure but as the human Jesus; nor is this manifestation a semblance for something more "real" underneath. In one sense then his full identity was established on the cross; in another sense, in the resurrection. The two forms, in their dramatic transition, constitute a unity. In both one may say, "here he was most of all himself" and mean by this expression not a mythological figure but the specific man named Jesus of Nazareth. That seems to be the import of the accounts in the synoptic Gospels.

In view of this assertion of the unity of the crucified and risen savior as one and the same Jesus of Nazareth, it is all the more important to stress the directness of the connection between the two events. The accounts are terse and tense in their rendition of this transition. One might almost speak of dramaturgic unity in the sequence. Christ resurrected is far from being a mythological figure in the accounts. He is most fully historical at this point in the narrative, if by "historical" we mean that he is regarded as an unsubstitutable individual in his own right. His actions and manifestations do not have a symbolic or purely representative character; they do not gain significance through being in an exalted or elevated sense typical of human or divine activity *par excellence.* They fit, at this point, neither the classical tragic nor the mystery account. They are more nearly like a novel or a short story. They are, whether fictional or real, a specific set of particular actions and reactions for which no other could plausibly or fittingly be substituted—just as in a novel the actions of the principals upon each other gain their peculiar and significant character by being these particular and no other actions, wrought by these and no other interactions of events and persons. That is why and how they are the embodiment of his unsubstitutable identity. And similarly, all the acts and sufferings are to be ascribed to him. No one else than he, Jesus, is manifest as the central agent or patient of them. In these actions he emerges as who he is.

Stages of the Identification of Jesus

Let us put the assertion of the unity of cross and resurrection in the accounts into the broader context of the identification of Jesus as the unsubstitutable subject that he is. It is doubtless true that the task of writing a life of Jesus, especially one including as its pivotal point his "inner" life, is difficult if not impossible—whether it is undertaken as a reconstruction from the recorded data or by entering by imaginative reiteration into his self-understanding, or both. But if the Gospels do not lend themselves easily to this sort of enterprise, they do manifest another kind of structure, indeed perhaps a series of (not mutually exclusive) patterns, as literary works often do. And these, in turn, lend themselves to interpretive ordering or to a series of such orderings.

If we may take the liberty of treating the synoptic Gospels as one composite account (with individual variations), at least one possible sequential arrangement or three-part pattern seems to emerge.[17]

1. There are in the first place the pre-birth, birth, and infancy stories—including, we ought not forget, the genealogies. In Matthew and Luke this first phase comes to an end with the transition to the next, Jesus' baptism at the hands of John (which begins the whole story in Mark). The striking fact about this first stage is that both in the story (or stories) and its liturgical or poetic decorative material the person of Jesus is identified wholly in terms of the identity of a community, the people of Israel. He is not the individual person, Jesus, certainly not "of Nazareth." He is not even an individual Israelite, but Israel under the representative form of an infant king figure. He is a representative person in barely individuated form. In his being and in the events surrounding him and focusing on him, we get a cross section, a summing up through miniature reiteration of that whole history of events which in its total transpiring makes up the people of Israel. The crucial events that happened to the people happen symbolically and in miniature to and about him, but in such a way that in connection with him there is a symbolic completion of what was originally left unfinished. In Matthew his identity is determined by cumulative reference to Abraham, Israel's single progenitor; to Jacob, the eponymous figure first called Israel; to Judah, the father of his tribe; to David, the great representative King. In Luke his identity is located by means of Adam in whom Israel, mankind, and God are all directly connected. (Luke's procedure is reminiscent of Paul's juxtaposition of the first with the second Adam who is Christ, a theme in turn reminiscent of some of the Gnostic religions as well as of some Jewish themes.) This is who Jesus is: not an individual in his own right, but Israel—even (to some extent) mankind. They lend their identity to, they bestow it upon him.

2. With the account of Jesus' baptism, the story undergoes a break, or rather a decisive transition to a second stage. Far more than in the first part he appears as an agent, an individual in his own right. Yet this is correct only to a limited extent. Certainly he is no longer in representative form the people as a whole and its history. He now performs mighty deeds, the signs of the kingdom of God. He proclaims its advent and teaches its marks and those of life in it. Nonetheless he retains something of the symbolical or representative quality that he had in the first part of the accounts. But now it is not the past of which he is representative. Instead it is the immediately pending rule of God. In short, he does indeed begin to emerge as an individual in his own right, and yet it is as witness to and embodiment of the kingdom of God that he does so. It is perhaps precarious to make the claim, but it does seem that at this stage he is identified by the kingdom, rather than the kingdom by him. Even the titles—Son of man, Son of God, Christ, King, etc.—serve to represent him as the representative of that kingdom and his identification by means of it.

In the earlier stage we find so obvious a proliferation of legends, symbolic events, and myths that history, understood either as lifelike representation or as events that actually took place, can hardly arise as a pertinent idea to be applied to the understanding of the reports. In the second stage, on the other hand, the lifelike representation of the specific individual in specific situations raises the question of historical veracity in acute fashion, since the individual here represented is generally agreed to have lived. We are bound to ask at certain points, "Did this actually take place?" "Was this actually his teaching?" Nonetheless, the specific individual's identity and the situations in which it is enacted are at this stage so often tied to a more ultimate referent, the kingdom of God, that it is frequently (probably in the majority of instances) at least a matter of great ambiguity, if not useless, to try to sort out what is actual happening and what serves stylized depiction, illustrating his representational character.[18]

3. It is worth emphasizing these matters in order to stress the contrasting situation when we turn to the next transition and the third stage in the story. It is in the first place the part generally taken most nearly to reflect actual events—at least in part. But even more important from our present perspective, it is the part of the story most clearly historical in our narrower use of the term. It clearly describes an individual in his own right and in connection with him as central character a series of events which, whether fictional or real, are what they are in their own right. Neither person nor circumstances can be abstracted from each other. They are not symbolic but

unsubstitutably what they are and gain all their significance from being this specific set and no other, and from the interconnection between this unsubstitutable person with these circumstances. He alone is at their center and lends them their character, so that they can focus neither on any other hero, human or divine, nor on that "everyman" for whom he might mistakenly be thought to be a symbol.

The transition to the third stage comes with Jesus' brief announcement to his disciples that he and they would now go to Jerusalem, and his prediction concerning the Son of Man's fate. (As a possible alternative place of transition I would suggest the events connected with the Last Supper and immediately subsequent to it.) The atmosphere becomes heavy and fraught with a troubled anticipation which is all the more effectively conveyed for its cryptic description, ". . . and they were amazed, and those who followed were afraid" (Mark 10:32). We are still at a point where the stylized characterization of Jesus in terms of his mission (i.e., his identification by means of the enactment in him of the Kingdom of God) holds good. Nonetheless, that very identification from now on becomes increasingly problematical and tenuous. Especially beginning with the arrest, or just before it, the connection with the Kingdom of God becomes loose. The figure of Jesus emerges more and more as one whose mission it is to enact and suffer his singular destiny, while the Kingdom of God and the Son of man who embodies it with its authority fade into the background. There is an increasing tendency to use the titles of that authority (Christ, Son of God, King, etc.) with an ironic and pathetic twist, when they are applied to Jesus. It indicates the apparent incongruity between them as well as the kingdom they represent and the figure supposedly embodying them. By means of this ironic or pathetic detachment or ambiguity (in the midst of which, however, we remember the traces of his yet abiding power!) between the figure of Jesus and the kingdom, the focus of the last part of the story falls more and more on him in his unadorned singularity. He is simply himself in his circumstances, truly a person in his own right. Everything else about him which has hitherto served to identify him and make him a representative figure or symbol of something more than himself now becomes ambiguous.

What is important for us now is not the question, did Jesus apply messianic titles to himself or was it the early church that did so? What is important instead is to understand that the ambiguity of the relation between Jesus and these titles is foursquare in the account of Jesus and of the relation between him and those who had followed him up to this point, and that the ambiguity is one that stretches beyond the printed page and is bound to raise a question concerning this man in the reader's mind. No doubt, indeed quite obviously, the writers themselves had no question concerning the identity of Jesus and the complete coincidence between him and the kingdom with its titles. But as an account or integral part of the story the ambiguity presented is real and remains at this point to be resolved. Its resolution, when it comes, must also be presented as *enacted* in the course of genuine transpirings, though at the same time, of course, it must be the enactment of the *true manifestation* of Jesus, telling us decisively who he is. Jesus must become who he is. He must gain, in enacting it, his own identity in which he is truly manifested as the one who is in some specific way related to the Kingdom and the messianic titles.

Now the story gradually begins to accelerate into an increasingly terse and spare climactic telling, virtually unimpeded in its final stages (beginning with Jesus' arrest) by any and all didactic material (until the resurrection appearances). Such material had hitherto been strongly to the fore, assuming some very somber hues after the entry into Jerusalem. But now it would be an encumbrance. The story's focus remains on the action by which the destiny of Jesus is accomplished. It remains on Jesus as the unsubstitutable person he is his own right through passion as well as resurrection. In terms of the movement that we have traced, from a symbolic or representative person to an individual in his own right, we have reached the last stage of the story. There is no further focusing of his identity. In this respect the passion and resurrection represent, in the very transition from one to the other, not two stages but one. In both, he is equally himself, none other than Jesus of Nazareth. In the unity of this particular transition, passion to resurrection, he is most of all himself, most historical (in our narrower sense of the term) as an individual in his own right. The difference is that whereas in passion and death this identity is *enacted* in the particular circumstances in which he is most of all himself, in the resurrection his identity is presented to us as that same one now ambiguously and rightfully *manifested* as who he is. Yet the difference is not absolute. For, as we have seen, the very question of who he is is ambiguously present and unavoidable in the very midst of the action beginning with his arrest. Conversely, the resurrection is not simply the true manifestation of the crucified Jesus but also the veiled action of God. The identity through act and subject manifestation of Jesus becomes, through distinction as well as identification, closely linked with the veiled activity and subjectivity of God.

In the descriptive account the matter is perfectly natural and in that sense not difficult. For any conceptual ordering it is mysterious indeed, and such ordering is at its best if it does not take us beyond the narrative description to an independent explanation of its own. The rising curve of God's activity increasingly supersedes Jesus' self-enactment in the passion story. But just at the point where the divine activity reaches its climax in God's resurrecting action it is Jesus and not God who is manifest as the presence of God. It is a complex sequence, but nonetheless a sequence in unity. The unity is the sequence of Jesus' identification. In the resurrection he is most nearly himself as a person who is an individual in his own right. He above all others is totally at one between manifestation and the identity manifested. And if, the writers seem to tell us, this one has a genuine identity so that we know who he is, how can we possibly say that human destiny is loss of identity or alienation, or even that alienation and identity are mysteriously and finally identical in the mythical savior-man figure? For it is he and none other, Jesus the Son of God, who is the representative man, the second Adam, representative of human identity and not alienated in his very singularity. Because he has an identity, mankind has identity, each man in his particularity as the adopted brother of Jesus.

Clearly the story of this redeemer is no ordinary dying and rising god story, no matter what the facts were and how deeply dyed the story was in the vat of syncretism. Its climax is that now, for the first time, Jesus is manifested as the true ascriptive subject of the hitherto ambiguously ascribed descriptions and prophecies concerning the Son of man. The ambiguity is resolved, and furthermore it is Jesus who manifests himself in the resolution. He imposes his identity on the mythical figure as well as on that history which is the substance of the community of Israel. It is, therefore, fitting that for Luke the climax of those steadily repeated predictions of the Son of Man's sufferings (which at the time of their pronouncement referred only veiledly or at best ambiguously to Jesus; cf. Luke 9:22; 9:44–45; 17:25; 18:31–34) should *now* and only now receive their proper ascriptive reference and that at this crucial juncture they should receive it from Jesus himself, who alone is capable of manifesting his identity rightfully and securely. Walking with two of his disciples toward Emmaus, he asks them, "Was it not necessary that the Christ should suffer these things and enter into his glory?" (Luke 24:26). Now that the ambiguity, which had appeared at the outset of this stage, is resolved, the author is in a position to say for the first time that "beginning with Moses and all the prophets, he interpreted to them in all the scriptures the things *concerning himself*" (Luke 24:27). Here then the elusive ascriptive subject is identical with his manifestation; the ambiguity is resolved. And not only his own history but all of the past of Israel receives its ordering by reference to his manifestation. The wheel has, in one sense, come full circle. Now that he is fully manifest in the absolute coincidence of his manifestation with his unsubstitutable individuality, the identity between him and the community is also restored. But whereas at the beginning, in the first stage of the account, it was the community which served to identify him, the reverse is now true. He, Jesus, provides the community and its whole history with his identity, just as he imposes it on the mythical savior figure.

Myth, Gospel, Story, and Fact Claim

Myths are convincing or true by virtue of their embodiment or echo of universal experience "Universal" may be too strong a term. But myth surely is the external, expressed mirroring of internal experience which is both elemental and, at the same time, a common possession of a whole group, possibly a whole culture. New Testament students, echoing a gradually growing trend in Romantic philology, learned from D. F. Strauss that where myth appears to be the key to the meaning of an account, no question concerning the factuality of the story need arise. Myth as the unconscious poetizing of a folk consciousness is a sufficient explanation. I do not wish in this context to call into question this claim. But in view of its prevalence, it seemed well to examine the gospel account of the resurrection, to see if its structure is that of myth. At the very least, a positive answer to that question would have to be heavily qualified. In point of fact, the evidence points in the opposite direction. The literary structure of the account, especially that in Luke, seems to me to point in favor of the thesis that the resurrection account (or better, the passion-resurrection account as one) is a demythologization of the dying-rising savior myth. For quite in contrast to the substance of a myth, the substance of the passion-resurrection account is about an unsubstitutable series of transpirings concerning an unsubstitutable individual, whose unique identity is, for the description, not ineffably behind but directly in and inseparable from the events related in the story.

A myth's capacity to convince lies in its echoing a widespread inner experience which cannot be directly or univocally expressed. "Did this happen?" or even "Could this have happened?" are not appropriate questions to ask in the presence of a mythical account. We must rather ask concerning a myth, "What elemental aspirations or emotions does it express?" or "To what transcendent dimension of truth does it unite us?" The truth of myth is religious or primordial rather than factual or historical. But the resurrection account, by virtue of its exclusive reference to Jesus and by virtue of its claim that here he was most truly manifested to be who he was in his human particularity, allows, even forces the question: "Did this actually take place?"

It *allows* the question. For this above all is one thing that novelists and historians have in common, that they deal with specific actions and specific human identities. And if a novel-like account is about a person who is rightly or wrongly assumed to have lived, *the question of factuality is bound to arise precisely at the point where his individuality is most sharply asserted and etched.* I have argued that both by virtue of the meaning of identity in general and in regard to the location of Jesus' identity in the Gospel account in particular, his individual identity is not given in an inferred inner state behind his teachings, but directly, i.e., in the report of the transpiring of an actual series of occurrences in which he was what he did and in which he was manifested. It is at this point then that the transition from literary analysis to historical affirmation or denial as well as to theological truth claim should be made. And this point is the complex unity of the passion and resurrection account, not the account of his earlier ministry.

I also said that the passion-resurrection account *forces* the question concerning its factuality. For what the authors are in effect saying (once again Luke in particular, though this time he is joined by John and by Paul in I Cor. 15) is that the being and identity of Jesus in the resurrection are such that his nonresurrection is inconceivable. (This does not mean that his resurrection *is* conceivable, any more than saying that God is that than which a greater cannot be conceived means that he *is* the greatest conceivable, or than saying that God cannot be conceived as not existing means that his existence *can* be conceived.)

In a sense (if I may put it in a manner totally uncongenial to them) the synoptic Gospel writers are saying something like this: "Our argument is that to grasp what *this* identity, Jesus of Nazareth, is, is to believe that, in fact, he has been raised from the dead. Someone may reply that in that case the most perfectly depicted character, the most nearly life-like fictional identity ought also in fact to live a factual historical life. We answer that the argument holds good only in this one and absolutely unique case where the described identity (the 'WHAT' of him) is *totally* identical with his factual existence. He is the resurrection and the life; how can he be conceived as not resurrected?"

It may be dubious wisdom to make Luke or John speak like a late eleventh-century theologian. Yet something like this argument seems to me to be present in the resurrection account. All that one leaves out in putting it this way is the fact that the affirmation of Jesus' resurrection is not like that of an ordinary fact, i.e., simply denotative, but rather overwhelmingly affective ("existential"), as befits a unique fact which is unlike other facts in being at the same time an absolute personal impingement. But I see no reason for trying to validate either the meaning or the truth claim concerning Jesus' resurrection by an elaborate description of its existential appropriation. That this is the only way to grasp it, I do not doubt, and in another context the fact might well have to be underscored; but that the elaborate description of the appropriation makes it or discourse about the resurrection in any way more intelligible does not seem to be the synoptic authors' point. The passion-resurrection account tends to force the question of factuality, because the fact claim is involved as part of the very identity that is directly enacted and manifest in the story as an event sequence. One could presumably still see this as a literary feature or part of the description of the account, and therefore either leave the fact question suspended or answer it separately in the negative.[19] But one cannot deny that for the authors or, perhaps better, in the story and as part of it, the fact question was inescapable and bound to be answered the way that they did answer it. It seems difficult, further, to deny that in that case the question of fact *tends* to be raised beyond the literary analysis of the account. And how might one come to answer it in the affirmative? Presumably by a kind of movement of thought similar to and reiterative of that of the original authors. But we have gone somewhat afield in these few remarks, for we have given some reflections concerning the transition from a literary description to historical (in the wider sense) and theological argument and affirmation.

I return to the description of the account, nonmythical and clearly involved in stating that in the case of this singular individual, manifestation of his identity involves his actual living presence. Who he was and what he was, did, and underwent are all inseparable to the authors from the fact *that* he was or is. (The reverse is obviously equally true: that he is brings with it the manifestation of who he is and what he did. The affirmation of the particularity of Jesus, together with stress on its importance, accompanied by the denial that any significant cognitive content is given with this particularity seems to me a silly game.) Once again, if in his resurrection he was most of all his identity as Jesus of Nazareth, then it was here most unequivocally that they could say that he lives. The authors, particularly Luke, are saying that as raised from the dead he exists. And saying this is for them inseparable from saying that as raised he is most clearly Jesus of Nazareth, whose being it is to be and to be unambiguously the embodiment and redeemer of Israel, he that should come, the Christ, the Lord, the Son of man, the manifestation of God.

Such seems to be the significance of the words spoken by the "two men" to the women at the empty tomb, even before Jesus himself was manifest. "Why do you seek the living among the dead?" (Luke 24:5) they ask, as though it were a matter of self-evidence, a direct implication of who he is, that he is alive; as though instead it were startling not to think of him who is "one who lives" (New English Bible) as living but as dead. The fourth Gospel, as though commenting on this perspective, extends Luke's identification of Jesus' being alive with his very identity to an all-embracing generalization: "I am the resurrection and the life" (John 11:25). He defines life. He is life. How can that which or he who constitutes the specific defining difference of something be conceived to be the very opposite of what he thus defines—except through sheer contradiction in the conception? To conceive of him as dead is the equivalent of not conceiving of him at all. Hence the question, "Why do you seek the living among the dead?" constitutes a startling reversal of what we would ordinarily expect to be self-evident and what most stunning. (The difference between Luke and John is that Luke stresses that Jesus is his being, i.e., "to live," only in the transition or bond of events constituting his being, from life to death to resurrection, whereas in John, Jesus' being as the resurrection underlies or encompasses his every manifestation and its acceptance. There are no crucial events or transpirings in time sequence in John, for whom history is subject manifestation. The transitions are from veiledness to manifestation or glorification, and from unbelief to belief, "death" to "life," "darkness" to "light.")

In explanation of what they have just said, the two men add immediately: "Remember how he told you, while he was still in Galilee, that the Son of man must be delivered into the hands of sinful men, and be crucified, and on the third day rise" (Luke 24:7–8). The reiteration of this prophecy, first spoken in anticipation and now in fulfillment, accompanies all the Gospels like a steady refrain (in this chapter of Luke alone it occurs three times in various forms: 24:6 f., 25 ff., 44 ff.). It is the primary content of what little we have in the way of description of Jesus' life in the earliest preaching of Christians. In the present context the saying is obviously designed to serve as commentary explanation for the question, "Why do you seek the living among the dead?" Had he not foretold them what would come to pass? But I think one may safely say that it is designed to do more than that. It focuses his identity as one who lives, who is life and not death. He lives as the one who cannot not live, for whom to be what he is, is to be. But who or what he thus is, is unambiguously Jesus of Nazareth; and as Jesus he is the Son of man, the one whose history, whose being as self-enactment in his unique circumstances it was to be delivered into the hands of sinful men, to be crucified, and to rise again. The prophecy (here taken as fulfilled) is the content of his identity as the one who lives. The content of the prophecy is not synthetically but analytically related to the question, "Why do you seek the living among the dead?" Who and what he is, what he did and underwent, and that he is, are all one and the same.

The relation between these verses (Luke 24:5 and 6, 7, and 8) is

similar to that between Exodus 3:14 and 15. In response to Moses'
query after his name, God tells Moses to convey to the children of
Israel that "ɪ ᴀᴍ" had sent him unto them. Immediately, as though
in explanation which says the same thing over again, God adds,
"Say this to the people of Israel, the Lord, the God of your fathers,
the God of Abraham, the God of Isaac, and the God of Jacob, has
sent me to you. . . ." The reference to God's "ɪ ᴀᴍ" is not synthetically but analytically related to the reference to him as the God of
Israel's particular history. For him to be, and to be this specific one,
are the same. Similarly, for Jesus to be and to be as Jesus the Son
of man and Israel's redeemer are one and the same thing. Once
again: his identity is so unsubstitutable now that he can bring it to
bear as the identifying clue for the community which becomes
focused through him. Indeed, the New Testament will ask just this
of men: to identify themselves with the identity, not of a universal
hero or savior figure, but of the particular person, Jesus of Nazareth, the manifest presence of God in their midst, who has identified himself with them.

What kinds of affirmation would be involved in belief in Jesus' resurrection? I think it would mean much more nearly a belief
in the inspiredness of the accounts than that they reflected what
"actually took place." I have directed attention all along to the
descriptive structure of thc accounts and not the historicity of their
contents. But at one point a judgment of faith concerning the inspiration of the descriptive contents and a judgment of faith affirming their central factual claim would have to coincide. The New
Testament authors, especially Luke and Paul, were right in insisting that it is more nearly correct to think of Jesus as factually raised,
bodily if you will, than not to think of him in this manner (even
though the qualification "more nearly . . . than not" is important in
order to guard against speculative *explanation* of resurrection). This
judgment that they were right is in part at any rate a matter of a
particular understanding of what identity means, what and where the
identity of Jesus is to be found most directly in the Gospel accounts
(i.e., in the crucifixion-resurrection sequence) and where the transition from the literary description to factual, historical, and theological judgment is to be made: precisely in that sequence. I think further that both because what is said to have happened here is, if true,
beyond possible verification (in this sense unlike other "facts"), and
because the accounts we have and could most likely expect to have
in testimony to it are more nearly like novels than like history writing, there is no historical evidence that counts in favor of the claim
that Jesus was resurrected. This is a good thing, because faith is not

based on factual evidence. To what historical, natural occurrence would we be able to compare the resurrection for purposes of cognitive assimilation? On the other hand I believe that, because it is more nearly fact-like than not, reliable historical evidence *against* the resurrection would tend to falsify it decisively, and that the forthcoming of such evidence is conceivable. In other words, if true it is unique, but if false it is like any other purported fact which has been proved false—there is nothing unique about it in that case. Again this is a good thing, because if it were not so, in what genuine sense could Christian faith be said to be historical and to involve a historical risk? Until such evidence comes along, however, it seems to me proper to say (despite St. Thomas and Hume who insist that every fact, without exception, can be doubted until shown to have taken place, which in turn is a matter of evidence rather than logic) that there is a kind of logic in a Christian's faith that forces him to say that disbelief in the resurrection of Jesus is rationally impossible.

Whether one actually *believes* the resurrection is, of course, wholly different matter. "God raised him on the third day and made him manifest, not to all the people, but to us who were chosen by God as witnesses . . ." (Acts 10:40–41a).

Excursus: Hermeneutics, Identity, and "The Historical Jesus"

The recent literature on the twin problems of our knowledge of the Jesus of history and the transition, historical as well as existential, from there to the kerygma involving his name, is extensive and growing. By fairly general consent the latter-day discussion received its heaviest single impulse from Ernst Käsemann's essay, "Das Problem des historischen Jesus," *Zeitschrift für Theologie und Kirche*, 51 (1954), 125–53, translated in E. Käsemann, *Essays on New Testament Themes*, trans. W. J. Montague, Studies in Biblical Theology, 41 (Naperville, Ill.: A. R. Allenson, 1964), pp. 15–47. The focal discussions in the American literature are: James M. Robinson, *A New Quest of the Historical Jesus*, Studies in Biblical Theology, 25 (Naperville, Ill.: A. R. Allenson, 1959), revised and expanded in a German edition, *Kerygma und historischer Jesus* (Zurich: Zwingli Verlag, 1960); and a critical review of Robinson's book by Van A. Harvey and Schubert M. Ogden, "How New Is the 'New Quest of the Historical Jesus'?" in C. E. Braaten and R. A. Harrisville, eds., *The Historical Jesus and the Kerygmatic Christ* (Nashville: Abingdon Press, 1964), pp. 197–242, originally published in a German translation as "Wie neu ist die 'neue Frage nach dem historischen Jesus'?" *Zeitschrift für Theologie und Kirche*, 59 (1962), 46–87. For surveys of the literature and problems see Hugh Anderson,

Jesus and Christian Origins (New York: Oxford University Press, 1964) and W. G. Kümmel, "Jesusforschung seit 1950," *Theologische Rundschau, Neue Folge* 31, 1 (January 1966), 15–46.

The reader should be cautioned that Harvey and Ogden's essay is exclusively critical and systematic in nature and in no sense a review of Robinson's monograph in the light of an independent examination of the New Testament. Harvey and Ogden neither argue any generalizations about the shape of the gospel accounts of Jesus' life, death, and resurrection, nor do they examine any specific texts. The result of their general procedure is that, whatever the hermeneutical problem(s) of the New Testament may be, it is in one sense declared to be insoluble; in another sense, it is solved before it arises.

I do not wish to engage in any lengthy discussion of the actual status and significance of the "hermeneutical question" in New Testament and theological studies. However, I should like to raise the question if the whole problem has not perhaps been exaggerated altogether out of proportion to its actual significance. The reason for that possibility lies in the fact that off and on now for 150 years or more, theologians in the traditions of German Idealism and now Existentialism, who have carried on the discussion on hermeneutics have been accustomed to take for granted two assumptions: (1) That the written word (especially in the case of the New Testament writers) represents not the proper expression but the frozen "objectification" of the mind that lies behind it; (2) that the proper way to grasp one's own intention, indeed identity, as well as that of others, is by entry into the basic self-reflective act of the self, into that which is never "merely given."

The dominant (often wholly unqualified) scheme of understanding involved in this conception is the one I have labeled the "subject-alienation" polarity. The adoption of this descriptive scheme, as a device for the examination of the principles of biblical interpretation, if it is not balanced or supplemented by some other analysis of human intention, identity, and their accessibility, obviously has built into it a guarantee that its very question can never be answered. How *can* the "objectified" written page actually bring us in contact with the "unobjectifiable" subject-reality in back of it, if the relation between them is in principle one not only of difference but of contrast? The endeavors to ameliorate or modify the statement of this gap have been many and earnest, as for example in the recent "post-Bultmannian" discussion carried on in the shadow of the later Heidegger's ontology by such scholars as Gerhard Ebeling, Heinrieh Ott, and Ernst Fuchs; but in principle the gap remains. It is this built-in guarantee which accounts for the fact that even though the *terminology* of the hermeneutical discussion has changed appreciably— becoming ever more complex, esoteric, and abstruse as the endeavors in recent decades to "overcome the subject-object split" have become linguistically more and more difficult—its *substance* has hardly changed at all since the days of its theological inception through Schleiermacher. How could it be otherwise, given the fundamental fact of the ongoing similarity of the understanding of the self that informs the whole discussion? Given a one-sided and absolutely consistent description of the self as nonobjectifiable self-reflexiveness, or at best as a subject concretized only in a "word event," and hence given an ever doubtful conjunction of public and personal meanings on the written page, the hermeneutical discussion can obviously be guaranteed an ongoing, indeed indefinitely perduring status. Even if we discount the possibility that the seriousness of this issue has been exaggerated, it does not seem likely that it represents a "new frontier" in theology.

Now, if we do indeed suppose that there is a serious hermeneutical issue, it is presumably before us when two differing conceptual schemes are to be brought into one common context for the conveyance of meanings contained in each. In the case of theological-biblical exegesis the common context is apparently agreed by many commentators to be that of self-description. Concerning the hermeneutical issue, two things may be said about Harvey and Ogden's essay. (1) They do not question the inherited scheme of *existentiell* understanding of the self (hence agreeing at least in principle to the importance of the hermeneutical problem), though they quite properly see the insurmountable difficulties which the scheme offers for the "historical" picturing of anybody, including Jesus of Nazareth—difficulties which Robinson had completely overlooked in his original adoption of this "new concept of the self." (2) Since they do not examine the New Testament itself, Harvey and Ogden never get into the position of having to pose even the possibility of independent conceptual patterns of the New Testament, which might, or on the other hand might not, then become problematical for the modern reader. The first point enables them to suggest that the hermeneutical problem with regard to the knowledge of the intention of the "historical Jesus" is insoluble. The second point enables them to solve the hermeneutical problem before it arises. For, though they disagree with Robinson over practically everything else, they are perfectly willing to adopt his (and other existentialist theologians') oversimplified and at the same time ineffable principle of "self-understanding" as the common and proper context for self-description, the understanding of man in the New Testament, and its account of Jesus' significance. The only difference between them and Robinson at this point is that he thinks that this principle makes "the Jesus of history" accessible to us, whereas they are properly dubious with regard to the direct accessibility of anyone (even to himself) on the basis of this principle, let alone the direct accessibility of Jesus. But whatever the remote *existentiell* selfhood may be for them (and however it may be grasped, inferentially or in some other way), it is clear that for them as for Robinson the true identity of a person lies in *existentiell* self-understanding, whether clear and accessible or obscure and inaccessible. It is this mysterious and (for Harvey and Ogden) remote "someone" that is addressed by the "kerygma" and lies somewhere in the depths of the self-reflexive life.

But surely there is no reason why we must declare ourselves bound, a priori as well as exclusively, to this understanding of identity, let alone assume it equally simply and without question to be applicable wholesale to the New Testament. To do so provides a clear instance of the ease with which the unmodified alienation or "non-objectifiability" schemes turn into a "ghost in the machine" position, especially when used in connection with examination of narrative material.

Van A. Harvey's recent *The Historian and the Believer* (New York: Macmillan, 1966) may move in the direction of a modification of the position on identity assumed in his and Ogden's essay. However, since the issue is not directly addressed it is obviously difficult to assess his position. In any case, despite the author's skillful analysis of the pertinence of different kinds of historical explanations for theological argument and his departure from German thought forms, it is not clear that he works with any other notion of identity. His use of the "perspectival image of Jesus" (pp. 268ff.), for example, functions in a way surprisingly similar to the claims of those engaged in "the new quest for the historical Jesus," who bring together Jesus, the kerygma, and ourselves by the common concept of *existentiell* selfhood. Here as there we find the same ambiguities, especially that of relating a basically undeterminable historical occasion to what appears to be a mysteriously and privately self-originating perspective of faith, i.e., a perspective for which it is extremely difficult to specify any external impulse, either from an actual historical occasion or from the transcendent source of that and all other occasions. To what extent this self with its perspective is basically characterizable as an agent self is also difficult to see. In other words, Harvey appears to leave carefully ambiguous the question if the self of faith is ever so genuinely in the public domain that narration of a historical or literary kind would be absolutely indispensable either to its own determination or to its connection with a wider spectrum of public events. The same ambiguity, by extension, characterizes the issue whether the God who reveals himself as trustworthy does so in any way remotely analogous to public and teleological activity that would have to be narrated in order to be understood.

What Harvey carefully leaves ambiguous, Ogden clarifies beyond possible doubt. All crucial action, human or divine, becomes for him reduced to "self-understanding," the really constitutive factor of our being and that "act" in the depths for which external instantiation in word or deed is a merely secondary and separable expression. Here God becomes the transcendent ghost in the historical or worldly machine and man the ghost inside the cells of his body. The characterization of either as historical agent in this context is obviously a totally Pickwickian use of the phrase. See Schubert M. Ogden, "What Sense Does It Make to Say, 'God Acts in History'?" *Journal of Religion* 43 (January 1963), 1–18.

Notes

Previously published in the Christian Scholar, vol. 49, no. 4 (Winter 1966), pp. 263–306.

1. On this point as it affects style of presentation, see Erich Auerbach, *Mimesis: The Representation of Reality in Western Literature*, trans. Willard R. Trask (Princeton: Princeton University Press, 1953, chap. 2.

2. See the excursus on hermeneutics, etc., at the end of this essay for some remarks on the issue, pp. 87–91.

3. Gilbert Ryle, *The Concept of Mind* (New York: Barnes & Noble, 1962), p. 23.

4. Ibid., p. 40.

5. Quoted in S. Barnet, M. Berman, and W. Burto, eds., *Aspects of the Drama* (Boston: Little, Brown and Company, 1962), p. 242.

6. In these reflections, constituting section 1 of this large section on "Identity," I have been helped by the analysis of Robert H. King in his unpublished doctoral disseration, "The Concept of Personal Agency as a Theological Model" (Yale University, 1965), chap. 1, and (in the last paragraph) by a formulation of my own suggestions by John C. Robertson, Jr. See also R. H. King, "The Concept of the Person," *Journal of Religion,* 46 (January 1966), pp. 37–44.

7. Ryle, p. 188.

8. Cf. P. F. Strawson, *Individuals* (New York: Doubleday, 1963), p. 84.

9. Ryle, p. 195.

10. Strawson, p. 96.

11. Ryle, pp. 197 f.

12. In literary art Kafka is, I take it, the great representative of this perspective. In philosophy its proponents are Schelling, Hegel, Marx, and the existential phenomenologists. In psychology their name is legion. In theology Tillich, Bultmann, and some of Bultmann's students represent it in different ways. The affinity of this outlook with the subtle movement of late antiquity called gnosticism has often and rightly been noted (though, of course, there are differences, especially in the tendency of Gnostics

to become pure escapists from the world). The parallel was first noted by Ferdinand Christian Baur in *Die christliche Gnosis* (Tübingen: C. F. Osiander, 1835). In our day it has been pointed out again in Gilles Quispel's brilliant interpretation of *Gnosis als Weltreligion* (Zurich: Orego, 1951). Cf. also the illuminating descriptions of Gnosticism by Hans Jonas, including especially his methodological or hermeneutical suggestions in *Gnosis und spätantiker Geist*, II, 1 (Göttingen: Vandenhoeck & Ruprecht, 1954), pp. 1–23. In describing the journey of the subject away from and toward identity through the historical world of alienation, several alternative forms of the subject-alienation scheme may be developed. The world is said by some commentators to be the medium by which the self is alienated from itself. Others suggest that the self is alienated not from itself but from the world. Hannah Arendt's profound criticism of Marx's typically modern onesidedness in this respect is instructive because her critique involves, among other things, a view of the world as both historical and yet also material in a strictly nonhistorical sense. For that among other reasons she can say: "World alienation and not self-alienation as Marx thought, has been the hallmark of the modern age" (*The Human Condition* [Chicago: University of Chicago Press, 1958], pp. 231, 364f. The evident parallel of the sense of alienation of perceptive folk in an advanced capitalist and a relatively advanced socialist society where, at least according to some interpretations of the rules of the dialectic of self-alienation, the phenomenon should not exist might well be evidence in favor of her thesis.

13. Karl Barth, *Church Dogmatics*, vol. 3, pt. 2 (Edinburgh: T. & T. Clark, 1960), p. 56.

14. Idem.

15. It is evident that I regard intention-action description and subject-self-differentiation description as closer to the kind of procedure we find in the New Testament than subject-alienation description. This is especially true of the synoptic Gospels, in which something like the first two kinds of description prevail (as we shall see). I have noted the applicability of the second, the subject–self-differentiation scheme, to the fourth Gospel. Whether or not the third, subject-alienation scheme, is at all applicable to the New Testament is a matter I cannot here try to determine. It would depend largely on an exegesis of Romans 7, and on an examination of the complex history of the exegesis of this chapter. Limitations both of space and technical knowledge prevent my undertaking such a task here.

16. Consult the excursus on hermeneutics, etc., pp. 87–91.

17. The outline to be followed is largely, thought not exclusively, that of Luke. The same type of analysis could have been applied if Mark had been used as the focal narrative, though the formal structure of the story is obviously somewhat different. The resurrection is just as indispensable in Mark as in Luke. But whereas it is the climax of the Lukan account and the preparation for Acts, in Mark it is the veiled center toward which the action moves, the open mystery not actually included in the narrative, which nonetheless serves as the narrative's mainspring.

18. In all that I have said here I do not mean to prejudge the relative success (or lack of it) attending specific historical endeavors to reconstruct

the setting of Jesus' preaching and acts in his own life and in the cultural matrix of his time. Nor do I wish to make *a priori* pronouncements concerning the significance of some such specific historical endeavors for judgments of faith and theological truth claims. On both matters I find myself sympathetic to the position adumbrated by Nils A. Dahl, "Der historische Jesus als geschichtswissenschaftliches und theologisches Problem," *Kerygma und Dogma*, 1 (1955), 104–32; translated in C. E. Braaten and R. A. Harrisville, eds., *Kerygma and History* (Nashville: Abingdon Press, 1962), pp. 138–71. I agree with Dahl's remark, ibid., p. 161, "That faith is *relatively* uninterested in the historical Jesus research does not mean that it is *absolutely* uninterested in it. To draw this conclusion would be a kerygma-theological Docetism." On the other hand such a cautiously affirmative position obviously does not entail any one particular argument for tracing the identity of Jesus proclaimed Messiah with Jesus of Nazareth who preached and was crucified, certainly not an argument from the historical evidence concerning Jesus' "self-understanding."

With respect to this particular problem, viz., the identity of Jesus as both crucified and Messiah, as it is presented in the particular shading of the New Testament sources, the position set forth in this paper again bears resemblance to that of Nils Dahl in his essay, "Der gekreuzigte Messias," in Helmut Ristow and Karl Matthiae, eds., *Der historische Jesus und der kerygmatische Christus* (Berlin: Evangelische Verlagsanstalt, 1960), pp. 149–69.

19. This seems to me to be the upshot of the intriguing first part of George Santayana's *The Idea of Christ in the Gospels* (New York: C. Scribner, 1946). Santayana seems to be saying that even if one must understand the Gospels as poetry, they have to be seen as unique poetry in which miraculous facts are indissolubly wedded to ordinary events. The endeavor to demythologize the story or to transcend its mythology ontologically would, for Santayana, spell the ruin of the story. For it is not mythology in the first place. To raise the question of fact concerning the story is likewise to do it damage by separating out fact from the poetry that embraces fact and indeed makes untranscendably miraculous fact part of itself. On the purely and prosaically historical level, of course, one would have on these grounds to enter a judgment against the credibility of these events.

3

Theology and the Interpretation of Narrative: Some Hermeneutical Considerations

For a number of years the religion department of Haverford College has invited two distinguished scholars in the field to a joint presentation in which each would respond to the other's paper. In 1982 the lecturers were Paul Ricoeur and Hans Frei.

This essay is a revised version of Frei's presentation. It provides an excellent introduction to Frei's thinking in the last decade of his life, ideas developed further in "The 'Literal Reading' of Biblical Narrative in the Christian Tradition: Does It Stretch or Will It Break?" and in Types of Christian Theology. *He begins here with the two ways of thinking about Christian theology that form the organizing principle of* Types of Christian Theology: *as a philosophically based part of what the Germans would call* Wissenschaft *and as a particular activity within the Christian community. Both this essay and* Types of Christian Theology *then argue for a modest but not exclusive emphasis on the second way of understanding theology as the theological method most likely to preserve faithfully the* sensus literalis *of Scripture as that has been generally understood in the Christian tradition. The argument favors a certain kind of methodological independence for theology, and yet Frei makes it in running informal dialogue with contemporary literary criticism and descriptive anthropology.*

* * *

I

For centuries the institutions of higher learning in Western culture were governed by the organization of learning into the study of the liberal arts—the trivium and quadrivium—and the study of specialized subjects, medicine, jurisprudence, and theology on top of them. The arrangement is a useful point of departure for looking at a long-standing ambiguity concerning the study of Christianity, the majority (should one say: the former majority?) religion of that culture. Christianity provided a vast yet simple narrative that in turn served to integrate a coherent view of truth, of the universe, of human nature and destiny—in fact of all things conceivable and inconceivable. That ambitious undertaking, strangely grown out of a small body of texts and a fragile tiny organization, has been the source of Christianity's grandeur and, in secular contexts, its misery. In omnibus undergraduate courses on Western civilization we still make a bow toward it by taking a look at selections from Thomas Aquinas: They represent the study of theology seen as the pinnacle of the structure of integrated knowledge, the queen of the sciences. Theology in that context is discourse about a concept, "God," and the usual assumption has been that part of what the inquiry is about is whether or not or how the concept "refers." On the one hand, then, theology has a generally accessible subject matter, broadly based both as a technical concept and as a wider cultural one, "God" and perhaps God, even if there may be arguments about distinctive conditions required to enable one to get into a position to study it. On this view, theology and philosophy are bound to be closely if perhaps oddly related, especially when philosophy is regarded not only as having its own contents (metaphysics, ontology, ethics, epistemology, anthropology, etc.) but in addition as being the "foundation" discipline providing all-fields-encompassing arguments and criteria for meaning and certainty, in the light of which philosophy arbitrates what may count as meaningful language, genuine thought, and real knowledge.[1]

On the other hand, Christianity is a specific religion among many others, a religious community called after its founder, whose name (Jesus of Nazareth) is linked to the title embodying the claim his followers made on his behalf (the Christ). "Theology" in this context may be said to be working from a number of ultimate and perhaps ultimately different "visions" or designs concerning the manner of God's presence implied by this religion and its sacred text—visions that have much more of an imaginative and aesthetic than philosophical character.[2] But more than that, in this view "theology" is not religions-encompassing, at least not necessarily. It is a problematic characteristic of Christianity, one specific religion.

Whether and how the term applies to the description of other religions would have to be determined case by case, and so would the
question of the extent to which their version of "theology" would
bring them into relation to what we, in our culture, recognize as
philosophy. In this way of speaking, "theology" is not part of that
general mapping out of the intellectual universe, the natural academic offshoot of which is the liberal arts curriculum replete with
graduate studies. "Theology" here is an aspect of the self-description of Christianity as a religion rather than *Christian* theology
being one instance of "theology" as a general class. It is an inquiry
into the coherence and appropriateness of any given instance of the
use of Christian language in the light of its normative articulation,
whether that be Scripture, tradition, the Christian conscience, a
mixture of these and other candidates.

The ambiguity may be a blessing, a curse, or a bit of both. In
any event, it is probably built into the religion itself, with its well-
known, problematic penchant for making universal truth claims,
establishing normative guidelines for interpretation, etc., and it is
at the same time a particular, social phenomenon rather than a
metaphysical construct or an ontological apprehension. In the second context "theology" is a characteristic of Christianity; it is a
second-order discipline dependent on the first-order language of the
religion and has been given nearly, or fully, institutional status.
When looked at that way, "theology" often becomes awkwardly
related to independent criteria for intelligibility and rules for interpretation that "foundational" philosophers think they can and "nonfoundational" philosophers think they cannot provide for it. It just
doesn't fit the rules or the categories terribly well, just as in days
past when it seemed more akin to a metaphysics it was difficult to
place it precisely among others and even more difficult to articulate its own without flaw or confusion.[3]

In the second way of seeing theology it is closer to the social
sciences than to philosophy, though certainly not identical with
them. Christianity is a religion, a social organism. Its self-description marks it typically as a religion in ways similar to those given
by sociologists of religion or cultural anthropologists. It is a community held together by constantly changing yet enduring structures, practices, and institutions—the way religious communities
are, e.g., a sacred text, regulated relations between an elite (overlapping but not identical with a professional group) and a more general body of adherents; and by a set of rituals—preaching, baptism,
the celebration of communion, common beliefs and attitudes, all of
these linked—again typical of a religion—with a set of narratives
connected with each other in the sacred text and its interpretive
tradition. All of these are, for social scientist and theologian (qua

adherent or agent of the self-description of the religion) not the *signs* or *manifestations* of the religion, rather they *constitute* it, in complex and changing coherence. A sensitive social scientist—neither positivistic nor completely governed by single theories such as structuralism or sociology of knowledge—one who is eclectic in theoretical resort, will give descriptions of religious communities that are rich, complex, methodically reflective, and yet neither reductionist nor method-ridden.[4]

More generally, it seems to me that the Christian theologian has more in common with the socioscientific tradition that originates with Max Weber than with the descendants of Emile Durkheim. For Durkheim society becomes a reified fact or power, external to the individual, controlling him coercively though, of course, on both sides unconsciously. The social facts manifesting themselves in the consciousness and actions of individuals are the latter's collective causes. Thus, not only does religious self-description have to be decoded, but the interpretive clue at the same time furnishes the causal explanation for the foundation and distinctive character of the religious phenomenon. Religious experience is based on the conscious or conceptual/experiential distinction of the world into sacred and profane realms, but the *real* meaning of the distinction is that between society and the world of empirical objects. And society, the true meaning-referent, is also the real or actual power responsible for the phenomenon and its peculiar character. Regional and local variations aside, the universalizing character of this interpretive/explanatory move involves assertion that religion is basically the same, always and everywhere, and therefore that explanation of it includes the predictability of how it will function in any society. The model for explanation and for the relation between interpretation and explanation is that of the natural sciences.[5]

Weber's much more complex theoretical enterprise has German historicism for its immediate background, and so the model for it is not the natural sciences. Even though his work on the major religions aimed at comparison, it was not based on a generalizable and therefore predictive causal schema, nor on a universalizable description of the essence of religion, nor yet on the self-perpetuating functioning of society as an independent collective phenomenon. Instead, Weber focused on what we would today call intentional personal agency in a social context (he defined it as human behavior to which the acting individual attaches a subjective meaning), and he applied the concept to an "ideal type" on the one hand and to a hypothetical "average person" on the other. The reflective stance appropriate to this unitary complex and to its highly specific character in each instance must be able to identify the subject matter as belonging to a distinct genre. Weber called that stance "understanding" (and meant only partially what Dilthey meant by it). Religiously governed action *within* the social world is analogous to the characterization of divine action *on* the world in religious self-description, though, of course, this does not mean that Weber accepted the latter as *true* description. It simply meant in the first place that intentional human actions, describable under the reasons that govern them, are an appropriate pattern both for the self-description of religion and for its redescription by the sociologist. Second, causal explanation in this arena is not *tout court* different from the description or redescription of intentional agency. Obviously, this is quite different from appeal to "social facts," for which the "real" meaning of religious self-description is identical with the nonreasoning collective forces that explain it, the bridge between meaning and cause, between self-description and explanatory description being a theory such as unconscious projection.

Weber did not oppose sociological resort to other descriptive or explanatory devices—including collective uniformities—functional reference frames, as well as internal and external "conditions, stimuli, furthering or hindering circumstances of action."[6] But he had no integrating—and in that sense explanatory—hypothesis that would unite these various theoretical strands under its own overarching heading, and intentional agency maintained a certain unsystematic primacy in the complex. Apparently he did not think that this incompleteness prevented adequate use of theoretical guidance in the interpretation of actual religions and other social traditions.

Conceptual redescription of religious self-description under the primary, though not exclusive, rubric of intentional personal agency in a social context obviously demands a much more complex theoretical accounting than the sharp and simple cleavage between (1) a "nonreductionist" view that restricts the real meaning of religious phenomena to the perspective of the religious participant and thus to their own irreducible, universal realm of meaning, such as the experience of "the sacred" (Eliade) or "faith" (Wilfred Cantwell Smith), and (2) "explanatory reductionism" for which the real meaning of religious phenomena (i.e., their meaning beyond conceptual description, in which the adherents' own description must be honored) is the normative explanatory hypothesis, the "ideal type" of which is presumably one that results from an accumulation of theory neutral or hypothesis-untainted uniform, empirical data all falling into place. I am not suggesting so much that this sharp cleavage between "description" and "explanation" at the level of theory is probably a naive oversimplification of a much more complicated and mobile sliding interaction between kinds or levels of reading— though I believe that it is—as that this return to the tradition exemplified by Durkheim is not the sort of social-scientific analysis of religious phenomena with which Christian theology, seen as part of the self-description of the Christian community, can have much in common.[7]

On the other hand, there is the other extreme that, having accepted the cleavage, claims that the socioscientific explanation of religion is not that at all, but simply an alternative description that simply mistakes some secondary phenomena of religion for its essence. The essence that social scientists cannot capture is indelibly bound to its self-expression in adherents' experience and description. For some who espouse this view, description is all, and there is no "essence"; the very notion is a conceptual error. But for most of the proponents of the irreducibility of religious self-description, that uniqueness is a function of linguistic as well as prelinguistic experience, and understanding them is conditional upon understanding the circular relationship between the experience and its meaning-referent, the essence of religion (e.g., the "realm of the sacred"). This is the phenomenological view of religion.

In effect, we have here a theory as foundational and exclusive as that of the opposite extreme. Because the "essence" or "realm of meaning" to which religious self-description refers is universal (whatever its logical or ontological status), the espousal of this view demands universal consent: We *all* have a participant's awareness of this experience given with our humanity, even if we are not aware of that awareness. In principle we can be brought to it without having—as in the explanatory hypothesis view—to undergo a transposition to a different underlying interpretive frame of reference. Therefore, to understand religion is to be, to an indeterminate extent, a participant. "Indeterminate" because we may find ourselves treating some nontraditional or not "officially" religious ideology as a surrogate religion or because we may find that the basic, hidden religious meaning-referent is only tenuously symbolized for us by the specific religious tradition through which alone it is accessible to us.

For this view the price of coherence and irreducibility is, as its opponents claim, isolation from other and obviously plausible theoretical frames for the description of religion, except to the extent that the latter buy in on phenomenology. This is especially true in regard to the social sciences. Indeed, the public and accessible character of this interpretive stance is precarious (as its conflict with Structuralism and Poststructuralism tends to confirm), resting solely on the justifiability of the foundational status of the theory as such. For the Christian theologian adoption of this view of the description of religious phenomena will finally amount to a commitment that theology must be grounded in a, or more specifically, this foundational philosophical theory in order to be intelligible; and that the interpretation of Christian self-description will never be more than a "regional" embodiment of this more comprehensive undertaking.

As a contrast to both extremes, the equation of adequate interpretation of religion with an explanatory hypothesis that both integrates and judges all partial interpretive frames and possesses superior adequacy to the data, and the confinement of interpretation to a reiteration of participant description under a foundational hermeneutics or theory of meaning-and-understanding, one may cite Clifford Geertz's view of ethnography, or cultural anthropology, as "thick description." It is a view that obviously shares more with Weber than Durkheim. More than phenomenology and more than the explanatory-hypothesis position, this outlook shares common ground with theology in the second mode.

It is striking that theologians as divergent as Friedrich Schleiermacher and Karl Barth are agreed that Christianity, precisely as a community, is language forming,[8] not purely, of course, but sufficiently so that that language as embodied in its institutions, practices, doctrines, and so on, is a distinctive and irreducible social fact. The language is religion-specific, and theology is the constant testing of the way it is used in a given era, against a norm that consists not only of *some* ordering of the paradigmatic instances of the language (such as the sacred text), but also the cumulative tradition and the most supple and sensitive minds and consciences in the community past and present. No theologian here speaks for himself without first speaking for the community, and his first task is, therefore, to give a normative description rather than positioning himself to set forth or argue Christian truth claims. This common outlook kept Barth, to whom Schleiermacher's theology was largely uncongenial, from wholesale antagonism against his great predecessor's thought.

In practice, of course, the definitional waters between the first and second instances of theology are more muddied than I have indicated because of the ambiguous character of the Christian religion. To take the most obvious instance: The concept "God" has customarily been used referentially and not simply as one concept related to others in the complex of Christian language, the Christian community, and the Christian life. Christian discourse because it is not merely a coherent abstract of specific linguistic conventions but the discourse of persons using them has hauntingly elided "God" as concept, as proper if elusive name, as designating "real" presence, though not in the way ordinary objects are present: "God" and God and, cognately, first-order religious and second-order technical discourse have become elided, and yet the theologian may insist on the importance of these distinctions in the very act of transgressing against them. So whereas "God" is very much a concept governed by the community's language, it is asymptotically related to other senses of the same word, including some that are the fruit of philosophical speculation.[9]

Caught between two ways of doing theology, practitioners of the craft have to order their priorities. They can do so in one of two ways. The first is to find themselves a supertheory to mediate the two and explain both as autonomous contents undergirded by a single structure. In our day "hermeneutics" as the theory of a unified and all-embracing process of understanding is a strong candidate. These efforts are usually called theologies of "correlation." The second way is to order their priorities without the aid of such a theory, either by denying one side or the other, or by maintaining the ambiguity but subordinating one side to the other without a very strong warrant for their choice, except that it allows them to say more of what they want to say.

The theologian putting first the general culture setting of Christian language and relating theology primarily to philosophy will, of course, give strong emphasis to general theories whether of culture and human nature or of meaning and understanding. Theologians emphasizing the distinctive and irreducibly social functioning of Christian language, including the Bible, will be much more cautious about explanatory generalization. They will stress the functional, varying, and context-dependent character of concepts and words. Generalizing concepts like "meaning" and "understanding" to them are analytical tools that likewise function in context-dependent ways, parasitic on first-order language, and not as unitary, context-invariant universals describing either translinguistic essences or transsituational internal processes or events.

For the first outlook, understanding or interpreting a text is a universal transcendental condition of possibility that integrates such indispensable features as the distinctively "textual" status of the text in and for consciousness; the fusion of horizons between the text's traditioning history and the present unity of linguisticality and understanding; the hermeneutical circle between the "forestructure" of understanding and the actual understanding of the text; and finally the irreducibly diachronic location of understanding both to pose and solve the problem of relating past text to present understanding. For the second outlook, understanding is an ability rather than a process or internal event, a capacity to follow an implicit set of rules unintelligible except in the examples of text or discourse in which they are exhibited. You do not ask how understanding is possible but what rules govern a particular linguistic operation such as the functioning of concepts in a Christian context. Understanding is the competence to follow and the judgment to apply or not to apply them.

II

There is a strong family relationship between the second understanding of Christian theology—normed description of the Christian religion and of its language as a social phenomenon—and a theological interpretation of the community's Scripture that gives priority to the *sensus literalis,* including the "literal sense" of its narrative portions that have dominated the Scripture in its interpretive tradition in a way not true for the parent religion, Jewish Scripture and its tradition.

One can distinguish three senses of "literal sense," the third of which is especially closely related to theology in the second mode. But more generally it is the case that description of the Christian religion, especially in the West, has included a description of its sacred text in which at the very least certain portions regarded as central were to be read not allegorically or spiritually but literally. Another reading may be allowed, but it must not offend the basic literal sense of those crucial sections. It is clear now that this view was much more deep-seated even in the Middle Ages than we used to think, although the cost of that realization is the knowledge that the *sensus literalis* varied much more through the ages than we used to think.[10]

First, *sensus literalis* may describe the precise or fit enactment of the intention to say what comes to be in the text. The intention may be that of the human author, in which case the construal of the text by the original audience has to be added. Or it may be the intention of the divine "author" or "inspirator" in the community's construal of the text as sacred or the coincidence of human and divine intention. If there is a theory of divine inspiration, the "literal" sense may be extended to overlap with the figurative or typological sense that may be part of the literal sense for God, though not for the human author.[11]

The appeal to the author's intention has had odd effects. On the one hand, it is an encouragement to historical criticism that wants to learn what the human author meant, through textual and extra textual devices—though, of course, the critic wants to know many other things also. On the other hand, the text taken as divinely inspired had some devastating effects. Since a text is an intelligibly enacted project, a unitary continuum rather than two separately intelligible acts, one mental, the other physical, the reader can detach it from its author: After all, grammatically, semantically,

stylistically, and conceptually it is the realized intention, and therefore there is no need to go behind the text. These are the means by
which the intention was enacted; they *are* the enacted intention.
The bibliolatry and sheer equation of Bible and doctrine by Protestant orthodoxy were the logical heirs of this constriction and sev-
erance of enactment from intention, and so were fundamentalist biblical literalism and factual inerrancy. Both shared a mechanical
notion of inspiration.

Second, literal sense refers to the descriptive fit between *verbum*
and *res*, sense and reference, signifier and signified, "Sinn" and
"Bedeutung," between grammatical/syntactical and conceptual sense,
between the narrative sequence and what it renders descriptively.
Centrally, in the Christian interpretative tradition of its sacred text,
the signifier of the New Testament narrative was taken to be the
sequence of the story itself, and what was signified by it was the identity of the agent cumulatively depicted by it. By extension this narrative was joined with others to make one temporal sequence that
cumulatively rendered the identity of God or his self-identification as
an agent in this storied context. Although the picture is confusing and
confused I take it that until modem times this "fit" between signifier
and signified was largely at an intralinguistic or semiotic rather than
epistemological level. Whether or not the story "referred" in a more
than storied way (i.e., what its truth may have been), it served
adequately as depiction or story, and thus what was depicted by it
needed no other conveyance—either linguistic and imaginative or
nonlinguistic—to bring story and meaning together. The question of
the "real" reference or truth of the sacred text, particularly its central
narrative, was one that was beyond interpretation (i.e., beyond
determining the sense, whether literal or spiritual). It meant that something else was brought into play. I am now oversimplifying a complex matter that I can only treat cryptically: Seen one way, namely,
from the vantage point of a *principled* difference between the linguistic "meaning" of narratives and their translinguistic "reference,"
hermeneutical inquiry is—in the second way of doing theology—
confined to description and conceptual use of the narratives, and it
eschews going further to the point of indicating the manner of their
true reference. But for this same way of doing theology this "principled difference" is precisely one of those philosophical constructs or
conventions that may have to be subordinated and may not apply in
an ordinary way but only ambiguously when it comes in contact with
the self-description of the Christian religion. On that reading, the
question of "reference" is included in hermeneutical-theological inquiry because it is solved descriptively in the case of *this* narrative
(whatever may be true of others). The linguistic account, that is, the
narrative itself, renders the reality narratively. We have the reality

only under the depiction and not in a language-neutral or language-transcending way. Nor are we barred from the reality by language. No further knowledge is needed, none is available. The narrated world is as such the real world and not a linguistic launching pad to language-transcending reality, whether ideal essence or self-contained empirical occurrence. Whatever may be true of other instances of linguistic or narrative worlds and what they refer to, in this case the depicted story renders reality in such a way that it obviates the translinguistic reference question as a separate question. The reality is given linguistically; it is linguistic for us. It is as *Word* that God's presence is incarnate, and that Word is *incarnate* and not merely transcendent. That is the self-description of the Christian religion in the form of conceptual redescription of its sacred text's central narrative under the *sensus literalis*.

Parable and metaphor came to be not identical but connected with the literal sense. Of course, an author could literally intend a metaphor. Beyond that, however, metaphor had a strong descriptive component different from that of allegory because, although displacing a linguistic world through rearrangement, it shared its features. The innovative and expressive element was subordinate. Metaphor involved a different world, but it did so by descriptive embodiment of that world as at once distanced from, and yet reinventing, the world of common discourse.[12] The parables of the Kingdom are (in this interpretive tradition) more like metaphors than allegories. The implication is that the parables are seen in the light of the story identifying Jesus of Nazareth rather than (reversely) providing the clue for the theme of that story. In the context of the *full* narrative—pericopes together with passion and resurrection—Jesus identifies the Kingdom of God and is only secondarily identified by his relation to it: He is himself the parable of the Kingdom.

Finally, the *sensus literalis* is the way the text has generally been used in the community. It is the sense of the text in its sociolinguistic context—liturgical, pedagogical, polemical, and so on. This is the setting in which it is appropriate to reach for that saying of Wittgenstein that has so often and wrongly been given the status of a general principle: "Don't ask for the meaning; ask for the use." In the words of a recent writer:

> This literal sense—the "natural," "plain," obvious meaning which the community of faith has normally acknowledged as basic, regardless of whatever other constructions might also properly be put upon the text—is grounded in the community's own experience with the text. As those adjectives suggest, it is the sense whose discernment has become second nature to the members of the community. It is a grasp of this literal sense which permits one to understand through the text, rather than being forever preoccupied with the text itself.[13]

The tradition of this kind of reading is venerable, going back to the early interpretation of Jewish Scriptures. *Peshat*, Raphael Loewe has shown, was not taken to be the plain sense of the text corresponding to the author's intention but was often far removed from it. Rather, it is "that familiar and traditional teaching of Scripture which was recognized by the community as authoritative."[14]

The Western Christian use of Christian Scripture in its most important theological representatives was similar. Augustine, for example, understood the plain sense of Scripture to be that which conduces to faith, hope, and the twofold love of God and neighbor.[15] The *sensus literalis* therefore is that which functions in the context of the Christian life, and James Preus is right in proposing that for Augustine this edifying or normative literal sense is actually identical with the true spiritual reading of an unedifying literal sense.[16]

The greatest difference between the Jewish and Christian interpretive traditions was of course that the latter dropped halakhah altogether, focusing exclusively on the New Testament equivalent of haggadah, which became the literal sense in all of the three ways we have adumbrated.

One of the most impressive features of Christian continuity is the degree to which the *sensus literalis* still persists. After the growth of modern "representationalism" in epistemology, the literal sense came to be the text's accurate reference to truth or reality, whether temporal or essential in character. And given once again (and this time even more so!) the centrality of the story of Jesus in the interpretive tradition, the *sensus literalis* meant the correspondence between crucial elements of that story and some actual, historical state of affairs, either inward or outward. On the one hand, we learned to say that Jesus' self-consciousness consisted of his awareness of being uniquely related to God and thought of this as an actual historical description; on the other, we learned to speak of the indispensability of the "historical occurrence character" of the event Jesus of Nazareth for a Christian interpretation of the New Testament. The recent complex corrective theory that tries to identify text and historical reference without reconstruction of the "personality" behind the text, by turning certain supposed authentic sayings of Jesus into the speech-event constituting him is further, perhaps even stronger corroboration of the tough persistent character of the *sensus literalis*. It claims not only the identity of language and being in the case of Jesus, but also the accessibility of the person so depicted. One may be skeptical about the way it uses the literal sense, its turn from descriptive to a purely inwardly performative (attitudinal?) theory of language and so on, but we still have here a version of the *sensus literalis*. That sense predominates heavily throughout the Western Christian history of interpretation, usually where the biblical-hermeneutical enterprise has been part of theology functioning as an aspect of normed self-description of the Christian religion.

Despite its variations, the *sensus literalis* has customarily been used to further not an obscurantist anticritical reading of the text but that reading Professor Ricoeur has perceptively characterized as a second or postcritical naivete. A good way to put it into sharp perspective is to set forth a powerful contrasting view.

Frank Kermode in *The Genesis of Secrecy* makes a great deal of "narrative shock," of the quality of the occult, of the inexhaustible hermeneutical potential of a text—in short of the sense that the New Testament parables, especially the earlier versions in Mark, with which he is largely concerned, are riddles that divide insiders from outsiders. They actually succeed in turning us all into outsiders, for they "may proclaim a truth as a herald does, and at the same time conceal truth like an oracle."[17] These narratives are in any case not "transparent upon history," but whether they are or not, they may be enigmatic or even fortuitous in plot, so that closure or fulfillment is something we impose upon them.[18] Like all "good enough" texts they have the capacity to subvert obvious expectations and manifest senses, and "good enough" readers will exploit the fact.[19] Kermode then presents us with a nice inversion: It is not only that the insiders turn out to be outsiders but that the external reading capitalizing on the enigmatic character of the text, which excludes us from its concealed truth, is actually the nearest thing to true "inside" reading. Subverting the obvious, carnal sense and turning instead to a hidden spiritual one is the way the then new insiders, the Christians, treated (and violated) the Torah. The very character of the New Testament (Mark!) invites us to do the same thing to it[20] and rid ourselves of the "myth of transparency" that has governed modern biblical exegesis.[21] A "good enough" text not being "transparent upon a known world," "interpreters lose the possibility of consensus, and of access to a single truth at the heart of the thing." For all except the most reactionary hermeneutics, "the pleasures of interpretation are henceforth linked to loss and disappointment,"[22] as the torch of inquiry passes from the most recent insiders, the professional biblical scholars who took the place of the earlier ecclesiastical interpreters, to the latest outsiders who divine the literary structure of the text on the secular model.[23] And what they divine makes a perfect fit with the symbiosis of illumination and concealment; divination is an avenue into what remains basically an unfollowable world or text.[24] We follow up veiled hints such as the translation into narrative of schematic oppositions like silence and proclamation, election and rebuke, clean and unclean, the things of God and the things of man.[25] We get a Gospel of Mark structured as a narrative line that is continuously enhanced through plotted disruptions, cultivated oppositions, or "intercalation or analeptic narrative constructions" into which even the interpreters themselves become intercalated.[26]

Kermode has given us a nice, nondogmatically structuralist reading of the text. Nondogmatic because the structures are the yield not simply of synchronic analysis, communications theory, the plotting of phonemic curves, and so on, but at least incipiently of a moment of discovery—a decidedly unstructuralist notion. There is the moment of divination, of understanding as momentary illumination occasioned by some "impression point" within the narrative that becomes emblematic of the whole.[27] Professor Ricoeur has suggested that the real business of interpretation begins where structuralist analysis leaves off. By contrast Kermode, although he says he agrees with this view,[28] seems to correlate the two horizontally or dialectically rather than hierarchically; the structures occasion—and are occasioned by—understanding as an inner event or process in time. They come as close to a "content" as the illumination can have. But no new world of discourse, no new linguistic universe is constructed (for Kermode) in "understanding." In his workshop of interpretation we are not pressed toward that convergence of limit experience and limit expression for which metaphor and parable are the verbal hoists, and in the service of which the innovative semantic function of parable and metaphor is accorded primacy. In that view the religious horizon of experience—perhaps one should even say "transcendence"—is linguistically yet transconceptually disclosed in parable and metaphor as symbols or instantiations of the convergence.[29] Kermode does not share this outlook any more than he does its obverse side, namely, the "ordinariness" of the world of the parable within which this metaphoric "extravagance" or "oddness" appears.[30] For Kermode, a structuralist reading is attractive in large part because it rids you of the illusion of "reference," of the truth, of "what is written about rather than what is written." Neither objective reality—whether historical occurrence or eternal metaphysical essence—nor transcendentally grounded understanding or mode-of-being-in-the-world-in-a-limit-way is the referent of narrative. Denied all of that in our interpretive moves, we stand transiently in our moment of illumination—dare I say that "lighting of being"?—where we perceive rather than merely see, understand and not merely hear, only to find that the illumination is also the concealment, except in (but perhaps even in) the moment of passage. "It is a momentary radiance, delusive or not."[31] Standing in it we cannot judge between revelation and deception, and for the long run we know simply that we are barred from the truth. The text is an unfollowable world. We are all outsiders and that is our secret insiders' knowledge. So "understanding" a text is neither a

hermeneutically circular process or event referring to limit-experience
or expression, nor the conceptual competence to follow the text in
the appropriate context. The dialectic of disclosure and concealment
dissolves into the latter, for which the intercalation or analeptic narrative constructions are the perfect occasions or objective correlatives.
For what do they tell us but that the content of the disclosure is—
concealment and disruption?

It is precisely the reverse of a similar dialectic between outsider
and insider in the Christian interpretive tradition in the West. The
relation between "letter" and "spirit," whatever it is, is not equivalent to that between manifest and latent sense. The primacy of the
sensus literalis is in effect an assertion of the fitness and congruence of
the "letter" to be the channel of the spirit. It is the assertion that the
text is more nearly perspicuous than not and that, therefore, the dialectic insider/outsider as well as disclosure/concealment must end in
the asymptotic subordination of the latter to the former in each pair.
Indeed, the *tendency* is more radical yet. It is that the dialectic of the
first pair—though not the second—is in principle dissolved, just as it
is for Kermode, but in the opposite direction. For the Protestant
Reformers, governance by the *sensus literalis* in the reading of Scripture as well as its perspicuity entailed that in principle there is no
interpretive outsider. We are all insiders, even if that affirmation is
made chiefly in hope and with an eschatological edge rather than in
present realization. Calvin has it that our hearts and minds may need
illumination, the text does not. It is plain for all to read. The odd, philosophically ambiguous status of "reference" in this tradition, for which
literal and historical, word and thing were congruent in a semiotic
rather than epistemological or representational way meant that the
text did not communicate—as though by way of a channel of
absence—the presence of God. The text did not refer to, it *was* the
linguistic presence of God, the fit embodiment of one who was himself "Word," and thus it was analogous to, though not identical with,
Incarnation. The literal sense was therefore the fit and appropriate way
to read the text. "Theology," Luther said, "is the grammar of the Holy
Spirit." He was talking about the interpretation of Scripture. Here, to
use Wittgenstein's words, "grammar is essence." We are not barred
from truth though we might well be if the relation between text and
truth is of the sort Kermode proposes and then says we do not have.
But for the Christian interpretive tradition truth is what is written,
not something separable and translinguistic that is written "about."

A more drastic and dramatic way of putting part of Kermode's
position comes in the wake of Jacques Derrida's *De la Grammatol-
ogie*, claiming connections between ontological presuppositions of
the dialectic of exile and Western philosophy's traditional notion of
language as mimesis. A metaphysical concept of truth as "Presence"

underlies both the Judaeo-Christian metaphor of man as an exile "outside" or absent from God and the theory of language as an imitation of something essentially unlike language, something that is often conceived spatially, as if behind or beyond the medium that imitates it. "An 'inside/outside' dichotomy governs both the exile and the writer who sees his words as the imitation of things *(res)*, whether physical objects or concepts. . . . As long as language is seen as an imitation or transportation of significance, metaphor is seen as a home away from home, a detour in the road whose goal is union or reunion with truth."[32]

It is difficult to respond in a short space. Christian theology does not present the finite condition of human being as identical with its fall, and hence thinks neither of the original state as metaphysical union with God, nor of the fallen state as metaphysical separation or "dispersal" in contrast to union. Rather, the created state is that of "contingent independence" (Austin Farrer), not easy to state by way of any metaphysical scheme, but certainly not accurately portrayed as separation, dispersal, or fall from union. Creation is not the fall in Christian doctrine. This is a confusion of Christian belief with whatever Neoplatonism, gnosticism and the existentialist heritage derived from German Idealism have in common. Obviously, then, language is, for Christians, a created good and not in principle fallen, and therefore it is not "absent" from the truth. In fact, the whole scheme of "inside/outside" relations to truth—when it is systematically connected with this metaphysical *mélange*, language being "outside" and meaning-as-translinguistic-essence "inside"—is misleading so far as Christian thought goes: Being external to God is not evil or being out of relation with or absent from him; and being internally related to him metaphysically is, for Christians, a very odd notion, indeed, and certainly not what "divine presence" means.

Language is not fallen, not absent from truth or meaning—that supposed essence which is unlike language and for which language merely furnishes the transportation. For Kermode we are outsiders barred from truth; for the more dramatic position it is not only that interpretation of texts should ignore the futile lure of meaning or truth, but also that the whole picture of language, on the one hand, and meaning or truth, on the other hand—whether accessible or not—is misleading. We have language and that *is all* we have, and to intercalate "meaning" into it is the very temptation we must resist. We have texts and intertextuality and no other realm. We are ready for deconstruction, and in deconstructing we shape the text as our universe. Kermode has language refer but do so always in vain. The more astringent position gets rid of reference, but unlike Kermode it retains the innovative function of metaphor that can only be liberated when reference is done away with.

But the diagnostic description is wrong in the first place, and the prescription is for a nonexistent patient. For the Christian tradition, language is not fallen and the "transport" metaphor is therefore inappropriate; thus the argument that ends up with the solitary character of language in the absence of the transport to meaning cannot be generated in the first place. Moreover, since meaning, whatever the correct uses of that term, is not a translinguistic essence; and therefore since meaning is not to be conceived as heterogeneous or in principle absent from language, language is not only not solitary, but also not all-encompassing. If one has to talk in these large, abstract terms one ought to say that from the beginning language is such that meaning or truth can be linguistic or verbiform.

III

The *sensus literalis*, I have suggested, is deeply embedded in the Christian interpretive tradition of its sacred text, and in that way embedded in the self-description of the Christian religion as a social complex rather than as a set of phenomena cohering in, and manifesting, an underlying essence. Especially the third way of understanding the literal sense, as the customary use to which a text has been put in the context of the community's belief and life—for example, Augustine's appeal to love of God and neighbor as the aim of the literal sense—shows the convergence of interpretation and communal self-description. No other portion of Christian Scripture has had so nearly an identical applicative use in the Christian communal context as the story of Jesus, understood both as his narrative identification, the enactment of who he is, and in its emblematic function for the life of the community. Indeed, one may suppose that this narrative identification became the paradigm for combining into one sequential whole from creation to eschaton that disparate set of stories from Jewish and Christian Scriptures that in modern Christian theological interpretation has been termed "salvation history." It was St. Paul who turned the Adam of the Torah into the first Adam prefiguring the new one.

The *sensus literalis*—not only as use-in-context but as unity of grammatical/syntactical sense and signified subject—also found its clue or focus in this development. The amazing abandonment of halakhah in favor of haggadah in the Christian interpretive tradition (surely not wholly, though largely explicable from the antilegal sentiment accompanying the transplantation of Christianity to gentile soil) involved a further specification of very early vintage. The subject matter of the Christian equivalent of haggadah became in the first place a diachronic narrative rendering of an intention-action sequence rather than sets of individual, cryptic metaphoric tales. Thus, the parables of the Kingdom of God, whatever their original intent, were soon used as figurations of Jesus that substantiated his messianic identity as enacted in his story so that their point of signaling the "limit experience" of the Kingdom of God, although very real, was not logically independent of that other theme. Jesus, proclaiming, describing, and proleptically presencing the Kingdom of God was himself the subject of what he said in the use of the parables by the interpretive tradition. The identity of the messenger became the clue to the character of the message and this, in turn, was due to the priority of his identification in agency or enactment over his identification as speech act, linguistic performative or embodied, innovative metaphor.

In view of the centrality of the story of Jesus in the interpretive tradition from the earliest days forward and its crucial part in the rise of the *sensus literalis* to eventual predominance, one may well see a connection between this story and the fascinating blurring between allegorical and figural or typological interpretation that one soon observes in Christian scriptural reading, for typology is in fact a not easily specifiable and yet definite bridge between allegorical and literal reading.[33] The development is obvious in the Christian use of Jewish Scripture as Old Testament, but it may also be observed within the New Testament itself to the extent even of structuring the gospel accounts themselves, so that the parables, for instance, become figures of the intention-action pattern embodied in the passion and resurrection of Jesus.

The literal sense is a paradigm case of what Professor Ricoeur has so wisely called the hermeneutics of restoration in contrast to the hermeneutics of suspicion. For in its way of depicting the realization of a theme through the interaction of character and circumstances, the literal reading does two things: (1) It comprehends together under "literal" both the grammatical/syntactical sense *and* the storied sense, "literal" thus meaning both syntactical and *literary*-literal (in contrast to allegorical) use; (2) it renders for us by way of the story a common world of discourse, the world we need to understand the story—the same kind of world as ours, the world in which persons and circumstances shape each other and their stories cannot be told without that interaction, nor can that interaction be schematized into a dialectic substitutable for the account itself. Whatever else we are and whatever may be hidden about us, our surface story has its own density, and it is the literary or narrative linguistic world that we all inhabit. We may inhabit other worlds also, and for certain purposes it may be illuminating and even essential to subvert this diachronic world of ageney and suffering—by "deeper" accounts—deep synchronic structures, the unconscious, or economic infrastructures—but it will have to be *subverted*, for we must return to it again and again. That world is at once read sensitively along the surface of its diachronic specificity, but its specificity also reaches into the mode of our reading it: It governs our "depth grammar." We are embodied agents and understand what we do, suffer, and are in the contexts in which we are placed as the world is shaped upon and by us. In that way the gospel story and we ourselves inhabit the same kind of world.

I am not proposing or arguing a general anthropology. I am precisely *not* claiming that narrative sequence is the built-in constitution of human being phenomenologically uncovered. That may or may not be the case. Rather, I am suggesting that it is narrative specificity through which we describe an intentional-agential world and ourselves in it If there *is* a "narrative theology," the meaning of that term in the context of the self-description of the Christian community is that we are specified by relation to its particular narrative and by our conceptual redescription of it in belief and life, not by a quality of "narrativity" inherent in our picture of self, world, and transcendence at large.

Perhaps, indeed, the *sensus literalis* is congenial to a hermeneutics that describes or explains the possibility of understanding as a unitary process or event, mayhap as a linguistic event, so as not to pull language and selfhood apart. Language, being, and meaning are closely linked here. Such a hermeneutics is closely, probably necessarily connected also to a general anthropology of selfhood as subjecthood or consciousness. However, this is a view for which it seems most likely that language is basically neither descriptive nor performative because it is basically preconceptual and expressive. The text is the projection of a world, and so are we readers. In that case what the text "signifies" is likewise pre- or transconceptual (i.e., that intimation of transcendence that is projected in the convergence of limit experience and limit expression). Here, "metaphor" as innovative thrust disrupting ordinariness is precisely fit to identify both Kingdom of God and Jesus. Moreover, "metaphor" or human being as innovatively linguistic consciousness will finally have to become the clues to the "meaning" or "reference" of depicted action: The interaction of person and circumstance in which his/her identity is rendered will have to be embraced by a more profound, nonagential or preagential view of the person as linguistic self-expression rather than embodied self-enactment. For the *sensus literalis*, however, the *descriptive* function of language and its conceptual adequacy are shown forth precisely in the kind of story that does not refer beyond itself for its meaning, as allegory does, the kind of story in which the "signified," the identity of the protagonist, is enacted by the signifier, the narrative sequence itself. It is an instance of literary literal sense.

The meaning of the gospel story for the *sensus literalis* is, then, that it is *this* story about *this* person as agent and patient, about its surface description and plot. A unified theory of understanding that conceives of understanding as a process or event and is in turn an aspect of an anthropology of consciousness is unlikely to do justice to the character of human being as agent-enactment or to the descriptive, conceptual adequacy of language in the depiction of such a story.

To the extent that theology is undertaken as part of the self-description of the Christian religion and the *sensus literalis* is at the heart of the Christian interpretive tradition of its sacred text, "understanding" involves a capacity combining a variety of skills rather than a single unitary phenomenon. Understanding texts may differ in accordance with different texts and their differing contexts. Didactic letters may demand different skills from realistic narratives, and parables may differ from both. This does not necessarily mean that "to understand" is many things, but simply that it may not be of the sort for the unity of which an explanatory theory is available.

Still one does not therefore have to reject wholesale the other side of the ambiguous status of theology, viz., its philosophical relationship. One will have to subordinate the philosophical relationship to the Christianly self-descriptive one without eliminating the former. This will obviously mean a humbler hermeneutics for rather low-level guidance in interpretation than we have become accustomed to. It will raise doubts about a theory or the possibility that is logically prior to the actuality of interpretation, and it will be a theory of descriptive elements that *go into* but do not *constitute* a unified description of "understanding"—elements of methods if you will. In a way this is a return to eighteenth-century hermeneutics, but a sober and chastened one, instructed by a long, exciting story of profound search and yet failure in the intervening epochs. Yes, we shall have to continue to ask what it is to understand, but it should be a technical question that is not only second-order to (and upon) actual practice, but relativized because its first order of business is to realize the urging of the *sensus literalis* that between the Christian narrative and the interpreter there is the nexus of the common linguistic world, which is rendered by the diachronic, agential, i.e., narrative web of that world.

The descriptive elements of hermeneutics will thus be something like Karl Barth's proposal of three stages that shade into each other, yet keep their logical if not practical distinction:[34] (1) *Explicatio*, the sheer retelling of the story or other texts, together with the philological and other aids that go into that activity for the more technically trained; *(2) meditatio*, the conceptual redescription or (more generally) refraction of the text through the structures of our minds—whether we think of this as taking place by virtue of a unified phenomenon, an internal process, or through the discovery of deep structures shared by synchronically ordered texts into which the interpreter himself becomes intercalated, or other forms of what this autonomous intellectual activity might best be described to be; and finally (3) *applicatio* or use, which is in its own way as inclusive as the second stage. It is the skill to relate the story (or other texts) to the context, the judgment that we do or do not share a world with the text and with the community in which it has functioned since its first telling. The text is meaningful by appropriation, its meaning is performatively or existentially realized.

Yet the latter is not all that is involved in conceptual mastery, and it is important therefore to keep the logical distinction between the second and third stages even though in practice they shade into each other. But both of them are in one way subordinate to, though distinct from, the first stage: For the first stage, humdrum though it be, signals the insistence that we can and do read together in the Christian linguistic community and that the text governs us all—in that context. In interpreting conceptually and existentially, we are governed first by the story and, in the second place, by the way it functions in the Christian religion

Notes

1. A recent proposal typical of this outlook is Gordon Kaufman, *An Essay in Theological Method* (Missoula, Mont: Scholars Press, 1975).

2. David H. Kelsey among others has made this suggestion. *The Uses of Scripture in Recent Theology* (Philadelphia: Fortress Press, 1975), pp. 162ff.

3. This awkwardness of placing Christianity and its theological articulation philosophically becomes even more fascinating when philosophers become unsure of placing philosophy itself. Richard Rorty, *Philosophy and the Mirror of Nature* (Princeton: Princeton University Press, 1979) differs from "foundational" philosophers in allowing traditional religion a passport to go on as an independent conversational enterprise, yet warning it that there is just enough cultural foundation from the past in our present outlook that it must not expect nonfoundational support in any struggle against the character it has had assigned to it ever since the Enlightenment, namely, that it is a hollow, purely "in-group" kind of undertaking. See also Jeffrey Stout, *The Flight from Authority: Religion, Morality and the Quest for Autonomy* (Notre Dame: University of Notre Dame Press, 1981), pt. 2.

4. One thinks of Clifford Geertz's sensitive descriptions of Islam, for example, in *Islam Observed* (New Haven, Yale University Press, 1968).

5. For a very useful comparison between these two approaches to sociology, see Reinhard Bendix, "Two Sociological Traditions," in R. Bendix and G. Roth, *Scholarship and Partisanship: Essays on Max Weber* (Berkeley: University of California Press, 1971), pp. 282–98. For a more than adequate summary of the theoretical portions of Durkheim's *The Elementary Forms of the Religious Life* (Glencoe, Ill.: Free Press, 1954), see the sections excerpted in Roland Robertson, ed., *Sociology of Religion: Selected Readings* (Harmondsworth; Penguin, 1969), pp. 42–54.

6. See Max Weber's essay "The Fundamental Concepts of Sociology," in M. Weber, *The Theory of Social and Economic Organization* (New York: Oxford

University Press, 1947), edited with an introduction by Talcott Parsons, see esp. pp. 88–112. The quotation is from p. 100. For the contrast with Durkheim see the essay by Bendix "Two Sociological Traditions."

7. I have relied in my account on an elegant statement of this simple and straightforward cleavage in the first part of an essay by Wayne Proudfoot, "Religion and Reduction," *Union Seminary Quarterly Review* 27 (Fall/Winter 1981–82), esp. 13–17.

8. Friedrich Schleiermacher, *On the "Glaubenslehre"* (Chico, Calif.: Scholars Press, 1980), p. 81; Barth, *Church Dogmatics* (Edinburgh: T. & T. Clark, 1936), vol. I, pt. 1, p. 1.

9. I would only protest the purist who confines "theology" completely to the first, that is, philosophical option, and for good measure makes the social language of the Christian community simply a function of the language of a more inclusive construct such as "Western culture." For an example, see Kaufman, *Essay in Theological Method*, pp. 3 ff., 53 f., where the concept "God" on the one hand is a product of that culture, and on the other hand its efficacy as a construct is dependent on the meaningfulness of another construction involving a permanent feature of the world and the general human condition, namely, its being relativized and its being humanized at the same time.

10. Cf. Brevard S. Childs, "The Sensus Literalis of Scripture: An Ancient and Modern Problem," in H. Donner, R. Hanhart, and R. Smend, eds., *Beiträge zur Alttestamentlichen Theologie: Festschrift für Walther Zimmerli zum 70. Geburtstag* (Göttingen: Vandenhoeck und Ruprecht, 1977), pp. 80–93.

11. See Thomas Aquinas, *Summa theologiae I*, 1, 10.

12. The description of metaphor, connected with the *sensus literalis*, is close to one rejected by Paul Ricoeur on the ground that metaphor is a tension between all the terms in it, resulting in semantic innovation. "Paul Ricoeur on Biblical Hermeneutics," *Semeia 4*, pp. 76 ff.

13. Charles M. Wood, *The Formation of Christian Understanding* (Philadelphia: Westminster Press, 1981), p. 43. I am deeply and generally indebted to Professor Wood's book, particularly in pt. III of this paper.

14. Childs, "Sensus Literalis of Scripture," pp. 80 f; Raphael Loewe, "The 'Plain' Meaning of Scripture in Early Jewish Exegesis," *Papers of the Institute of Jewish Studies in London* (Jerusalem, 1964), vol. 1, 140–85.

15. Saint, Augustine, *De doctrina Christiana*, I, 36, 40; II, 6, 8; II, 9, 14.

16. James Preus, *From Shadow to Promise* (Cambridge, Mass.: Harvard University Press, 1969), p. 14.

17. Frank Kermode, *The Genesis of Secrecy: On the Interpretation of Narrative* (Cambridge, Mass.: Harvard University Press, 1979), p. 47.

18. Ibid., pp. 63–65.

19. Ibid., p. 14.

20. Ibid., pp. 18 ff.

21. Ibid., pp. 118 ff.

22. Ibid., pp 122 ff

23. Ibid., pp. 136 ff.

24. Ibid., p. 126.

25. Ibid., p. 140.

26. Ibid., pp. 127, 133.

27. Ibid., pp. 14, 40, 136.

28. Ibid., p. 41.

29. Ricoeur, "On Biblical Hermeneutics," pp. 107 ff., esp. p. 127: cf. David Tracy, *Blessed Rage for Order* (New York: Seabury Press, 1975), chap. 6.

30. Kermode, *Genesis of Secrecy*, p. 99.

31. Ibid., p. 144.

32. Margaret W. Ferguson, "Saint Augustine's Region of Unlikeness: The Crossing of Exile and Language," *Georgia Review*, (Winter 1975), 843 f.

33. I agree with Erich Auerbach on this placement of figural interpretation (cf. *Mimesis*, trans. Willard R. Trask [Princeton: Princeton University Press, 1953], chaps. 2 and 3; and "Figura" in *Scenes from the Drama of European Literature* [New York: Meridian Books, 1959]).

34. Barth, *Church Dogmatics* (Edinburgh: T. & T. Clark, 1956), vol. I, pt. 2, pp. 722–40, 766–82.

4

The "Literal Reading" of Biblical Narrative in the Christian Tradition: Does It Stretch or Will It Break?

This essay was originally read at a conference on "The Bible and the Narrative Tradition" held in May 1983 at the University of California, Santa Barbara. Harold Bloom, Frank Kermode, and James M. Robinson also presented papers at the conference. These were then published with others in The Bible and the Narrative Tradition, *edited by Frank McConnell (New York: Oxford University Press, 1986).*

Frei's earlier work had often drawn upon literary critics influential at the time, Erich Auerbach and the New Critics in particular. This essay reflects his reading in more recent literary criticism: Kermode, Bloom, and various deconstructionists, among others. It also continues the debate with Paul Ricoeur and David Tracy that he had begun the year before in "Theology and the Interpretation of Narrative: Some Hermeneutical Considerations." Frei had previously argued for the peculiarly narrative character of biblical texts at a time when that was too often overlooked. Ricoeur, however, had certainly paid attention to narrative, yet Frei thought he was still somehow missing the point in a way that illustrated deep flaws in the whole tradition of "hermeneutics." Ricoeur and Tracy, Frei maintained, were still finally treating the Gospel stories about Jesus as presentations of a certain mode-of-being-in-the-world rather than first of all as narratives about the singular person of Jesus. Further, they still understood Jesus' selfhood primarily as an internal consciousness more or less expressed in words and deeds rather than as constituted by his enacted intentions.

This essay also reflects the increasing importance Frei assigned to the Christian community as the "cultural linguistic" setting in which the biblical texts have most frequently been read. He consistently urged attending to the biblical texts as realistic narratives, not only because that was most faithful to the character of the texts themselves, but also because that was the way the Christian community had read them for most of its history. Frei's earlier work had emphasized the first of these consider- ations. Here the second comes more to the fore. If the priority of the lit- eral reading is made dependent on some theory about the nature of narratives, Frei feared, the argument may "break" in the face of dis- putes about that theory. But the informal rules that have traditionally guided the Christian community in its reading of these texts will "stretch" to accommodate a wide range of theories about narrative texts, history, and human persons.

* * *

An outsider to the lively, cacophonous discussion among contempo- rary theorists of literature is bound to wonder whether the very term "narrative tradition" isn't one more among the hypostatized constants, like the "canon" of literature or the notion of "literariness," which some of the discussants want to consign to dissolution. As a Christian theologian rather than a literary or biblical scholar, I shall not try to position the Bible in relation to this putative tradition; instead, I will comment on what I perceive to be a wide, though of course not unani- mous, traditional consensus among Christians in the West on the primacy of the literal reading of the Bible, on its connection with narrative, on its present status and future outlook.

Much of the essay will be taken up with "hermeneutics," the theory of the interpretation of texts and of the character of under- standing going into that activity. The exposition will be complex because both the theory itself and the criticisms often mounted against it today are complex, not to say esoteric. But the reason for the exer- cise is as simple as the exercise itself is difficult: In the midst of a mounting crescendo of dissent from thematic readings of narratives, including scriptural stories, as normative guides for living and believ- ing as well as reading, hermeneutical theory is the most prominent contemporary champion of the embattled tradition. So if one comes to the conclusion that the value of this sustained and subtle effort is in the end questionable, one had best go through the paces of argu- ing the negative case. In sum, I believe that the tradition of the *sensus literalis* is the closest one can come to a consensus reading of the Bible as the sacred text in the Christian church and that current herme- neutical theory defends a revised form of it; but I also believe that the defense is a failure, so that, in the words of the essay's title, the literal reading will break apart under its ministrations. One may well hope that the *sensus literalis,* a much more supple notion than one might at first suspect, has a future. If it does, there will be good reason to explain what it is about with a far more modest theory—more modest both in its claims about what counts as valid interpretation and in the scope of the material on which it may pertinently comment.

This essay is therefore a strictly second-order affair, commenting on theories pertinent to the past as well as present and future *conditions* for the literal reading as a religious enterprise; it is neither an exercise within that traditional enterprise, nor even an argument in behalf of its continued viability. That viability, if any, will follow excellently from the actual, fruitful use religious people continue to make of it in ways that enhance their own and other people's lives, without the obscurantist features so often and unhappily associated with it. And even if, as may be expected, there is a continuing decline of the felt pertinence of this way of reading among those who do not make a direct religious use of it, this in no way alters the case for its viability in principle to Christian people, no matter how distressing it is bound to be to them as an actual cultural fact.

The association of narrative with religion generally and Christianity in particular has always been close, although the self-consciously systematic use of the concept "narrative" in Christian theology is a modern invention. Reference to "the sacred story" or "sacred" or "salvation history" as a category to describe what was taken to be the dominant content of the Bible did not arise until the seventeenth century.

Most, if not all, religions contain tales of creation, loss, quest, and restoration which symbolize reality and allow the readers or listeners access to the common identifying patterns making up that symbolized world, and to the communal ways of inhabiting it. It is generally assumed that such tales are originally oral in character, with no particular author, and that they are perpetuated by a tradition of authoritative narrators or singers. These tellers adapt the content and pattern of a common story in their own individual ways usually under formulaic constraints imposed both by linguistic conventions and by the absence of all ironic distance between narrator, story, and audience. Tellers and listeners are part of the same symbolic and enacted world, so that the conditions for self-referencing authorial or listening perspectives are lacking.[1]

Not all oral epics can become candidates for the status of "sacred stories" within "sacred texts," especially if one accepts the speculative theory that the distinction between "profane" and "sacred" is universal as well as primitive,[2] so that "folktales" come to be distinguished from "myths," which are of the same narrative order but include sacred themes.[3] However, the easy and natural fusion of historical tradition, myth, and social custom in ancient folktales makes for the natural inclusion of some of them in sacred texts, once the transition from oral to literate culture takes place.

However one speculates, in this or other ways, about the origins of sacred stories—and speculation it remains—most literate cultures have them and include them in their sacred texts. Contact and conflict among religions within the same demographic area or cultural family typically result in a parasitic takeover in altered form of the elements of one such text by a later, or even a contemporaneous, religious group as part of its own scripture. So it was between Hinduism and Buddhism, between Hebrew and Christian Scripture, and between Hebrew and Christian Scripture and the Qur'an. Sacred stories are obvious targets for such scriptural transformation. The adherents of Jesus did not obliterate the story of John the Baptist, assigning him instead the role of forerunner and witness in the story of Jesus and thus a secure, if subordinate, place in the Christian New Testament.

The Primacy of the Literal Sense in Christian Interpretation

The most striking example of this kind of takeover in the history of Western culture is the inclusion of Jewish in Christian Scripture by means of "typology" or "figuration," so that not only "Old Testament" narrative but its legal texts and its prophetic as well as wisdom literature are taken to point beyond themselves to their "fulfillment" in the "New Testament." The Jewish texts are taken as "types" of the story of Jesus as their common "antitype," an appropriating procedure that begins in the New Testament, notably in the letters of Paul, the letter to the Hebrews, and the synoptic Gospels, and then becomes the common characteristic of the Christian tradition of scriptural interpretation until modern times.

Two features in this process are especially striking. First, in contrast to Hebrew Scripture and the Rabbinic tradition, in which cultic and moral regulations tend to be at once associated with and yet relatively autonomous from narrative biblical texts, Christian tradition tends to derive the meaning of such regulations—for example, the sacraments, the place of the "law" in Christian life, the love commandment—directly from (or refer them directly to) its sacred story, the life, teachings, death, and resurrection of Jesus the Messiah. This narrative thus has a unifying force and a prescriptive character in both the New Testament and the Christian community that, despite the importance of the Exodus accounts, neither narrative generally nor any specific narrative has in Jewish Scripture and the Jewish community.

Second, it was largely by reason of this centrality of the story of Jesus that the Christian interpretive tradition in the West gradually assigned clear primacy to the literal sense in the reading of Scripture, not to be contradicted by other legitimate senses—tropological, allegorical, and anagogical. In the ancient church, some of the parables of Jesus—for example, that of the Good Samaritan (Luke 10:25–37)—were interpreted allegorically as referring latently or spiritually to all sorts of types, and more especially to Jesus himself, but this could only be done because the story of Jesus itself was taken to have a literal or plain meaning: He was the Messiah, and the fourfold storied depiction in the gospels, especially of his passion and resurrection, was the enacted form of his identity as Messiah. Thus, by and large, except for the school of Origen in which the Old Testament received a kind of *independent* allegorical interpretation, allegory tended to be in the service of literal interpretation, with Jesus the center or focus of coherence for such reading. In that way, allegory remained legitimate up until the Reformation, even in its supposed rejection by the school of Antioch. Typological or figural interpretation, which was applied not only to the Old Testament but to the meaning of extrabiblical life and events, including one's own, stood in an unstable equilibrium between allegorical and literal interpretations. An event real in its own right and a meaning complex and meaningful in its own right are nonetheless understood to be incomplete, and thus "figures" of the event-and-or-meaning that fulfills them in the story of Jesus or in the universal story from creation to eschaton, of which it was the effectually shaping centerpiece.

The title of James Preus's important book on the history of Christian Old Testament interpretation, *From Shadow to Promise*,[4] points out a basic distinction between two kinds of allegorical and typological interpretations in Christian "Old Testament" reading. The "Old Testament" could be understood as "mere" letter or shadow, a "carnal" figure in the most derogatory sense, to which the "New Testament" stood in virtual contrast as the corresponding "spiritual" or genuine reality, and the all but direct contrary of its prefigured representation. There is often considerable similarity between orthodox Christian allegorical reading of the Old Testament and its hostile, negative interpretation on the part of Marcion, even though the orthodox, in contrast to Marcion, insisted on retaining the Old Testament as part of Scripture. However, other Christian exegetes thought they were honoring the Old Testament texts for their mysterious, many-sided, and spiritual profundity in reading them allegorically. For others yet, allegory and thus the "carnal" tales of the Old Testament were an educational means by which God accommodated himself to an early, crude, and temporary human condition—a theme that resurfaced during the Enlightenment era.

Whenever the Old Testament is seen as "letter" or "carnal shadow," spiritual and literal reading coincide, and figural and allegorical reading are one. "Spiritual reading" in this context is that of those who are in the first place privy to the truth directly rather than "under a veil," and who know, secondly, that the reality depicted is "heavenly," spiritual or religious, rather than earthly, empirical, material, or political. But since it is the story of Jesus taken literally that unveils this higher truth, the "literal" sense is the key to spiritual interpretation of the *New Testament.* In this as in some other respects, "letter" and "spirit" turn out to be mutually fit or reinforcing in much orthodox Christianity, despite the superficially contrary Pauline declaration (2 Cor. 3:6).

On the other hand, rather than as *shadow,* the Old Testament could be understood as *promise,* that is, as pointing to a state of affairs literally meant but only incompletely or not yet actualized at the time it was written, such as the prophecy in Jeremiah 31:31 ff., "The days are coming when I shall make a New Covenant with the house of Israel and with the house of Judah: After those days, saith the Lord, I will put my law in their inward parts and write it in their hearts." Not only was this saying taken to indicate the fulfillment of an earlier by a later historical event in a chronological sequence, but earlier and later are at the same time related as trope to true meaning; tablets of stone are a preliminary, imperfect figure for their *telos,* tablets of flesh. Much Reformation and orthodox Protestant exegesis was governed by this outlook. Figure and fulfillment, or type and antitype, are related along a temporal as well as a literary or metaphorical axis.

Interpretive traditions of religious communities tend to reach a consensus on certain central texts. We have noted that the literal reading of the gospel stories was the crucial instance of this consensus in the early church. What is striking about this is that the "literal" reading in this fashion became the normative or "plain" reading of the texts. There is no a priori reason why the "plain" reading could not have been "spiritual" in contrast to "literal," and certainly the temptation was strong. The identification of the plain with the literal sense was not a logically necessary development, but it did begin with the early Christian community and was perhaps unique to Christianity. The creed, "rule of faith" or "rule of truth" which governed the Gospels' use in the church asserted the primacy of their literal sense. Moreover, it did this right from the beginning in the *ascriptive* even more than the *descriptive* mode. That "Jesus"—not someone else or nobody in particular—is the subject, the agent, and patient of these stories is said to be their crucial point, and the descriptions of events, sayings, personal qualities, and so forth, become literal by being firmly predicated of him. Not until the Protestant Reformation is the literal sense understood as authoritative—because perspicuous—in its own right, without authorization from the interpretive tradition.

The upshot of this ruled use of the New Testament stories was of course bound to entail the expropriative rules for the interpretation of Jewish Scripture which we have noted, and all three cases of the procedure—shadow and reality, prophecy and fulfillment, metaphorical type and literal antitype—came to present modern Christian biblical reading with two enormous problems. First, how is one to acknowledge the autonomy of the Jewish scriptural tradition without a collapse of Christian interpretation? Even if you brutalized it, you needed Jewish Scripture; for what is a fulfillment without antecedents that need to be fulfilled? Christians could neither do without Jewish Scripture nor accord it that autonomous status that a modern understanding of religions calls for. The second problem is a natural extension of the first, and it has been mentioned by commentators from Gotthold Ephraim Lessing to Frank Kermode, by some in an upbeat, by others in a deeply pessimistic mood: Suppose now that the literal sense of the New Testament only prefigures a still newer reading that displaces it in turn, developed by a new set of inside interpreters who transcend the now old (i.e., New Testament), exoteric, or carnal to reach a new spiritual sense which, because it refers to the truth in its real and not veiled form, is identical with the *true* literal sense. That new reading could be a new religion, with a new story ranged onto the old—who knows, perhaps the Unification Church. On the other hand, it could already be history, for example the Ottoman Turks carrying the Qur'an westward, except that their hermeneutical triumph stopped short at the gates of Vienna. The new reading could also be the product of a vision of a new humanity in which the previous difference between insiders and outsiders, esoteric and exoteric, or spiritual and carnal reading would disappear: All humanity would be the true new church, reading past Scriptures in the light of their eternal and universal transformation. As Lessing envisioned it: "It will surely come, the time of a new eternal gospel, which is promised us even in the primers of the New Covenant itself." We will all be insiders on that climactic day.[5]

On the other hand, such a new reading could involve the discovery that the only inside information we have is that, Lessing notwithstanding, we are all outsiders to the truth, and the only point at which literal and true spiritual senses coincide therefore is not—as Christians have claimed—in the Gospel narratives, nor in any later substitute, but in the shock of recognition that, the road to truth being barred, there must be an end to the literal sense. Rather than all humanity being insiders, we are all outsiders, and the only thing

we know is that the truth is what we do not know.[6] The very notion
of a true referent of the narrative texts of the New Testament—
historical or ideal, accessible or not—and of the textual meaning as
possible truth in that sense is an illusion. For Kermode it is a persistent and haunting, perhaps even inescapable, illusion, since readers
of narrative texts are forever caught up in their dialectical alternation
of divinatory disclosure and foreclosing secrecy. For Deconstructionists,
by contrast, the discovery of the illusory character of linguistic meaning as truth is liberating, and with that liberation comes a way of
reading a text which reverses the prior belief that texts open up a
world, into the conviction that the world (or a world) must be seen
as an indefinitely extended and open-ended, loosely interconnected,
"intertextual" network, a kind of rhetorical *cosa nostra*.

Hermeneutical Theory, Deconstruction, and the Literal Sense

This destruction of "normative" or "true" reading means an end,
among other things, to the enterprise called "hermeneutics." Right
from the beginning of that enterprise in the early nineteenth century,
the notion of a unitary and systematic theory of understanding (contrasted to the older view of hermeneutics as a set of technical and ad
hoc rules for reading) had been anything but neutral with regard to
the Bible as a source of profound meaningfulness and truth. All texts
are "understood" in accordance with their "meaning," and "meaning"
in turn is a systematic and dialectical partner or counterpart to "understanding," rather than a textual equivalent of a Kantian thing-in-
itself. To include the Bible under this polar subject-object pattern for
interpretation was no problem in the systematic hermeneutical tradition, for the Bible belonged in this view to a certain class of texts that
illustrated the structure paradigmatically. Indeed, it was often taken
to be *the* text above all others whose "meaning" raised "understanding" to its very limit at the edge of mystery, to its diacritical self-ques-
tioning level, and thereby brought about in a single "event" the full
coincidence of disclosive textual force with the understanding self's
ultimate interpretive and self-interpretive act.

   The older tradition of hermeneutics had long since been trans-
mogrified. In one of its shapes it ended up in this century as
Anglo-American "New Criticism," denying all creative status to the
second-order activity which was now called "criticism" rather than
"interpretation," and banishing (usually, but not consistently)
the notion of textual reference to a contextual world, together with
intentional and affective fallacies. The literary text itself had an
unchangeable, almost sacred, status conferred upon it and became a
self-enclosed imagistic world, structured by such devices as paradox

and irony, which the second-order commentator must, above all, leave as they are and not translate into some didactic "meaning" by way of prose paraphrase. For all its difference from hermeneutical theory, this outlook shares with it a belief in the possibility of valid, if not invariant, reading and (despite itself) a sense of a common, humanistic world shared by the "literary" work and the reader. However, it is hermeneutical theory that has been the most recent, vocal defender of that tradition. A brief summary of that position, within which biblical narrative becomes a "regional" instance of the universally valid pattern of interpretation, looks like this:

(1) All texts are "discourse," even if, being inscribed discourse, they gain freedom from the person of the author. (2) The obverse side of "discourse" is "understanding," from which "discourse" and its meaning never gain freedom: The basic condition of the possibility of understanding texts is the transcendentally grounded universal dialectic between understanding and the subject matter to be understood. In other words, though the status of the text is one of freedom from the author, and it is therefore possessed of its own meaning—"utterance" meaning in contrast to "utterer's" meaning, in Paul Ricoeur's terms[7]— utterance meaning is inherently related to an appropriating understanding. "If all discourse is *actualized* as an event, all discourse is *understood* as meaning."[8] Understanding (or interpretation) is an internal event; it is nothing less than the centered self or transcendental ego in that particular and basic mode. The dialectic in which this event is operational is when the understanding stands "before" a text, so that the text is its equal or superior and not a replaceable phenomenon controlled by the ego's own interests or cultural location, such as historical inquiry into the social or psychological genesis of the text. (3) Language is, of course, indispensable to this discourse-and-consciousness process or event, but linguistic "sense," that is, the semiotic structures and semantic patterns of discourse, must also be related to its function as an expression of preconceptual consciousness or experience. (4) There is therefore a thrust within language and natural to it, both in utterance meaning and its appropriation, by means of which it transcends itself qua semiotic structure and semantic sense (beginning with the sentence) through such instruments as symbol and metaphor and "refers" to a real world. (5) But obviously it is actually *we*, the language users, who refer linguistically, so that the reality referent of language is at the same time a mode of human consciousness or of our "being-in-the-world." Language is the way of realizing or enacting self-presence in the presence of a world of meaning and truth, which is at the same time "distanced" from us having its own referential integrity. (6) By a natural extension, metaphor and symbol (i.e., "poetic" language) are

taken to be the modes in which language (and experience) can express the creative thrust of the centered self toward an absolute limit and the "world" espied at that limit. In other words, there is a "split reference" in symbol and metaphor, to self-presence and its being-in-the-world, and—through one of its modes, the mode of limit experience and language—to the disclosed presence of the transcendent as the limit or self-transcending instance of the "secondary" world accessible through poetic language. The "objective" world of "descriptive discourse" is consigned to a decidedly peripheral and ambiguous status in the situation of "limit disclosure." Theoreticians in this tradition of phenomenological hermeneutics tend to be as critical of "outmoded" views of metaphor that stress a descriptive rather than a creative role for it as they are of those who reduce metaphor to a rhetorical or decorative function. The "limit" and "disclosure" situation in which transcendence and understanding come together is the class to which biblical writings belong, and to which the concept "revelation" is at least "homologous."[9] This view is strikingly reminiscent of the "doctrine of revelation" of liberal and neoorthodox religious apologists a generation ago, who held that "revelation" is a "spiritual event" rather than a historical or metaphysical propositional claim; it is, in fact, the hermeneutical equivalent of this outlook.

One should note three consequences of this outlook when it is applied to a literal reading of the Gospels. First, if the literal sense means that the story of Jesus is above all about a specific fictional or historical person by that name, and therefore about his identification through narrative descriptions which gain their force by being ascribed to him and no one else as the subject of those dispositions, words, actions, and sufferings, then the hermeneutical position we have described entails a view of him as ascriptive subject chiefly in the form of consciousness, that is, of his selfhood as "understanding." Obviously, this view of what it is to be a person is consistent with, if not indispensable to, the hermeneutical scheme of "meaning-and-understanding." Like anyone else, Jesus is here not in the first place the agent of his actions nor the enacted project(s) that constitute(s) him, nor the person to whom the actions of others happen; he is, rather, the verbal expressor of a certain preconceptual consciousness which he then, in a logically derivative or secondary sense, exhibits in action. For example, *that* Jesus was crucified is not a decisive part of his personal story, only that he was so consistent in his "mode-of-being-in-the-world" as to take the risk willingly. One would not want to deny the latter as part of the story, but it is surely a one-sided simplification of what it is to be a person in a world or a character in a plot. The personal world in the hermeneutical scheme is one in which the status of happenings is that of carnal shadows of the true "secondary" world of "meanings" "understood" in "disclosure."

On a technical and specifically hermeneutical level, what is wrong with this scheme is simply its claim to inclusiveness and adequacy for the interpretation of all texts depicting persons in a world, quite apart from doubts one may entertain about the claims to foundational, inclusive, and certain status of any hermeneutical framework for the interpretation of all narrative texts. The hostility to all interpretation of narratives, in which "descriptive discourse" is not "subverted" in favor of "creative metaphoric discourse" "referring" to (or "disclosing") a "secondary world," is a natural, perhaps even necessary, consequence of this hermeneutics produced by a phenomenology of consciousness. By and large, the Christian tradition of literal reading, even in the late, liberal and historical-critical states of "reconstructing" the "actual historical" Jesus "behind" the texts, has resisted this reduction of the subject of the narrative to consciousness (and consciousness as "event") rather than agent-in-occurrence, and of descriptive to metaphoric discourse in the presentation of the way in which this subject was significantly related to a world about him.

Second, it seems that *any* kind of literal ascription of "meaning" to a personal subject within the narrative world is highly tenuous, if not simply dissolved, under this hermeneutical governance. The clearly and irreducibly personal focus within this scheme is constituted not by the "meaning" of the narrative but by the interpreter—that is, the "understanding" to which "meaning" is related. What narratives present (whether or not "literally") is not in the first place ascriptive selves that are the subjects of their predicates, not even really the self-expressive, centered consciousness or transcendental ego, but the "mode-of-being-in-the-world" which these selves exemplify and which is "re-presented" by being "disclosed" to "understanding." In the words of David Tracy, a theologian whose New Testament hermeneutics is a close reading and precise regional application of Ricoeur's general hermeneutics:

> One may formulate the principal meaning referred to by the historically reconstructed re-presentative words, deeds, and destiny of Jesus the Christ as follows: the principal referent disclosed by this limit-language is the disclosure of a certain limit-mode-of-being-in-the world; the disclosure of a new, and agapic, a self-sacrificing righteousness willing to risk living at that limit where one seems in the presence of the righteous, loving, gracious God re-presented in Jesus the Christ.[10]

Not that one can have any such "mode" without personal ascription either within the story or in appropriation (is that perhaps the point of the solecism, "the principal referent disclosed . . . is . . . the disclosure . . ."?), but the ascription in the story is simply a temporary personal thickening within the free-flowing stream of a general class of describable dispositional attitudes. "Jesus" in the statement quoted names a meaning, namely (the disclosure of) a generalizable set of attitudes (self-sacrificing righteousness, etc.), rather than these attitudes being referred to, held, or actuated, by "Jesus." What is being set forth here in technical language is a view of the Gospel narratives which is far closer to traditional allegorical than literal reading: Certain virtues or dispositions are hypostatized, that is, they are the significant referents of certain statements, but to maintain the narrative rather than didactic shape of these statements there has to be a personal embodiment, an "archetype" Kant called it, to exemplify them. But the archetype is identified by the virtues, not they by him through his self-enactment in significant temporal sequence. At best the link between meaning-reference and ascription to a personal subject within the story is tenuous in this view. At worst it is eliminated. The irreducibly personal element comes only in the "re-presented" "disclosure" situation, that is, in "understanding" appropriation of the text.

As with dispositional description and ascription, so with the "kerygmatic" verbal expression of consciousness "re-presented" by the Gospels. To "limit' *experience* there corresponds metaphoric "limit" *language*, and the two have the same "referent." Traditionally, "the Kingdom of God" in Jesus' preaching and Jesus himself have been understood to identify or "refer" to each other. By contrast, in hermeneutical theory one subsumes Jesus' preaching, especially the parables of the Kingdom of God, under a more general reference. In Ricoeur's terms, there is an "extravagance" in the denouement and the main characters that contrasts with the realism of the narrative and constitutes the parables' specific "religious" trait.[11] Religious language redescribes human experience: "The ultimate referent of the parables, proverbs, and eschatological sayings is not the Kingdom of God, but human reality in its wholeness. Religious language discloses the religious dimension of common human experience."[12]

Whether in the form of described dispositions, such as those exemplified by Jesus, or in the form of redescribed experience originally expressed in nondiscursive symbols or metaphorical discourse, such as Jesus' parables of the Kingdom of God, the narrative texts' meaning, that is, their referent, is a reality or world transcending the teller within the story, the character within the plot, and the descriptive dimension of the narrative language (in the case of the parables). "Human reality in its wholeness" will in one way or another be the subject matter instead each time, though perhaps a bit more obliquely and allegorically in the case of the narrated ascriptive subject called "Jesus," and more metaphorically and directly evocatively in the case of the parables and the experience they express.

Even Aristotle's *mimesis* has therefore to be understood as creative or magnifying rather than reduplicative imitation in narrative: It becomes "a kind of metaphor of reality."[13] Released from its moorings in or as descriptive world, historical or history-like fictional narrative, depicting and ascribing plot and character, refers actually to the general transcendental condition which constitutes the underlying possibility of such stories, namely, the "historicity" of humankind in general and of each self severally. And what is that? "We belong to history before telling stories or writing history." "Historicity" is finally neither reference to specific events, nor a pattern in specific stories; it is their ingredience in or unity with the logically prior general condition of self as consciousness within a diachronic frame, which stories—indispensable but logically subsequent—then bring to expression.[14] Once again, "meaning-as-reference" is not only not true but meaningless without its polar relation to "consciousness-as-understanding," but at this point (perhaps one of several), the polarity is actually transcended into the unity of the two. "Historicity" is the referential meaning *and* the consciousness or understanding of it. As personal, ascriptive subject "historicity" is at once (positively) particular and (transcendentally) general; it is at once irreducible (as understanding) and eminently transcendable (as universal, metaphorically subverted descriptive reference).

In sum, then, the view that the notion of being human is inseparable from that of being an agent becomes highly problematic in a general anthropology of consciousness and its hermeneutics; but the irreducibly *descriptive* as well as any irreducibly personal *ascriptive* character of literal reading is even more problematic in this hermeneutical setting. Yet one variant or another of this theory, more than any other, has been proposed as a general and foundational justification for a revised traditional reading of the narrative texts of the New Testament. Numerous warrants for doing so have been adduced by the theory's adherents: The applicability to these narratives of such concepts as revelation, uniqueness, and yet (simultaneously) generality of meaning; the significance of personal understanding and appropriation; the claim to normatively valid interpretation which transcends, without ignoring, the cultural setting of both texts and interpreters; and the claim to diachronic continuity between presently valid interpretation and a tradition of interpretation reaching back to the text itself, in particular the tradition of interpretation that assigns a distinctive status to Jesus in these stories.

Indeed, this last consideration has been particularly important to those Christian theologians who have adopted this general theory for regional hermeneutical application to the New Testament. They have been motivated by a desire on the one hand to claim the unsurpassability of the New Testament narratives' ascriptive reference to Jesus, so that they do not become exoteric or carnal shadows, in principle surpassable by a later and fuller spiritual "reference" or "disclosure," but on the other to deny that this unsurpassability involves the

invidious distinction between insiders and outsiders to the truth.[15] So
they try to maintain that Jesus is the irreducible ascriptive subject of
the New Testament narratives, while at the same time they make
general religious experience (or something like it) the "referent" of
these stories.[16] It is an uneasy alliance of conflicting hermeneutical
aims. The theory simply cannot bear the freight of all that its proponents want to load on to its shoulders. Whatever may be the case in
its other regional exemplifications, when it is applied to the New Testament narrative texts the result is that the tradition of literal reading
is not only stretched into a revised shape, it breaks down instead. It
may well be an eminently worthy goal to have a theology that is at
once Christian and liberal, but founding its reading of the New Testament on this general hermeneutical theory is not a good means for
achieving that aim.

The third consequence of appealing to the general hermeneutical
theory as a basis for a literal or revised reading of the New Testament
narratives is simply that, no matter how adequate or inadequate the
theory turns out to be in actual exegetical application, the very possibility of reading those narratives under its auspices has to stand or
fall with the theory's own viability in the first place. It is well to be
clear on what this does and does not involve. Paul Ricoeur, like many
others but in a more sensitive and systematic way, has drawn attention to certain distinctions that one may summarize as pre-critical,
critical, and post-critical stages in reading or, in his own terms, first
and second naïveté (with "criticism" in between). A similar (though
not identical) distinction is that between the "masters of suspicion"
and a "hermeneutics of restoration" or "retrieval." Post-critical reading, reading with that second naïveté which is done in correspondence
with a hermeneutics of restoration, is the kind of reading that might
well wish to be of a "revised literal" sort. It distances the text from
the author, from the original discourse's existential situation and from
every other kind of reading that would go "behind" the text and "refer"
it to any other world of meaning than its own, the world "in front
of" the text. And yet, this kind of reading has been through the mill
of critically transcending that (first) naïve literalism for which every
statement on the printed page "means" either because it refers not
only ostensively but also correctly, naming a true state of affairs each
time, or else because it shapes part of a realm of discourse whose
vocabulary one can finally only understand by repeating it and in that
sense (if sense it is) taking it at "face value." If the general theory of
hermeneutics is to stand, it must persuade us that its appeal to a second naïveté and to a hermeneutics of restoration constitutes a genuine option between reading with first naïveté on the one hand and
on the other reading with that "suspicion" which regards the linguistic "world," which text and reader may share, as a mere ideological

or psychological superstructure reducible to real or true infrastructures, which must be critically or scientifically adduced.

An indispensable part or assumption of the theory, especially in explaining the possibility of reading with second naïveté, is that there can be a coincidence, a "fusion of horizons," in H.-G. Gadamer's phrase, between the strange, distant, in a sense even timeless, world of the text detached from its temporal authorial origin, and the present reader who, though doubtless part of his world, is also the subject transcendental to it. This position is a strong revision of the "Romantic" hermeneutics Schleiermacher, for whom "understanding" was a direct dialogue between the reader and the spirit of the author, present in the latter's language. "If," writes Paul Ricoeur,

> we preserve the language of Romanticist hermeneutics when it speaks of overcoming the distance, . . . of appropriating what was distant, other, foreign, it will be at the price of an important corrective. That which we make our own . . . is not a foreign experience, but the power of disclosing a world which constitutes the reference of the text.
>
> The link between disclosure and appropriation is, to my mind, the cornerstone of a hermeneutic which could claim both to overcome the shortcomings of historicism and to remain faithful to the original intention of Schleiermacher's hermeneutics. To understand an author better than he could understand himself is to display the power of disclosure implied in his discourse beyond the limited horizon of his own existential situation.[17]

The kind of language used to indicate the link between "disclosure" and "understanding" in this theory invariably has a strong component that appeals to the experience of "historicity" or time consciousness, and the dimension of the link is always that of the present poised between past and future. Appeals to synchronic links or to spatial metaphors are either secondary or diachronically intended in the language of this theory, so that, for example, "present" is the antonym of "past" rather than either the synonym of "near" or the antonym of "far." "Distance" and "distanciation" have a clearly diachronic ring in the theory's use of them. In cases such as the interpretation of the New Testament narratives, this temporal outlook is very clear indeed. Their "meaning," we have noted, is "re-presented" to the understanding. There is no proper understanding of texts from the past, "distanced" or released from their original moorings, except on the model (or, rather, more than the model) of a temporally present event, an event in or of contemporary consciousness.

Why this absolute centrality of the link between disclosure through text and the world to which it refers, and the temporally present event of understanding? No doubt there are many reasons, but surely one of the chief is simply a set of conceptual needs: One *needs* to have the text refer to or open up a (usually diachronic) world, if it is not merely to function as an instance of an internally connected general semiotic system or code in which the specific linguistic content or message ("parole" in contrast to "langue," in Saussure's famous formula) is no more than a trivial surface phenomenon. Furthermore, one *needs* to have the text open up a world independent of the text's cultural origins and every other reductive explanation, if we are going to have a hermeneutics in which understanding a text entails normative and valid exegetical interpretation, in a word a hermeneutics for "second naïveté." One *needs*, finally and foremost, to have a text both atemporally distanced from its moorings in a cultural and authorial or existential past and yet also re-entering the temporal dimension at the point of the present, if it is going to have the capacity to inform an understanding that is itself essentially characterized as present, in a word a hermeneutics of restoration. And yet this present re-entry of the text must not be a function or predicate of the presently understanding self—else it is illusory self-projection. "Disclosure" is a term satisfying these needs: The text is normative, in fact it transcends present understanding *ontologically,* but only in such a way that it is in principle *hermeneutically* focused toward the latter. Textual "disclosure" means that the language of the text "refers," but refers strictly in the mode of presentness. It also means that language, especially metaphoric language, refers creatively without creating what it refers to. "Disclosure" answers the need for and reality of a genuine convergence into coincidence of referential meaning and understanding.

The language of the text in opening up a world is simultaneously opened up by it. That simultaneity prevents language from turning either into simple descriptive, that is, falsely representational ("objectivist") language, or into being captured by purely "subjectivist" and self-projecting understanding. We *must* have "disclosure" if we are to have a hermeneutics that respects Heidegger's affirmation that language speaks because it indwells a world, instead of a hermeneutics that is a linguistic replica of the Cartesian error of separating out a self-contained, self-certain ego of "understanding" from the understood world. In the case of our hermeneutical theory, the Cartesian error can be avoided only if the disclosure that fills this need of text and world "opening up" each other to present understanding is at least possibly true, in order to avoid the conclusion that understanding is simply the bedrock upon which it creates its own world in which it dwells and which it discloses to itself.

The world of the text's reference must be disclosed as a *possibly true* world. Meaning in disclosure has an ontological reference, and it is not clear whether the distinction between "possible" and "actual" truth is very sharp in "meaning as reference." In reference to general or possible truths, the matter is not significant, but only in individual instances, since "possible truth" is logically and ontologically dependent on the priority of "actual truth." In this respect as in others there is for the theory a real parallel to the claims of ostensive reference which, whether true or false in given instances, would make no sense except if there is an actual class of such items. Likewise, there must be ontological truth in the notion "textual reference to a world in disclosure" generally, if any particular case of it is to be possible and thus meaningful. I take this to be implied when Ricoeur writes: "The text speaks of a possible world and of a possible way of orienting oneself within it. The dimensions of this world are properly opened up by, disclosed by, the text. Disclosure is the equivalent for written language of ostensive reference for spoken language."[18]

Here, then, is the claim to a recovery of that view in which texts can in principle be normatively or validly interpreted because they refer to a truly possible world—a world Kermode declared to be either inaccessible through the text or illusory in the first place, and one which Nietzsche and Derrida have taken, if anything, to be worse than illusory because it is no more than the fruit of a wishful misuse of texts. Neither a set of conceptual *needs* arising out of a certain understanding of language as a sign system, say such critics, nor the supply of a set of *answers* to them are necessarily persuasive because the two, needs and answers, cohere. One might well expect them to do so, because that is the way to meet the need intrasystematically; but that very fact might strengthen the suspicion that this is a case of systematic legerdemain, which is bound to produce a built-in verbal solution for every real or imagined conceptual problem. The system is an all-encompassing structure in which "meaning-and-understanding" have set the foundational, inescapable terms, and "disclosure" is the equally inescapable, universal link between them.

"Disclosure" as an "event" in "understanding" is something of which many people testify they are ignorant. They say that this is not *their* model for what it is to understand, at least not one that holds pervasively. The advocates of the theory tend simply to respond that whether or not they understand that understanding is of this sort, that is in fact the case; and then they reiterate the theory in the hope that the reiteration will evoke the experiential correlate as an echo. And there the impasse remains.

Deconstruction, a deliberate subversion of this theory as of many others, is not identical with the strictly anti-hermeneutical procedure of "suspicion," with which hermeneutical theorists have understood themselves to be in sharp contention. The "masters of suspicion" simply dismiss the immanent, directly fitting *interpretive* structure which supports a textual reading of "second naïveté," supplanting it instead with an independent and wholly external *explanatory* frame. However, unlike Structuralist, Freudian, Marxist, and other theories of suspicion, Deconstruction is not *tout court* "a modern inheritor of [the] belief that reality, and our experience of it, are discontinuous with each other."[19] Deconstruction is an immanent subversion, rather than an external, all-embracing reductionist treatment of phenomenological hermeneutics, just as it tries to effect the same relation of immanent subversion to Structuralism, and so forth.[20] One may, in fact, see Deconstruction as an exuberant or desperate (depending on the mood) rescue operation designed to pry loose a linguistic humanism hopelessly caught between the Scylla of total captivity to the absolute truth and certainty of "self-presence," and the Charybdis of *anti-humanist* or "scientific" dissolution of that supposed certainty.

"Language," whether as discourse or text, is to be caught out and tripped up in its own metaphorical character precisely at the point where philosophical theorists claim recourse to a close relation between metaphor and technical concept or true meaning. In the case of the hermeneutical theory under discussion, an example of such metaphorical usage would be the phrase "'referent' basically manifests the meaning 'in front of' the text,"[21] a turn of phrase whose strikingly spatial character in what is actually a nonspatial pattern of overall thought highlights, through its contrast to "meaning 'behind' the text," at once the distinction and the coherence between "sense" and "reference." The "referent" "in front of the text" is precisely that restorative "sense" of the reading of second naïveté, for which text and reader come to share a common referential world ("that way of perceiving reality, that mode-of-being-in-the-world which the text opens up for the intelligent reader")[22] which they cannot share in critical reading of the "meaning behind the text." Meaning "in front of the text" is a centered world of meaning made accessible and viable to an equally centered self.

In the one case ("meaning behind the text") the spatial metaphor is intended to indicate mutual absence or distance between semantic sense, real referent, and the reader's world. By contrast, the other spatial metaphor ("in front of") is supposed to indicate the overcoming of that distance without a direct—either naïve or Romantic—*mergence* of the previously distanced partners. To someone like Derrida, it is clear that even if the one metaphor ("behind" the text) comes close to accomplishing what is wanted from it (which is not to be taken for granted) an indication of distance or absence, the other ("in front of") means simply by oppositional affinity with the first. Insofar as it is supposed to indicate a significant *conceptual* pairing (distance between two linguistic "worlds" which remains while nonetheless being overcome, the reading of second naïveté), it simply spins its wheels. It is a case of "absence" supposedly being "presence" at the same time, a virtual admission of the fault that Deconstructionists espy at the foundation of the edifice of the traditional "signifier/signified" relation. The natural affinity of the second metaphor is not that of a "signifier" with a consistent, intelligible, and normative "signified" but simply that of one signifier or metaphor with another, previous one: Any "meaning" that "in front of" may have is *deferred* along a loosely connected, potentially indefinite metaphorical axis, and in the meantime it is what it is simply by displacing that from which it differs ("meaning behind the text"). It is this displacement or divestment of a signified world into the intertextuality of an indefinite sequence of signifiers—a focal insistence of the Deconstructionists—that is so apt in their critique of phenomenological hermeneutics: The "worlds" that are supposedly "disclosed" actually have the subversive, deconstructing nonreferentiality of pure metaphoricity built into them. Phenomenological hermeneutics, to Deconstructionists, is *malgré lui* a celebration of that very nonreferential purity of textual metaphoricity that it sets out to transcend. Second naïveté, far from being explained and justified, is an illusion, a verbal pirouette.

Such instances of the hermeneutical theory's built-in susceptibility to deconstruction are crucial to the Deconstructionists' cumulative argument that the general bearing of hermeneutical theory is one for which "understanding" as self-presence is the indispensable and irreducible counterpart to textual "meaning" as linguistic presence, and vice versa. Language as signifier has life or spirit breathed into it by its immediate relation to self-presence, and that in turn allows it to take the shape of the signified, the means by which it attains meaning as referent or ontologically present truth. Conversely and simultaneously, "disclosure" is the bridge over which truth as presence in turn travels to present itself as meaning to self-presence now. To Deconstructionists, this linguistic polarity of self-presence and presence is equally endemic to hermeneutical theory when language is taken as discourse and when it is understood as written text. But, they say, precisely that polarity guarantees the actual priority of speech over writing in either version of the theory. The indispensability of understanding as self-presence builds the very notion of presence into language ineluctably and thus constitutes an assertion of speech rather than written text as the original and natural form of language, and of the text as a deformation of speech. What is already written is not a present event, as understanding what is written is; it must be raised to the level of present communicative event, and thereby the textuality of the text is reconverted (in obverse form) into speech.

To realize the deconstructive susceptibility of this self-enclosed, presence/self-presence, scheme is, Deconstructionists tell us, to learn with metaphorical force (or, to an outsider to the whole argument, exaggeration) the drastic difference between speech and writing, and indeed—in contrast to the absolute connection between speech as linguistic origin and the mode of self-presence in hermeneutical theory—

of the independent *priority* of writing over speech. Such metaphorical and rhetorical vehemence alone will suffice to indicate the chasm opened up by the immanent subversion of the phenomenological theory of hermeneutics. Not the unreachable goal of a particular strategy but the instability and emptiness of an entire categorical scheme in which mutually indispensable conceptual devices sustain each other —and nothing else, is being proposed by the deconstruction of phenomenological hermeneutics. The Deconstructionists simply deny the stability of the theory's presuppositions.

If "meaning" implies absence and *difference* instead of centeredness or presence, then self-presence or "understanding"—its indispensable polar correlate in the theory—is bound to be just as hollow. Not that Deconstructionists necessarily deny the "reality" of centered selfhood, or even of experienced self-consciousness as its basic mode, after the fashion of the masters of "suspicion." Rather, strictly and simply as part of a way of explaining and justifying "interpretive" textual reading, specifically in the mode of second naïveté, this ingredient simply dissolves; like "presence," self-presence turns into absence, the absence of centeredness and of its "now," in relation to textuality and intertextuality.

One may well be sceptical about Derrida's and his followers' consignment of the *whole* Western linguistic tradition to the supposed metaphysical or "ontotheological" prioritizing of "phonocentric," and "logocentric," discourse over text and writing. But deconstruction does provide a strong case against the theory at issue. Indeed, at times it seems as if Deconstructionists, in their enthusiasm to consign philosophy to an awkward ancillary status to their own kind of literary reading, believe that Western metaphysics and philosophy of language from pre-Socratic days on were a grand and connected conspiracy aiming all along to arrive at the thought of Husserl and Heidegger, with only slightly camouflaged detours by way of Plato, the New Testament, Rousseau, and Saussure, and that the Deconstructionist duty is to smoke it out, root and branch. In the process, and whatever its philosophical strengths and weaknesses, Deconstructionist association of Christianity (in contrast to Judaism) with ontotheology *tout court* has all the appearance of overkill, as sweeping generalizations usually do. Christianity, especially in its Reformation Protestant rather than liberal or neoorthodox forms, is very much a "religion of the text," for which the textuality of the Bible is not systematically or metaphysically, but only in quite informal fashion, coordinated with linguistic meaning of a logocentric sort. In fact, the grammatical literalism of the "unfallen" biblical text, together with its textual autonomy from and priority over the *viva vox* of the interpretive tradition—all of which the Reformers proposed—may bear a remote resemblance (doubtless no more!) to the Deconstructionists' "textuality" and "intertextuality," which the latter have so far apparently not discerned. On the other hand, the affirmation of the textuality of the biblical text does not preclude a self-dispositioning of Christian language in other contexts that makes traditional and heavy drafts on "ontotheology" (especially in its Platonic and Neoplatonic versions). The integrity of textuality does not involve a systematic denial of ontotheology as one fit articulation among others for Christian doctrinal language. In other words, a Christian theological observer will want to resist a tendency toward global and foundational claims on behalf of inclusive theories, which Deconstructionists seem to share in practice, whatever the theory, with other theorists.

I do not propose to claim a decisive victory for the Deconstructionist subversion of phenomenological hermeneutics, nor to claim that Deconstruction is the ultimate mode of literary theory (nor, I believe, do Deconstructionists of the saner variety). Furthermore, it is obvious that Deconstruction is anything but universally helpful to a Christian reading of Christian Scripture, even though it may be useful *selectively*, just as hermeneutical theory may be similarly and modestly appropriate. (One thinks, for example, of aspects of experiential selfhood and self-understanding in the Gospel of John, in the reading of which a phenomenological interpretive scheme might have limited but significant applicability.) It is doubtful that *any* scheme for reading texts, and narrative texts in particular, and biblical narrative texts even more specifically, can serve globally and foundationally, so that the reading of biblical material would simply be a regional instance of the universal procedure. The contrary hermeneutical claim is, as we saw earlier, doubtful enough when it is judged by criteria of coherence and adequacy in regard to restorative or revised-literal reading of *New Testament* narratives. But now one also has to add that its very claim to adequate status as a universal and foundational theory justifying the restorative reading of "second naïveté" has been rendered highly dubious by the immanent subversion of its philosophical into a metaphorical turn at crucial points.

The threat to hermeneutical theory is that *either* "second naïveté" is no concept but simply a misleading term, and restorative hermeneutics explains or justifies no way of reading, *or* that if one is to hold out for anything like it, one had better invent a more adequate theory to support the claim. (Even so global, astringent, and telling a critic of Deconstruction as John Searle concedes the pertinence of Deconstructionist critique of phenomenology, especially in its Husserlian form.)[23] There is of course another option: One may want to claim that a notion similar to "second naïveté" (though not necessarily isomorphic with it) is indeed meaningful, but not because it is part of, or justified by, any general theory. But that is a position which neither hermeneutical Phenomenologists nor Deconstructionists will tolerate.

Closely interwoven with the hermeneutics of meaning-and-understanding is a position in modern liberal Christian theology, for which proper theological articulation has always to be the fruit of careful coordination of present cultural self-understanding, that is, a phenomenology of the contemporary cultural life-world, with an interpretation of the normative self-understanding inherent in Christianity, its sources, traditions, and historically varying external manifestations.[24] A paradoxical challenge now awaits the attention of this theology. Its proponents are understandably anxious to grasp the present intellectual, cultural, and spiritual "situation" (understood as possessing a kind of cohesive, describable essence) in its distinctiveness and its latest shape, as it may just be crafting the future immediately ahead of us. Hence, there are frequent references to the present situation as "post-modern," "post-critical," "post-theological," and so on. One may well entertain serious doubts about the wisdom of this procedure as a basic and systematic theological strategy. But that issue aside, in the context of our discussion the challenge now to the advocates of this theology of coordination or correlation is to consider seriously the possibility that the present cultural situation is among other things a *post-hermeneutical* and no longer a hermeneutical situation, and to frame their hermeneutical outlook in accordance with it, both for the sake of the technical credibility of hermeneutical theory and for the broader purpose of the cultural credibility of the theology itself.

Up to now this challenge has gone unmet among the theory's theological advocates: they have seen no need for serious modification of their views. Characteristically, they consider the possibility of such powerful high-cultural symptoms as deconstruction, or Foucault's elimination of interior unity in historiography in favor of "systems of dispersion,"[25] as well as many other basic orientations toward the relation between selfhood and culture differing drastically from that proposed under the rubrics of phenomenology, only to return to their previous analytical fruits. One way or another, the normative permanence of unique, irreducible, and shared interior experience remains the basic ingredient in any cultural life-world they discover. The depictions offered by other options may be temporary interruptions in that field of vision, but they are never potentially basic disturbers or immanent threats to this remarkably assured view of the compatibility of self-understanding with an analysis of apparently any present cultural situation. In the end, drastically "other" options usually become coopted—illustrations despite themselves both of the need for the phenomenological agenda and its perennial discoveries.

Just as in hermeneutical and phenomenological theory "understanding" as an event of self-presence remains a basically unquestioned category, and a cultural world is always a particular collective understanding, so in the theory's cultural-theological version religious experience or something like it remains a serenely assured category with an ever pertinent, ever available cultural correlate in every situation, including that which is post-hermeneutical or post-religious. So, for example, in the words of David Tracy, "We must keep alive the sense of the uncanny—the post-religious, religious sense of our situation."[26] It seems never really to have been in question in the first place.

Prospects for the Literal Sense

What of the future of the "literal reading"? The less entangled in theory and the more firmly rooted not in a narrative (literary) tradition but in its primary and original context, a religious community's "rule" for faithful reading, the more clearly it is likely to come into view, and the stronger as well as more flexible and supple it is likely to look. From that perspective, a theory confined to describing how and in what specific kind of context a certain kind of reading functions is an improvement over the kind of theoretical endeavor that tries to justify its very possibility in general.

Hermeneutical theory obviously belongs to the latter kind, but so also do those arguments for and against the historical factuality of the (perhaps!) history-like or literal and (perhaps!) historical narratives of the Bible that have generated so much religious and scholarly heat since the eighteenth century. As arguments claiming general validity they have usually been governed on both sides by the assumptions that "meaning" is identical with "possible truth," and that if a story belongs to the genre of history-like or "realistic" narrative, its meaning qua possible truth belongs to the class called "factuality." The necessary obverse is that if stories are *not* judgable by this criterion, they are finally not realistic but belong to some other genre and therefore make a different kind of truth claim. (This is finally the cutting edge of the reading of the New Testament by the proponents of the "second naïveté" of "restorative" hermeneutics. In their reading, the "historicity" of human being and human narratives "discloses" the truth and reality of a secondary and transcendent world that differs totally from the narrative description, transforming the latter into metaphor instead. Hence their preference in the synoptic Gospels for the metaphorical and disclosive character of the parables over the realistic, literally descriptive character of the passion and resurrection narratives.)

A recent proposal in the argument about the mutual bearing of realistic narrative and historical fact claim in respect of biblical stories, especially the synoptic Gospels, represents a transition from a high-powered to a less ambitious kind of general theorizing. It holds that the Gospel stories as well as large portions of Old Testament narrative are indeed "realistic," but that the issue of their making or not mak-

ing factual or, for that matter, other kinds of truth claims is not part
of the scope of hermeneutical inquiry. "Meaning" in this view is logically distinct from "truth," even where the two bear so strong a family resemblance as the designations "history-like" and "historical"
imply. The factuality or nonfactuality of at least some of these narratives, important as it is no doubt in a larger religious or an even more
general context, involves a separate argument from that concerning
their meaning.[27]

Two related assumptions are implied when this move is made as
part of a plea on behalf of realistic or literal (as well as figural) reading. First, there is a suspension of the question whether "truth" is a
general class (over and above specific true items), to which all reasonable people have equal access as a set of proper conclusions drawn
from credible grounds, by way of rational procedures common to all
(except that, unlike myself, not everybody has found right reason yet).
But second, "meaning," unlike "truth," *can* be affirmed to be such a
general class allowing across-the-board access to all reasonable people
who know how to relate genus, species, and individual case properly.
One appeals first to a qualitatively distinct genus of text (and meaning) called "literary" and then argues both historically and in principle that within it there is a species called "realistic narrative" that is
quite distinct from, say, romance or heroic epic. To this species then,
biblical narrative is said to belong; indeed it is often said to be its original and paradigm.[28]

The resemblance of this view to Anglo-American "New Criticism"
is obvious and has often been pointed out. Both claim that the text is
a normative and pure "meaning" world of its own which, quite apart
from any factual reference it may have, and apart from its author's
intention or its reader's reception, stands on its own with the authority of self-evident intelligibility. The reader's "interpretation" can, and
indeed has to be, minimal, reiterative, and formal, so that the very
term "interpretation" is already misleadingly high-powered. "Criticism"
is a far more appropriate term because it is more low-keyed and leaves
the text sacrosanct, confining itself to second-order analysis, chiefly
of the formal stylistic devices which are the "literary" body of the text.
In the case of the "realistic" novel these are devices such as temporal
structuring, the irreducible interaction of character and plot, ordinary
or "mixed" rather than elevated style, and so forth. These devices are
said to be of the very essence of the text and of its quality as a linguistic sacrament, inseparable from the world that it is (rather than
merely represents), but also the means by which that world is rendered to the reader so that (s)he can understand it without any large-
scale "creative" contribution of his/her own.

This outlook is less high-powered than hermeneutical theory, not
only because it is confined to "meaning" as logically distinct from

"truth" but because the formal features of realistic narrative about which it generalizes are as often as not implicit rather than explicit, so that they must be *exhibited* in textual examples rather than *stated* in abstract terms. But even though less high-powered, general theory it remains: The Gospel narratives "mean" realistically because that is the general literary class to which they belong. But precisely in respect of generalizing adequacy this theory has grave weaknesses. First, the claim to the self-subsistence or self-referentiality of the text apart from any true world is as artificial as it may (perhaps!) be logically advantageous: Moreover, the view is usually not held consistently, for New Critics argue not only for the integrity but the truth of their approach when challenged by contrary reductionist views such as Historicism, Structuralism, or Deconstruction. Despite their anti- or non-philosophical bearing, in fact many of them espouse a theory of a purely aesthetic kind of truth in literature. Second, it is similarly artificial and dubious to claim a purely external relation of text and reading, which in effect sets aside the mutual implication of interpretation and textual meaning (as hermeneutical theorists would have it) or of reading and the textuality of the text (in terms of the Deconstructionists). If a narrative or a poem should "not mean but be," avoiding paraphrase as the proper means to the realization of this ideal comes close to enthroning verbal repetition as the highest form of understanding.

In short, the less high-powered general theory that upholds the literal or realistic reading of the Gospels may be just as perilously perched as its more majestic and pretentious hermeneutical cousin. There is a greater problem yet with the more modest view. The resemblance of New Criticism to, indeed its partial derivation from, Christian theology (especially Aristotelian modes of that theology) has often and rightly been pointed out. Endowing the text with the stature of complete and authoritative embodiment of "truth" in "meaning," so that it is purely and objectively self-referential, is a literary equivalent of the Christian dogma of Jesus Christ as incarnate Son of God, the divine Word that is one with the bodied person it assumes. Here is a general theory about texts of which the paradigm case is not only in the first instance not textual but, more important, is itself the *basis* rather than merely an *instance* of the range as well as cohesion of meaning and truth in terms of which it is articulated. It has always been clear in Christian tradition that if the truth of such a dogma as that of the incarnation is to be affirmed, it has to be done by faith rather than rational demonstration. Less evident but equally true is that if the dogma is to be held consistently, its very *meaning*, that is, its logical as well as ontological conceivability is a matter of faith, and therefore of reason strictly in the mode of faith seeking understanding. Suppose one affirms that a partial but fitting second-order redescription of the gospel narratives may be carried out under the general and distinct ontological categories of infinite or divine and finite or human "natures" (and there is no reason to think that this set of categories is either worse or better than a number of others for what may aptly, if modestly, be termed "interpretation" of the dogma): The implicit rule of religious use or "rule of faith" under which it will be done is that the conceivability of the unity of the two categories in personal ascription, without compromise to their distinctness qua categories, is dependent on the *fact* of that unity. Conversely, then, it has to be denied that the fact is logically dependent on the conceivability of the categories' unification. All descriptive endeavors to show didactically or abstractly, rather than to reiterate narratively, *how* the unity is such as not to compromise the categories' distinction, or how they are inherently fit for unification, will break down or else, a better alternative, remain incomplete. The "rule" for the statement of the dogma and the deployment of categories in the process will therefore always have a reserved or negative cast: Nothing must be said in the proper philosophical articulation of the dogma such that the rightful priority of the categories' coherence in unitary personal ascription over their abiding logical distinctness would jeopardize the integrity of the latter. The implication of this reserve is that the full, *positive explanation* of the rule's rational status, while not at all an inappropriate aim, will have to await another condition than our present finitude. For now, the faith articulated in the dogma is, under this assumption, indeed not irrational, "paradoxical" or "fideistic," but rather rational yet fragmentary. The formal statement of the dogma's logic is of a (modestly) transcendental sort.

The irony of New Criticism (and it is not the first instance of this kind) is to have taken this specific case and rule and to have turned them instead into a general theory of meaning, literature, and even culture, in their own right. Detached from the original that is the actual, indispensable ground and subject matter of its meaning, the specific rule is turned about instead into its very opposite, a scheme embracing a whole class of general meaning constructs, from a Christian culture (in the religiously imperialistic and more than mildly fantasizing visions of T. S. Eliot's cultural-theological writings) to genres of literature. They are all understood "incarnationally" or "sacramentally." As a result, the original of this process of derivation, the doctrine of the incarnation of the Word of God in the person and destiny of Jesus of Nazareth, has now become an optional member within the general class, in which those who subscribe to the class may or may not wish to believe.

There may or may not be a class called "realistic narrative," but to take it as a general category of which the synoptic Gospel narratives and their partial second-order redescription in the doctrine of the Incarnation are a dependent instance is first to put the cart before the horse and then cut the lines and claim that the vehicle is self-propelled. The realistic novel, in which history-likeness and history prey on each other in mutual puzzlement concerning the reality status of each and their relation (so that Balzac could claim that his novels are true history, while Truman Capote could invent a category called the nonfictional novel for his reports on a series of gruesome murders in rural Kansas) is, from the perspective of the rule of faith and its interpretive use in the Christian tradition, nothing more than an appropriate even if puzzling as well as incomplete analogy or "type" of their "antitype," the coherence between linguistic or narrative and real worlds rendered in the Gospel stories. In that tradition, the ascriptive literalism of the story, the *history-likeness* if you will, of the singular agent enacting the unity of human finitude and divine infinity, Jesus of Nazareth, is taken to be itself the ground, guarantee, and conveyance of the truth of the depicted enactment, its *historicity* if you will—if, that is, in the wake of the Enlightenment these are the categories of descriptive meaning and referential truth one wishes to employ. The linguistic, textual world is in this case not only the *necessary* basis for our orientation within the real world, according to the Christian claims about this narrative, and this narrative alone; it is also *sufficient* for the purpose. This is hardly the sort of claim which one would want to turn into one instance of a general class, either in historical theory or theory of the novel, even if it is an antitype to serve a host of imperfect, partial types.

Whatever one may think of the phenomenologists' hermeneutical theory, it *is* a general theory; however, under its auspices the literal reading of the Gospel narratives vanishes, both because in application the theory revises it into incoherence and out of existence, and because the theory qua theory cannot persuasively make good on its claim to be availability of the revisionary literalism of a "second naïveté." As for the New Criticism, a literal reading of the Gospels is appropriate under its auspices, but only because and to the extent that it is in fact a disguised Christian understanding of them and not a reading under a general theory, not even a more low-level theory of meaning than the general hermeneutical scheme.

Rather than an example of an explanatory theory of meaning at work on the status and possibility of a specific case under its auspices, what we have in the *sensus literalis* is a reading about which one needs to say first that it governs, and bends to its own ends whatever general categories it shares—as indeed it has to share—with other kinds of reading (e.g., "meaning," "truth," as well as their relation). It is a case-specific reading which may or may not find reduced analogues elsewhere. Second, it is not only case-specific but as such belongs first and foremost into the context of a sociolinguistic community, that is, of the specific religion of which it is part, rather than into a literary ambience. Both considerations involve lowering our theoretical sights yet further to the level of mere description rather than explanation, to the specific set of texts and the most specific context, rather than to a general class of texts ("realistic narrative") and the most general context ("human experience").

That exercise in self-restraint should not be difficult to state, despite the complexity of the exposition up to this point. Nor does it preclude inquiry into either the fact or the character of possible truth claims involved in the literal reading of the Gospels. It is simply an acknowledgment of the inescapably ambiguous or problematic *philosophical* status of such claims when they are analyzed under the auspices of general theories. The theoretical task compatible with the literal reading of the Gospel narratives is that of describing how and in what context it functions. In that regard we need to do little more than return to the beginning of the essay: Established or "plain" readings are warranted by their agreement with a religious community's rules for reading its sacred text. It is at best questionable that they are warranted, except quite provisionally, under any other circumstances: Theories of realistic narrative for example are not likely to be highly plausible except in tandem with an informal cultural consensus that certain texts have the quasi-sacred and objective literary status of "classics," which form the core of a broader literary "canon." The plausibility structure in this case is a literary imitation of a religious community's authority structure; it rests on a tradition, reinforced by communal, usually professional, agencies authorized to articulate the consensus about what is to be included within the canon and what is to be especially exalted within that privileged group as "classic." The pleas by advocates of phenomenological hermeneutics that the status of a "classic" is warranted when a work provides a "realized experience of that which is essential, that which endures"[29] is little more than a tacit acknowledgment that the temporary cultural consensus is already on the wane, and agreed upon or "plain" readings with it. As a warranting argument it is a last-ditch holding operation, no matter how sound it may be as a report of how people are likely to experience works that already (or still) have the cultural status of classics.

In the tradition of Christian religion and its communal life, scripture has played many parts; it has been a guide to life, an inspiration to heart and mind, a norm for believing. The (largely but not wholly) informal set of rules under which it has customarily been read in the community, in the midst of much disagreement about its contents, has been fairly flexible and usually not too constrictive. The *minimal* agreement about reading the Scriptures (as distinct from their status or scope) has been as follows: First, Christian reading of Christian Scriptures must not deny the literal ascription to Jesus, and not to

any other person, event, time or idea, of those occurrences, teachings, personal qualities and religious attributes associated with him in
the stories in which he plays a part, as well as in the other New Testament writings in which his name is invoked. This ascription has
usually also included the indirect referral to him of that "Kingdom of
God," the parabolic proclamation of which is attributed to him in the
texts, and of which he himself was taken to be (in a phrase of Austin
Farrer's) the "self-enacted parable" both in word and deed. Second,
no Christian reading may deny either the unity of Old and New Testaments or the congruence (which is not by any means the same as
literal identity) of that unity with the ascriptive literalism of the Gospel narratives. Third, any readings not in principle in contradiction
with these two rules are permissible, and two of the obvious candidates would be the various sorts of historical-critical and literary readings.

Whether or not there are exact parallels in other religions to this
sort of governed use of scriptures for the edification, practical guidance, and orientation in belief of the members, it is at least a typical
ingredient in a recognizably religious pattern.[30]

In days long past, observers used to put the practices and beliefs
of differing "high" religions side by side, in order to compare and
contrast discrete items such as the nature of the divine or the character of salvation. This procedure rightly came to be seen as naïve and
wooden because it ignored questions of the criteria for comparison.
The result of the quest for criteria was a rash of theories of the relation of religion to human nature, to the character of society, to the
course of human history at large (are religion and history evolutionary?) or to the specific host or guest cultures with which specific
religions intertwined (are religions unique and relative and therefore
incomparable because cultures are?). The strength of phenomenology
of religion has been to propose a new option: While there is an irreducibly self-identical, universal "essence" of religion, it is not found
in the empirically given surface data or manifestations of religion—
which remain culture-specific—but in the depth experience of which
they are the symbolic forms. That essence or quality has to be adduced
from them but is in fact logically prior to them. Religion is pre-cogni-
tive, it is at home in the transcendental dimension in which selves
apprehend themselves by way of the indispensable instrumentalities
of culture (art, ritual, myth, etc.). In contrast to other ways of seeing
religion, this outlook is able to appreciate both the unity and diversity in the spectrum of the world's religions, always of course on the
twin assumptions of the priority of the unity and its transcendental
or experiential character: To understand the unitary essence of religion is identical with being, in however attenuated a form, religious.

Scepticism about this view—its assignment of primordial status to the self and its experience, its claim to a native religious cohabitation of the self and "the sacred" or "transcendent," the unpersuasiveness of its hermeneutical ventures—need not entail a return to understanding religions as the products either of identical mechanisms in institutional behavior patterns or of distinctive and therefore incomparable cultures. With phenomenologists one may agree that religions (and cultures, for that matter) are personal and interpersonal activities— even if not perhaps primarily experiences—rather than impersonal or superpersonal entities with independent causal powers, without adhering to a strongly developed general theory of the self or of understanding in phenomenological fashion. At the same time one may agree with interpretive social scientists who hold that a "culture" (including a religion) is like a language, a multi-level communicative network that forms the indispensably enabling context for persons to enact both themselves and their mutual relations. As in the case of phenomenology concerning selfhood, so in the case of social science concerning culture, it is best to postpone the generalizing tendency that raises theory from the descriptive to the explanatory power. ("Reductive" explanation of cultures and especially religions may or may not be compatible with interpretation or exposition from a merely descriptive point of view; the point is that it is a transition to a very different and generalizing stage of reflection. One only has to take care that the integrity and complexity of the description does not get lost in the transition. Reductive theoreticians, or masters and disciples of "suspicion," are usually better at starting at a point past the transition and looking back than at actually making or explaining the transition.)

The descriptive context, then, for the *sensus literalis* is the religion of which it is part, understood at once as a determinate code in which beliefs, ritual, and behavior patterns, ethos as well as narrative, come together as a common semiotic system, and also as the community which is that system in use—apart from which the very term ("semiotic system") is in this case no more than a misplaced metaphor. Clifford Geertz calls culture an "acted document," and the term applies also to religion.[31] Geertz calls the low-level theoretical effort at describing culture, which we have also affirmed for religion, "thick description" (using a term of Gilbert Ryle's). It is, first, description of details as parts of "interworked systems of construable signs . . . within which they can be intelligibly . . . described."[32] Second, it is description from the actor's, participant's, or language user's point of view, yet without mimicry or confusion of identity on the part of the interpreter.[33]

Those who follow this low-level use of theory for "placing" religions as symbol systems are persuaded that the description and critical appraisal of a religion from within the religious community itself, and external "thick" description, while certainly not identical, are not wholly disparate. Yet their congruence does not require—on the contrary it eschews—the elaborate synthesizing requirements of a more general, explanatory theory. To understand a religion or a culture to which one is not native does not demand a general doctrine of the core of humanity, selfhood, and the grounds of inter-subjective experience. There is of course the need for normal human sensitivity and respect. But beyond that, in Geertz's words:

> Whatever accurate sense one gets of what one's informants are "really like" comes . . . from the ability to construe their modes of expression, what I would call their symbol systems. . . . Understanding the form and pressure of . . . natives' inner lives is more like grasping a proverb, catching an allusion, seeing a joke—or . . . reading a poem—than it is like achieving communion.[34]

This is understanding without "empathy" or "transcultural identification with our subjects."[35] George Lindbeck has called this low-level theoretical deployment in the analysis of religions a "cultural linguistic approach" to the topic,[36] and has used the term "intratextual" to describe the kind of theology—the "normative explication of the meaning a religion has for its adherents"—that is not identical but congruent with it.[37] The congruence lies in the persuasion that

> Meaning is constituted by the uses of a specific language rather than being distinguishable from it. Thus the proper way to determine what "God" signifies, for example, is by examining how the word operates in a religion and thereby shapes reality and experience rather than by first establishing its propositional or experiential meaning and reinterpreting or reformulating its uses accordingly.[38]

"Intratextuality" in many of the "high" religions is used not only in an extended or metaphorical but in a literal sense, for they are in varying degrees "religions of the (or a) book." "They all have relatively fixed canons of writings that they treat as exemplary or normative instantiations of their semiotic codes. One test of faithfulness for all of them is the degree to which descriptions correspond to the semiotic universe paradigmatically encoded in holy writ."[39]

The direction in the flow of intratextual interpretation is that of absorbing the extratextual universe into the text, rather than the reverse (extratextual) direction. The literal sense is the paradigmatic form of such intratextual interpretation in the Christian community's use of its scripture: The literal ascription to Jesus of Nazareth of the stories connected with him is of such far-reaching import that it serves not only as focus for inner-canonical typology but reshapes extratextual language in its manifold descriptive uses into a typological relation to these stories. The reason why the intratextual universe of this Christian symbol system is a narrative one is that a specific set of texts, which happen to be narrative, has become primary, even within scripture, and has been assigned a literal reading as their primary or "plain" sense. They have become the paradigm for the construal not only of what is inside that system but for all that is outside. They provide the interpretive pattern in terms of which *all* of reality is experienced and read in this religion. Only in a secondary or derivative sense have they become ingredient in a general and literary narrative tradition. The latter is actually not only a provisional but a highly variable set of contexts for these texts; it is not foundational for their meaning, and there is no intrinsic reason to suppose that any given general theory for their reading in that context, be it hermeneutical or anti-hermeneutical, ought to be assigned pride of place—including that of New Criticism with its logical dependence on Christian theology. Equally clearly it is once more a case of putting the cart before the horse—but this time the wagon is theological rather than literary—if one constructs a general and inalienable human quality called "narrative" or "narrativity," within which to interpret the Gospels and provide foundational warrant for the possibility of their existential and ontological meaningfulness. The notion that Christian theology is a member of a general class of "narrative theology" is no more than a minor will-o'-the-wisp.

"Meaning" in a cultural-linguistic and intratextual interpretive frame is the skill that allows ethnographer and native to meet in mutual respect; if they happen to be the same person, it is the bridge over which (s)he may pass from one shore to the other and undertake the return journey; if they are natives from different tribes, it is the common ground that is established as they learn each other's languages, rather than a known precondition for doing so.

To return to the beginning: The third of these tasks is perhaps the most immediately pressing for Christian interpretation and for the future of its use of the literal sense. For the next-door neighbor to Christianity in all its various forms is Judaism with its own diversity, and they share those parts of a common scripture which Christianity has usurped from Judaism. The most pressing question from this vantage point is not the fate of the literal sense in the event of a new, perhaps more nearly universal, spiritual truth that would also constitute a new literal reading and threaten to reduce the Christian reading of the New Testament to exoteric, carnal status. This is unlikely, for we have noted that religions are specific symbol systems and not a single, high-culture reproduction of symbol-neutral eternal "truth." Lessing's "eternal gospel" is a noble ideal, but his appropriation of a story form for the purpose of advocating historical and religious progress is not a supplanting of one scriptural narrative by a later and better one; it is instead the substitution of a philosophy of history for an intratextual interpretive scheme.

A far more urgent issue for Christian interpretation is the unpredictable consequences of learning the "language" of the Jewish tradition, including the nearest Jewish equivalent to Christian literal reading. To discover Midrash in all its subtlety and breadth of options and to understand *peshat* (the traditional sense)[40] may well be to begin to repair a series of contacts established and broken time and again in the history of the Church, whenever linguistic and textual Old Testament issues became pressing in intra-Christian debate. Perhaps the future may be better than the past as a result of the intervening period of liberal scholarship and the persuasion that the two religions, even though closely intertwined, are quite distinct, each with its own integrity. The convergence of distinctness and commensurability between them has yet to be discovered, and attention to Midrash and to the literal sense may play a significant part in the discovery.

In addition to the inter-religious enrichment for which one may hope from such joint inquiry, certainly for Christianity, the secular gains may be surprisingly large, even if strictly speaking incidental or secondary. The Protestant theologian Friedrich Schleiermacher called Judaism a fossil religion, in part at least out of the animus which many Rationalist, Romantic, and Idealistic thinkers bore toward Jewish particularism. And yet it is now conceivable that that "fossil" may bear more of the future of the culture of the West in its hands than Christianity, and its traditional, particularistic forms may not be adventitious to the fact. Cultural, religious, and historical parallels are dangerous and speculative. Nonetheless there may be a lesson here, at least to the effect that the relation between Christianity and Judaism— including the complex issues of the relation between their Scriptures and scriptural interpretations—may play an indispensable part in the process of Christian recovery of its own intratextual or self-description. Whether with or without the aid of such a discussion, the most fateful issue for Christian self-description is that of regaining its autonomous vocation as a religion, after its defeat in its secondary vocation of providing ideological coherence, foundation, and stability to Western culture. Beyond that, however, the example of Judaism in the modern Western world might be a beacon to a reconstituted Christian community. One never knows what this community might then contribute once again to that culture or its residues, including its political life, its quest for justice and freedom—and even its literature. If the priorities are rightly ordered, the literal sense may be counted on to play a significant part in such a less pretentious enterprise. It will stretch and not break.

Notes

1. Cf. Robert Scholes and Robert Kellogg, *The Nature of Narrative* (New York: Oxford University Press, 1960), pp. 50 ff.

2. Cf. Mircea Eliade, *Patterns in Comparative Religion* (Cleveland: World, 1963), chap. 1, *inter multa alia*.

3. Cf. Northrop Frye, *The Great Code: The Bible and Literature* (New York: Harcourt Brace Jovanovich, 1982), pp. 31 ff.

4. James S. Preus, *From Shadow to Promise: Old Testament Interpretation from Augustine to the Young Luther* (Cambridge, Mass.: Harvard University Press, 1969).

5. G. E. Lessing, "The Education of the Human Race," *Lessing's Theological Writings*, translated and introduced by Henry Chadwick (Stanford: Stanford University Press, 1967), p. 96. The same message is of course a large part of the parable of the rings in Lessing's *Nathan the Wise*.

6. Cf. Frank Kermode, *The Genesis of Secrecy: On the Interpretation of Narrative* (Cambridge, Mass.: Harvard University Press, 1979), pp. 18 ff., 45 ff., 143 ff., *passim*.

7. Paul Ricoeur, *Interpretation Theory: Discourse and the Surplus of Meaning* (Fort Worth: Texas Christian University Press, 1976), pp. 12 ff.

8. Ibid., p. 12.

9. Cf. Paul Ricoeur, "Toward a Hermeneutic of the Idea of Revelation," *Essays on Biblical Interpretation*, ed. Lewis S. Mudge (Philadelphia: Fortress Press, 1980), pp. 73–118.

10. David Tracy, *Blessed Rage for Order: The New Pluralism in Theology* (New York: Seabury Press, 1975), p. 221.

11. *Semeia 4: Paul Ricoeur on Biblical Hermeneutics*, ed. J. D. Crossan (Missoula, Mont.: Scholars Press, 1975), p. 32.

12. Ibid., pp. 127ff.

13. Paul Ricoeur, "The Narrative Function," *Hermeneutics and the Human Sciences*, ed. and tr. by J. B. Thompson (New York: Cambridge University Press, 1981), p. 292.

14. Cf. ibid., pp. 293 ff.

15. Tracy, op. cit., p. 206. For a statement of the issue, cf. *The Bible and the Narrative Tradition*, ed. Frank McConnell, pp. 102–15.

16. Tracy's statement of the matter, *Blessed Rage for Order*, pp. 205–7, is quite typical. If the tenor of the passage quoted above (n. 10) is to turn 'Jesus' into an allegory of "universal meaningfulness" in the shape of an event or disclosure (cf. ibid., p. 106), Tracy's subsequent *The Analogical Imagination: Christian Theology and the Culture of Pluralism* (New York: Crossroad, 1981), pt. 2, chaps. 6 and 7, tends to redress the balance and stress 'Jesus' as the unsurpassable ascriptive subject of the narratives manifesting and proclaim-

ing the "Christ event" as an event "from God." However, since that event qua event must always be a "present experience," the movement toward universal meaningfulness as the referent of the stories and thus toward the allegorical use of 'Jesus' begins again right away (cf. ibid., p 234, passim). It is not at all clear that Tracy's hermeneutical procedure manages to coordinate these two simultaneous referents, but what *is* clear is that if their coordination is indeed a problem and as a result one becomes the chief referent and the other its satellite, then it is the tendency toward allegorization that receives Tracy's favorable nod.

17. Paul Ricoeur, "The Model of the Text: Meaningful Action Considered as a Text," in P. Rabinow and W. M. Sullivan, eds., *Interpretive Social Science* (Berkeley: University of California Press, 1979), p. 98.

18. Ibid.

19. Terry Eagleton, *Literary Theory: An Introduction* (Minneapolis: University of Minnesota Press, 1983), p. 108.

20. Cf. Christopher Norris, *Deconstruction: Theory and Practice* (London and New York: Methuen, 1982), p. 31.

21. Tracy, *Blessed Rage for Order*, p. 51, passim.

22. Ibid.

23. John Searle, "The World Turned Upside Down," *New York Review of Books*, 30, 16 (October 27, 1983), 74–79.

24. Cf. Tracy, *The Analogical Imagination*, p. 340.

25. Michel Foucault, *The Archaeology of Knowledge* (Harper & Row, Torchbooks, 1972), pp. 37f.

26. Tracy, *The Analogical Imagination*, p. 362. For Tracy's remarks about Derrida, cf. ibid., pp. 117ff., 220ff. (n. 17), 361ff., passim.

27. This position is implied by the present writer in *The Eclipse of Biblical Narrative* (New Haven: Yale University Press, 1974), and made explicit in *The Identity of Jesus Christ* (Philadelphia: Fortress Press, 1975).

28. The classic statement of this case is Erich Auerbach, *Mimesis: The Representation of Reality in Western Literature*, trans. Willard R. Trask (Princeton: Princeton University Press, 1953).

29. Tracy, *The Analogical Imagination*, p. 108.

30. For an interesting parallel see Gerhard Böwering, *The Mystical Vision of Existence in Classical Islam* (Berlin and New York: Walter de Gruyter, 1980), pp. 140ff.

31. Clifford Geertz, *The Interpretation of Cultures* (New York: Basic Books, 1973), p. 10.

32. Ibid., p. 13.

33. Ibid., pp. 13, 27.

34. Geertz, "From the Native's Point of View: On the Nature of Anthropological Understanding," in Rabinow and Sullivan, *Interpretive Social Science*, pp. 240ff.

35. Ibid., p. 226.

36. George A. Lindbeck, *The Nature of Doctrine: Religion and Theology in a Postliberal Age* (Philadelphia: Westminster Press, 1984), pp. 32ff. I wish to acknowledge my profound indebtedness to this book and to its author.

37. Ibid., p. 113.

38. Ibid., p. 114.

39. Ibid., p. 116.

40. Cf. Raphael Loewe, "The 'Plain' Meaning of Scripture in Early Jewish Exegesis," *Papers of the Institute of Jewish Studies in London* (Jerusalem, 1964), vol. 1, pp. 140–85, esp. pp. 180ff.

5

Conflicts in Interpretation: Resolution, Armistice, or Co-existence?

In 1986 Frei gave the Alexander Thompson Memorial Lecture at Princeton Theological Seminary. Apparently, no manuscript of the lecture has survived, but Richard Burnett found a tape of it among Frei's papers in the Yale Divinity School Library and made a careful transcription of it. Mr. Burnett's efforts have recovered an important piece of Frei's work.

Frei's approach to the Bible has interesting affinities with the work of two biblical scholars who were his colleagues at Yale: Brevard Childs's canonical criticism and Wayne Meeks's sociological study of the earliest Christian communities. But many of those committed to historical critical study of the Bible found his work puzzling. This essay tries to reach out to the "guild" of biblical scholars. It also discusses with particular care the delicate relationship Frei saw between questions of meaning and truth and offers another example of his ongoing reflections on the work of Frank Kermode, which appear in a number of these essays.

* * *

I want to begin by reflecting on a story that, although too blatant to be characteristic, is nonetheless representative of its time, place, and social location: upper-class Victorian England. It could just as well have been upper-class early Augustan England, several generations back. The moral is the same though only the characters have changed. In Leslie Stephen's biography, Noel Annan describes an argument that pitted William Gladstone—Britain's great, liberal prime minister and an ardent high churchman and biblicist, who played a role somewhat like William Jennings Bryan in the fundamentalist controversy in America—against T. H. Huxley—agnostic and the most widely known scientist of the day, the man who more than any other succeeded in popularizing Darwin's theory of the evolution of species through natural selection. The argument was over how you judge what is true in history. The common ground between the antagonists, true Englishmen both, was that you study the evidence. And what was at stake was, of course, the historical veracity or accuracy of the Bible. The text was Mark 5:11–13, the expulsion of the Gerasene demon or demons ("Legion") into the herd of swine to be drowned.

Huxley declared that the faithful could not have it both ways. Either the Evangelists were fabricating a story when they spoke of Jesus casting out devils and permitting them to enter a herd of swine who immediately plunged into the sea or Jesus had wantonly destroyed other men's property. Gladstone rose to the bait. Roused by the suggestion that Jesus might have undermined the fundamental liberal principle of the sacredness of private property, he declared that this accusation against our Lord was intolerable. The destruction of the swine was legitimate, because Jews were forbidden under Mosaic law to keep pigs. Huxley replied at length. He examined the authorities and argued that Gadara was, in fact,

> a Hellenic and Gentile town and therefore the inhabitants had a right to keep pigs. Since we may assume that Christ would never have wrongfully harmed such men, we may dismiss the story as false—unless one chose to assume that Christ broke "the first condition of enduring liberty which is obedience to the law of the land." Further animadversions on pig-keeping habits in Galilee, the administrative boundaries, the social structure of Gadara, and Schurer's interpretation of Josephus, lead Huxley to declare that all the best opinion agrees that the synoptic Gospels are not independent but are founded on a common source and hence the story rests on legend or the observation of a single observer; and, while, pace Hume, there is no a priori objection against the miracle, such frail evidence for its occurrence is wholly insufficient. And Huxley added the singular prophecy: "Whether the twentieth century shall see a recrudescence of the superstitions of medieval papistry, or whether it shall witness the severance from the living body of the ethical ideal of prophetic Israel from the carcass, foul with savage superstitions and cankered with false philosophy, to which the theologians have bound it, turns upon their final judgement of the Gadarene tale."

As for the feeding of the five thousand, why should we "believe it to be so on contradictory evidence available?" Will Christians "boast that since faith is not in touch with fact at all it will be inaccessible to infidel attacks"?[1]

Beyond the agreement that you study the evidence, will you note one further agreement between the parties. It was best formulated much later by Stephen Toulmin in *The Uses of Argument* and utilized by such commentators on arguments about the Bible as Van Harvey and David Kelsey.[2] Suppose the question of evidence is not one of further supply of data or "What've you got to go on," but of legitimizing the passage from given data to a conclusion. In this case the claim to factual status, the bridge between data and conclusion is called a "warrant." Gladstone and Huxley agree that their respective cases depend on the issue of the admissibility of a particular warrant, in this case, the sacredness of the belief in private property. Would Jesus have to subscribe to it if he were to have any claim upon our allegiance? "Yes," says Huxley—tongue-in-cheek or seriously? Gladstone says, "No, the principle doesn't work in this instance." Huxley, tacitly, gives ground and changes warrants: In order for a story about Jesus to be true it cannot contravene the basic moral principle of obedience to the law of the land on which enduring liberty is founded. But this story does so. We know Jesus to have been "a" if not "the" supreme moral teacher of humankind; therefore, the story cannot be true. Right there, in packaging obedience to law with liberty and supreme ethical teaching, Huxley loses the liberationist constituency although the orthodox Gladstone doesn't capture it. Yet, note the character of the warrant. Huxley is not arguing against miracle, at least not straightforwardly. He's saying that a cock-and-bull story that violates universal moral principles cannot be attributed to Jesus. This critique is a little more subtle than that of his spiritual ancestor, David Hume, who thought much as Huxley did about miracle, but argued further that religious thinking in earlier days was generally a mass of primitive and superstitious fanaticism. Not so Huxley at this point. Note that the warrant about "liberty under law" plays for him another role, that of a hermeneutical principle. (In the next life, if I have any choice, there will be two terms that I shall eschew, one is "hermeneutics", the other is "narrative"!)

Let us say, for our purposes, that a hermeneutical principle is a judgment concerning any concept of meaningfulness that texts and their readers, contemporary or later, have in common. Further, that common concept must be of central significance to both and not peripheral or accidental to either or both, text and reader. "Liberty under law" will do quite well in this case. But then it seems that Huxley is queasy about his warrant, turned hermeneutical principle, and changes the character of the argument. That is, he turns from the credibility of a conclusion based not so much on certain data as on warrants for reading or not reading them in a certain way, to the other kind of argument in which neither warrant nor hermeneutical principle is involved. Evidence? Yes, but not evidence backed by warrant that is at the same time an assumption of an affirmation that Jesus and readers of this text would hold in common. Instead, the evidence becomes simply a matter of "What've you got to go on?" And so, Huxley turns to source criticism. The story rests on the report of a single observer and "such frail evidence for its occurrence is wholly insufficient," and so on. Amusement turns to chagrin over the trivialization of the text, and one is glad to leave the episode behind.

But before we go on our way, a couple of observations are in order. There is a distinction made by Paul Ricoeur (who cribbed it from somebody else: Jean Starobinski) between "what is written" and "what it is written about." Clearly what we have seen so far is a conflict over the "about what" of the text. Is the story true or false? Is it about something or nothing? We know the positions that were taken up in this conflict. There would be neither armistice nor resolution between rationalists of a fundamentalist or rationalists of a liberal kind. Conflict in interpretation, at least in this instance, involves common weapons and a common battleground on which the interpretive armies clash by night and sometimes, perhaps, by day.

Sometimes such direct clashes on a well-defined battleground are the worst, brooking neither compromise nor resolution. Like civil wars they tend to be very bloody. But there is another feature to them. The controversy of which we have seen a trivial instance has always been taken as a case of Christian interpretation fighting the infidel outsider. That is partly true. On the other hand, from the Enlightenment on, the very concept of "fact," historical or physical, was adopted in the vocabulary of Christian students of the Bible. It became a constitutive part of their own common or group thinking. At the same time, or rather, in the same century, we saw the growth of the core curriculum in the German Protestant theological faculties: Old Testament, New Testament, Church History, Theology, and Practical Theology. Institutionally as well as intellectually, the biblical–critical enterprise was not nearly so much a secularization as it was an ecclesiastical–academic enterprise. It was then, and to a large extent still is, a specialists' craft within the ecclesiastical academy (or, its equivalent, i.e., the theological faculty within the secular academy). Biblical criticism is church thinking adapted to Enlightenment and post-Enlightenment modes. By extension, the same observation may be made about the impact of literary-historical procedures and the history of religions on biblical studies (something that I have heard recently James Barr rightly stress) in the theological academy a century or more later. In short, biblical studies were largely an insider's craft and the arguments were well defined. When friendly, and technical, they were subject to the hope, if not the reality, of consensus within the broader institutional context. When unfriendly, they were well defined and did not often move to outright religious clashes except in cases such as Gladstone and Huxley or evangelicals and liberals in the later nineteenth and early twentieth centuries. But in neither case, friendly or unfriendly, did the participants to discussion completely misunderstand the terms of the discussion. There was not the sense of two sides talking completely past one another. But that in a sense is the situation that has obtained more recently.

It is not that structuralism or poststructuralism have not been picked up with almost unbridled enthusiasm by some members of the biblical-critical guild. Critical theory also does not lack for hermeneutical adherence in the guild, but I think there is a strong sense that, unlike the leap from historical judgment to existential reflection and commitment or phenomenological reduction, there is no confidence in the biblical guild of the compatibility between historical work and the other partner, literary theory and its constructs. One notes a sense of incommensurability rather than direct conflict or mutual supplementation. Members of the guild find that their technical work is trivialized or subverted. And the other side of the coin is that if members of the guild become enthusiasts for these newer literary theories, they seem largely to leave behind the technical crafts: source, form, redaction criticism—traditional hermeneutical methods that have shaped them in the formative stages in their careers. Under those circumstances, the outside discussion partner to the guild becomes a confusing figure to the insider. Far more confusing, let us say, than Karl Barth in the days of his dialectical attack on the biblical guild. Far more confusing than T. H. Huxley in his attack on Gladstone. Far more confusing than the benevolent, grandfatherly hermeneutics of Hans-Georg Gadamer with his reassuring word that "we are all linguistically incorporated into the effective history of our tradition," for the new outsider ad-libs. He appropriates at will from the very fruits of the guilds' investigations, though quite skeptical of the guild's framework and its aims or its canons of significant explanation. It is as though, to use Paul Ricoeur's useful, almost inescapable distinction, these outsiders are borrowing elements, even if not the whole agenda, from a "hermeneutics of suspicion," such as Marx, Nietzsche, and Freud, in which the guild's special vocabulary is made use of as a plausible superstructure, but then as a whole reinterpreted into a coherent pattern by being grafted on to a totally different infrastructure. And this transpires in contrast to the hermeneutics of retrieval of the likes of Barth, Huxley, Gadamer, Bultmann, and all the other previous discussion partners. Because for all these thinkers there is a single sense to a text, even if we find it only imperfectly at any given time or even if that single meaning varies in the reading of people of different eras, cultural settings, and, of course, ideologies.

I read somewhere in Juan Luis Segundo's *The Liberation of Theol-*

ogy that the meaning of the biblical injunction to "turn the other cheek" under present revolutionary conditions—i.e. post-Enlightenment thinking, late capitalist hegemony—is "Shoot 'em between the eyes!" (Or, at least, words to that effect.) Well, one envies him the hermeneutical instruments that enable him to do this. It has a long and honorable tradition.

I was unable to check a graduate student's claim that Luther interpreted the story of Legion passing into the herd of swine in the following way: They were not actually drowned. They swam. They swam and they swam and they finally went ashore—in Rome! Luther said some other things also, of course, but at this point I think there is a certain similarity between him and Segundo. The only difference being that Luther had a sense of humor.

But even then, even under Segundo's rubrics, for this era, *that* is the sense of the passage. Now obviously some "hermeneutics of suspicion" has to take place, for example, the change in the framework of interpretation, that is, to come up with this result and not simply a change in interpretation. And the frame has to be, to use a term of Frank Kermode, "transparent upon a known world," so that the text may be likewise, i.e., "transparent upon a known world." What I am saying is, before this more recent hermeneutical "surge," one has to say that all these earlier interpreters (Huxley, Gadamer, Barth, Bultmann, etc.) and even our sociocritical commentators agree, within limits at least, with the single-sense view of the meaning of texts, a single sense redolent upon a real world.

Now I want to take a contrast case. I choose it because I find it clear where much structuralism and deconstruction is flamboyantly and self-indulgently opaque, and also because I find it powerfully and poignantly seductive. And finally, I choose it because the same exorcism story of the Gadarene demoniac serves as an example in it. The book is Frank Kermode's *The Genesis of Secrecy: On the Interpretation of Narrative.* Here we read:

> There is a famous parable in Kafka's *The Trial.* It is recounted to K by a priest, and is said to come from the scriptures. A man comes and begs for admittance to the Law, but is kept out by a doorkeeper, the first of a long succession of doorkeepers, of aspect ever more terrible, who will keep the man out should the first one fail to do so. The man, who had assumed that the Law was open to all, is surprised to discover the existence of this arrangement. But he waits outside the door, sitting year after year on his stool, and conversing with the doorkeeper, whom he bribes, though without success. Eventually, when he is old and near death, the man observes an immortal radiance streaming from the door. As he dies, he asks the doorkeeper how it is that he alone has come to this entrance to seek admittance to the Law. The answer is, "this door was intended only for you. Now I am going to shut it." The outsider,

though someone had "intended" to let him in, or anyway, provided a door for him, remained outside.[3]

And, of course, the moral of the lesson for Kermode is that we are all finally "outsiders" to the truth.

> K engages the priest in a discussion concerning the interpretation of this parable. He is continually reproved for his departures from the literal sense, and is offered a number of priestly glosses, all of which seem somehow trivial or absurd, unsatisfying or unfair, as when the door-keeper is said to be more deserving of pity than the suppliant, since the suppliant was there of his own free will, as the porter was not. Nevertheless it is claimed that the doorkeeper belongs to the Law, and the man does not. K points out that to assume the integrity of the door-keeper, or indeed that of the Law, as the priest does, involves contradictions. No, replies the priest: "It is not necessary to accept everything as true, one must only accept it as necessary. "A melancholy conclusion," says K. "It turns lying into a universal principle."[4]

Next, Kermode observes, quoting some analytical philosophers of history, that history like story has to have the property of "followability," that a history is a narrative structure imposed upon events. Such narratives will have the logical structure of other stories though their purpose is to provide explanations by establishing connections other than those immediately suggested by a chronicle sequence. Under those rubrics, "a convincing narrative convinces mainly because it is well formed and followable, though sometimes for other reasons also."[5]

At this point, Kermode concludes as follows: Having said that when history writing is, as it were, a replication of a story redolent upon a transparent world (in other words, if followability occurs by reason of transparency upon the real and if the real is the "followable" in that it has sequence and aim in it) and when this is the heart of the interpretation of stories, then all we do is "re-cognize" what we have already said.

And then he comes to this conclusion. And for me, this is of striking significance and, I must say, I tend to identify myself with it: "All modern interpretation" (speaking of himself and, I think also, of deconstructionists, though he doesn't like them)—"All modern interpretation that is not merely an attempt at 're-cognition' involves some effort to divorce meaning and truth." (Notice that is precisely what our previous arguers never did. Certainly not Gladstone and Huxley. They were united in that.)

> This accounts for both the splendors and the miseries of the art. Insofar as we can treat a text as not referring to what is outside or beyond it, we more easily understand that it has internal relationships independent of the coding procedures by which we may find it transparent upon

a known world. We see why it has latent mysteries, intermittent radiances. But in acquiring this privilege, the interpreters lose the possibility of consensus, and of access to a single truth at the heart of the thing. No one, however special his point of vantage, can get past all those doorkeepers into the shrine of the single sense. I make an allegory, once more, of Kafka's parable; but some such position is the starting point of all modern hermeneutics except those which are consciously reactionary. The pleasures of interpretation are henceforth linked to loss and disappointment, so that most of us will find the task too hard, or simply repugnant; and then, abandoning meaning, we slip back into the old comfortable fictions of transparency, the single sense, the truth.[6]

In the process, of course, Kermode has explicitly denied the difference that Christian interpreters have both inherited and been troubled by, that is, the difference between inside interpreters (biblical critics plus the right religious hermeneutics) who know the truth esoterically and outsiders who know it either not at all or exoterically. And he has denied its strongest, earliest, Markan form, which is even more ironic since the book is largely on Mark; "To you has been given the secret of the kingdom of God, but for those outside everything is in parables so that they may indeed see but not perceive and may indeed hear but not understand, lest they should turn again and be forgiven" (Mark 4:11–12). That is our situation as interpreters and we are all, according to Kermode, outsiders.

But then, in his last chapter, Kermode draws his own conclusions about interpreting narrative in the Gospel of Mark. He proposes very tentatively that the pattern in Mark is one of "intercalation" or "analeptic story-telling", that is to say, of interrupting one sequence with another that strengthens the earlier sequence by being a contrasting supplement to it. And this pattern is neither moral nor thematic in content, that is to say, it has no didactic aim. Nor is it in any other way a mirror of a followable world. In this he follows another Swiss literary-historian, Jean Starobinski. Let me return back to the text:

> The demoniac, presumably gentile, is possessed by an unclean spirit named legion, who, as is the custom of unclean spirits in Mark at once recognizes Jesus as the Son of God. Mark emphasizes the enormous strength of the madman. Matthew leaves that out. In Mark he haunts tombs and no fetter or chain can bind him. When legion is expelled he or they occupy a herd of swine which promptly destroys itself. This cure promotes terror among the Garazenes who implore Jesus to go away. He does so leaving the madman cured and docile. But he tells the man, whom he will not allow to accompany him, to proclaim his cure. The Garazene displayed a demonic excess of male strength, but his violence leaves him with the demonic spirit. That it goes into pigs merely confirms its uncleanliness. The man is now ordered and civil. Formerly naked, he is now dressed. Formerly dangerous in his strength he is now fit for society.

And then Kermode refers back to two earlier interpretations in adjoining chapters, which he previously discussed, namely, the woman with the issue of blood and the raising of Jairus's daughter.

> In the case of the woman with the hemorrhage, the going-out of power into the unclean was effected by a garment; here the going-out of strength with spirit [this time unclean] is signaled by the adoption of clothes. The tombs are unclean; the man, now healthy, leaves them. He is free of the unclean spirit and from the unclean place and wears an unsoiled garment. This is a Gentile cure, as the other was Jewish (Jairus was a "ruler of the synagogue"). In both there is an emission of spirits, clean and unclean. One is followed by an injunction to proclaim, the other by a command to silence. One cure is of an excess of maleness, the other of related effects of femaleness. The lake divides the two like a slash, and the cured demoniac is forbidden to cross it.[8]

And then he takes a similar interpretation from Starobinski, one that is interested in the conflict with Legion:

> It seems useless therefore to predict the fate of Starobinski's method or mine which is different but which depends equally on the effectiveness of its difference from the methods of the insiders. I have been proposing that the device of intercalation [supplementation, interruption, and supplementation] in Mark's narrative is an emblem of many conjunctions and oppositions which are found at all levels of the discourse. I think these should be attended to and not dissolved by re-cognitive hermeneutical tricks. For these conjunctions and oppositions reflect something of what the Gospel presupposes of its own structure and the structure of the world.[9]

In short, what is written, not what is written about, above all, no structure of the gospel patterned upon chronology whether in the text, in the world, in the human constitution, or any of them in conjunction, above all, nothing that is redolent of historicity.

Here then we seem to have incommensurabilities between insider and outsider interpretation. Let me simply suggest a few of them. First, many senses are possible of which insiders perceive only one and not the basic. Although the Markan Messianic Secret is noted, it is simply one more instance of such an intercalated contrast case. Second, there is no relationship—neither of clash nor of congruity—between the meaning or textuality of the text and its truth. Text and truth are simply incommensurable. Third, a resuscitation occurs of something like that fourfold method of pre-modern ecclesiastical hermeneutics that had been so alarming to the Reformation and equally alarming to Enlightenment or critical interpretation. There is, first, the literal sense, but equivalent with it is, second, the allegorical sense, and third, if you wish (and, of course, he does not, because he is a literary critic and not a moral interpreter) there is the tropical or moral sense, and finally (and I don't have time to quote it), there is also a forlorn, sober aspect of the anagogical sense. There is the literal sense (what the text says), the allegorical sense (what we believe), the tropical sense (what we must do), and there is the anagogical sense (what we must hope—or not hope). The latter is actually the one to which Kermode holds: "Hope," he says, "is the fatal disease of the interpreter," just as it is for "the person with terminal tuberculosis."

Let me return to one of the themes obliterated here, the relationship between meaning and truth. The textuality of the text goes down the drain when "what it is really about" is identified as the meaning of the text—to which all the rest, its semantic sense and its semiotic structure, is simply subservient. This is a tricky problem. For instance, we may say that a text like Mark 5:1–20, or especially vv. 11–13, possibly contains history-like elements—perhaps not the demons, but the maniac behavior of a man sufficiently possessed to frighten a herd of swine into a stampede (so Holtzmann and Weiss, a long time ago). "History-like" here means possibly historical rather than having a textual shape like a historical account, that is, the linguistic form of verisimilitude. What counts is the possible truth, not the textual form.

If I have a continuing theme in my reflections from here on, it is that I agree with structuralists and post-structuralists, that we should treat textuality (what is written) and the referent or truth of the text (what it is written about) as two different things and that we be cautious about saying that one is in principle more important than the other. I do not say, finally, that they have no bearing on one another. I do not even say that they are wrong categories. I do want to suggest that what has distinguished most recent secular interpreters of the Bible from their Christian counterparts (I am not all sure about rabbinic readers in this connection) is that the former want to emphasize the text itself and that they do not wish its interpretation to be governed by a criterion of meaning that is strongly connected to one of truth. Rather than risking that connection, they would drop the very notions of meaning and truth. This is certainly the case with deconstructionists, and Jacques Derrida's hyperbole, "There is no outside to the text," is a drastic summary expression of it.

And there is a point here even (if I may now turn to myself) for Christians to note, even though they may ultimately want to dissent. In the period of modernity interpreters have been so ardent, so hot in pursuit of the truth of the text, that texts were often left little "breathing space." And I would suggest that a good interpretation of a text is one that has "breathing space," that is to say, one in which no hermeneutic finally allows you to resolve the text—there is something that is left to bother, something that is wrong, something that is not yet interpreted.

The history-likeness of a text as equivalent to its possible histori-

cal truth is only one of a number of similar moves. What is so striking about the hermeneutics of Paul Ricoeur and such theological disciples of his hermeneutics as David Tracy or Sally McFague is the very
strong connection they see between the language, for example, of the
parables (the Great Supper [Luke 14:16–24] is a frequent example)
and its extravagance, its built-in intentions, its metaphoric character,
and therefore, its own thrust beyond itself, beyond the literal shape
to a re-description of reality. Because reality and language are united
in human beings as bearers of metaphor, one may call reality also "a
mode of being in the world." The ineluctable movement from meaning to truth, or their natural affinity, is not, in this case, the movement from the history-like shape to possible historical referent, but
from textual language to ontological referent. The text means as possible truth. It means as the world of which it is the text. Of course,
Christians want to live and speak truth or speak truthfully, but we
ought to be careful at what point and in what way. There may be
Christian reasons, if no other kinds, to exercise reticence about the
transition. The move from text to truth or from language to reality,
which ever form it takes, is almost always premature and some of us
have found the secular literary readers of the Bible very helpful in
reminding us of the fact. At the very least, the Christian reader has
to stop soberly in front of a barrier that in its own way is as impenetrable as the "death strips" that separate two countries at cold war with
one another.

The Reformers tell us that the text is the Word of God: "Do not
seek God beyond the text," for you may find, instead of the God of
grace, the *Deus absconditus* or *Deus nudus* on the other side of the "limit,"
that sinister force of devouring consummation rather than enlightenment. Alternately, to have a limit-language expressing limit-experience is to reach beyond ourselves to where we hope to espy transcendence but may well end up discerning our own mirror image. And
the two things, our mirror image and the *Deus nudus* or *absconditus*
may not be that far from each other.

But the Reformers also propose that even though the text is "sufficient," we ought not to worship it. And so it is I think rightly proposed that they also implied that the text is "witness" to the Word of
God and that its authority derives from that witness rather than from
any inherent divinized quality. And is that Word which is witnessed
to, is that not the truth, at once ontologically transcendent and historically incarnate?

Karl Barth is the modern theologian who has asserted this dual
claim regarding Scripture. For Barth, following the Reformers, this dual
affirmation has meant the primacy of the literal sense. What is written is the Word of God. The divine touch on it is not that extravagance by means of which what is written, the word, might be trans-

formed into that about which it is written. Christians do have to speak
of the referent of the text. They have to speak historically and
ontologically, but in each case, it must be the notion of truth or reference that must be re-shaped extravagantly, not the reading of the
literal text. Any notion of truth such that that concept disallows the
condescension of truth to the depiction in the text—to its own self-
identification with, let us say, the fourfold story of Jesus of Nazareth
taken as an ordinary story—has itself to be viewed with profound
skepticism by a Christian interpreter. The textual world as witness
to the Word of God is not identical with the latter, and yet, by the
Spirit's grace, it is "sufficient" for the witnessing. Perhaps I hammer
this theme too vigorously. If I do so, the reason is that in much
modern theology the primacy of the subject matter, the referent or
the truth, over the text has usually meant that the text is adequate
to the task by virtue of pointing to the subject matter—that is to say,
by what is hidden within or implied by the text and not by the literal
sense. My own view of the matter then is that those who want to
preserve Luther's fine, tense balance between Scripture as witness and
as literal sense may well actually and in effect today be giving up one
side of it. In modernity, or as they like to say in Chicago, "post-
modernity," the temporary condition of the balance is to stress the
sufficiency of the literal sense, without, of course, the "fundamentalist"
correspondence between the literal and its ostensive reference.

I plead then for the textuality of Scripture, the importance of
its linguistic-depictive shape this side of metaphor (or better, with
metaphor as a secondary instrument under the governance of the
literal sense rather than the other way around). The difficulty of uniting thematically the preaching pericopes of the synoptic Gospels with
the accounts of the Passion is a notorious one. One will read either
the parables of the kingdom and the Passion disparately or else one
will either read the Passion through the parables or reversely, the
parables in light of the Passion. Neither of these latter two ways is
adequate. A residue of puzzlement, of the fit being less than perfect
at best remains, and those interpretations are best that allow the fit
to remain in large part a matter of puzzlement. But, choice is something one has to make—unless one is, literally, a deconstructionist.
The identification of Jesus through his self-enactment in suffering,
obedience, death, and resurrection is not unresidually identifiable with
the identification with the Kingdom of God in his preaching. The
crucial form of the primacy of the literal sense, nonetheless, is that
the parables are to be seen more in the light of the identification of
Jesus than the reverse. Though they are descriptively metaphorical,
they contribute indirectly to the identification of the person who spoke
them "with authority." Their meaning in this procedure is primarily
ascriptive. (I take that to be the basic sense of what one means in the

tradition of pre-critical New Testament interpretation as the "literal sense." That is, is it literally "about" Jesus? Are certain descriptions literally ascribed, not are they literally descriptive, appropriately or rightly, but do they have for their subject matter this storied person, Jesus, and none other or no person but a concept? It is the literal ascriptiveness that is the basic sense of the literal it seems to me in the Christian tradition.) Our reading of the parables' description of the Kingdom of God must be consonant with their being part and parcel of the identification of this storied person and not of someone else or of no one in particular, that is to say, of having some meaning without any need for ascription to the bearer of that meaning. And that ascriptive literalism has descriptive consequences.

The marvel or miracle of at least some of the parables is not that their ordinary and everyday referential descriptions are subverted by a metaphorical extravagance that provides us and them a new secondary referent (which is what Professor Ricoeur suggests when that reference becomes transcendence or "a-mode-of-being-in-the-world"), but rather the reverse, namely, the reign of the One who is beyond all description, beyond all metaphorical thrusts, is depicted fitly by ordinary, realistic, literally referential language: "The kingdom of heaven is like leaven which a woman took and hid in three measures of meal." The text does not say "unlike." Metaphorical extravagance? Of course, but subordinate to, and in the service of, literal, ordinary descriptive language within the text. That is the marvel of at least some of the parables, although not without residue, as part of the indirect identification of Jesus, an ordinary man who was the presence of God. In the one interpretive way, Jesus is identified through the parables as "parable of God" (to quote Sally McFague), in the other the parables are finally coherent because he chooses them as part of the way in which he identifies himself or veils himself from his hearers. Is there an irresolvable conflict between these two ways of going either from the parables to the Passion or going from the Passion to the parables? Not necessarily. It is irresolvable; it becomes warfare only if it becomes systematized into a parody of two mutually exclusive approaches. Instead one has constantly to ask oneself which of these can more easily accommodate the other in a subordinate position, that is, keep on using it and not leave it behind in the deployment of the more dominant procedure.

The point I want to make is that in such complex cases as the parables, singularly or as genre, or set of overlapping genres, the best reading is the reading in which the text is not interpreted without residue, i.e., where a surd or problem of reading always remains. Does the text resist being totally resolved by any hermeneutical solvent applied to it? That is a good reading of the text, and my suggestion is that to do that and try to keep the two things together, one moves better from the self-identification of Jesus through the Passion and Resurrection stories toward the parables rather than the other way around. As for the rest, it seems to me then, that close attention to the textuality of the text would I think allow one to suggest (and this is the only point at which I would disagree with the Reformers) that if the literal ascriptive sense that has been the tradition of the Church is guarded, then why not a recrudescence of other internal textual devices? Why then cannot the critic and the ordinary reader accommodate himself to such purely textual modes as structuralism or post-structuralism, that is to say, those modern versions of the allegorical sense?

I plead then for the primacy of the literal sense then and, it seems to me, its puzzling but firm relationship to a truth toward which we cannot thrust. The *modus significandi* will never allow us to say what the *res significata* is. Nonetheless, we can affirm that in the Christian confession of divine grace, the truth is such that the text is sufficient. There is a fit due to the mystery of grace between truth and text. But that, of course, is a very delicate and very constant operation to find that fit between textuality and truth. The Reformers saw the place where that fit was realized in the constant reconstitution of the Church where the word is rightly preached and where the sacraments are rightly administered. *There* is where that fit takes place and there alone—and there without any guarantees. It is a very straight path. It is a tightrope walk toward a very narrow gate. One constantly has to look with unease to the right, where referential truth theories abound (or at a more humble level, where neo-conservatives beckon us), or to the left, where pragmatists tell us that we have no problem of truth (or, at a more mundane level, where liberationists explode). And in between, it seems to me, is the witness of the Church within the text of the Bible.

Notes

1. Noel Annan, *Leslie Stephen* (Cambridge: Harvard University Press, 1952), p. 311.

2. David H. Kelsey, *The Uses of Scripture in Recent Theology* (Philadelphia: Fortress Press, 1975); Stephen Toulmin, *The Uses of Argument* (Cambridge: Cambridge University Press, 1962).

3. Frank Kermode, *The Genesis of Secrecy: On the Interpretation of Narrative* (Cambridge: Harvard University Press, 1979), pp. 27–28.

4. Ibid., p. 28.

5. Ibid., p. 118.

6. Ibid., p. 123.

7. Ibid., p. 134.

8. Ibid., p. 135.

9. Ibid., p. 137.

6

Karl Barth:
Theologian

Karl Barth's theology inspired some of Hans Frei's best writing, as this essay readily attests. First presented at a Yale Divinity School symposium held on the occasion of Barth's death in 1968, the essay conveys much of what Frei found to be attractive in Barth. Like John Updike, who noted "the superb iron of Barth's paragraphs," Frei admired that "iron yet gay consistency" to be discerned in Barth's theologizing, with its uncanny potential "to haunt and comfort the rest of us." He also admired the "long, cool scepticism" with which Barth had appraised the history of modern theology and the ironic stance he then struck over against it. (This skepticism would perhaps in some ways be paralleled by Frei's own mildly ironic stance toward Barth that, for all its appreciation, seemed theologically more reticent and accommodating by contrast.) Above all, however, Frei seemed to admire Barth's unswerving focus on the singularity of Jesus. As the enactment and embodiment of "incarnate Reconciliation" between God and humankind, Jesus himself was aptly conceived as the "logical ground" for all subsequent Christian discourse about the actuality, possibility, and necessity of his saving significance—a conception Frei found it possible to admire without always employing it in his own typically more indirect forms of theological reflection.

* * *

Writing about his impressions of America, Karl Barth said that "fantastic" was the appropriate word for them. And, he went on, to do them justice he would have to reproduce them in fantastic language—adding parenthetically, ". . . if I had the spirit and means of non-objective art at my command."[1]

But he did not, though he was obviously open to doing things that way if one had the gift. It is perhaps a little bit of an exaggeration to say that he did not, because the second edition of his commentary on Romans, which first brought him fame, has some echoes of this way of doing things. It is not exactly non-objective, but the recurring metaphors certainly aren't mimetic. For the most part they are vaguely mathematical. There are points—tiny, disappearing points—instead of prepared Christian positions; there are lines, life and death lines bisecting each other; there is talk about empty space between temporally filled spaces, and so forth and so on.

But it came hard. It had more than a touch of flamboyancy about it, and Barth dropped it fairly quickly. It dramatized the large minus sign he saw around the whole bracketed human equation, but that's about as far as it went. It was really much more typical of Barth, even in that halcyon day of supposedly indirect dialectical talk when, in the middle of a terribly complex debate with Tillich about the "paradoxicality of the positive paradox," he suddenly asked Tillich why he was so terribly reticent about using the simple word "God."

The *Church Dogmatics* are quite different, and I believe they represent Barth at his most powerful and imaginative. After all, as for the commentary on Romans: Was it really so strange for a modern man, with his aversion to miracles and all the other supernatural paraphernalia and with the first world war fresh in his memory, to think of God as the negative limit to all human efforts, experiences and ideas? But now, consider the *Dogmatics* instead, where that same very modern writer increasingly reveals a quite different and, for this present age, much bolder imagination, because more mimetic or representational. In casting about for a comparison I am invariably drawn to some things Erich Auerbach has said about Dante. (I hasten to add that this is a comparison in kind, not in degree of greatness: It is obviously too early and a rather trivial exercise to speculate about Barth's stature.) The Dantesque element in Barth came to expression more and more fully as he worked his way through the materials of volumes 3 and 4 of the *Dogmatics*.

In an essay entitled "Figura," Auerbach makes a distinction between "allegory" and "figure." Allegory, we know, is the literary personification of abstract qualities, usually personal attributes—virtue, reason, faith, courage. At the opposite end from allegory there is the description of personal, earthly existence, which is just what it is and neither is nor "means" something else. And between them there is "figura," which is itself and yet points beyond itself to something else that it prefigures. Auerbach suggests that much of the *Divine Comedy*, including Virgil and Beatrice, is of this sort.

> Virgil in the *Divine Comedy* is Virgil himself, but then again he is not; for the historical Virgil is only a *figura* of the fulfilled truth that the poem reveals, and this fulfillment is more real, more significant than the figura. With Dante, unlike modern poets, the more fully the figure is interpreted and the more closely it is integrated with the eternal plan of salvation, the more real it becomes. And for him, unlike the ancient poets of the underworld, who represented earthly life as real and the life after death as a shadow, the other world is the true reality, while this world is only *umbra futurorum*—though indeed the *umbra* is the prefiguration of the transcendent reality and must recur fully in it. . . . For Dante the literal meaning or historical reality of a figure stands in no contradiction to its profounder meaning but precisely "figures" it; the historical reality is not annulled, but confirmed and fulfilled by the deeper meaning.[2]

For Barth the Bible was, in a manner, Virgil and Beatrice in one. The Guide who took him only to the threshold of Paradise, it was at the same time the *figura* in writing of that greatest wonder which is the fulfillment of all natural, historical being without detracting from it: The incarnate reconciliation between God and man that is Jesus Christ. He is not the incarnate Lord who, as a separable or added action, performs and undergoes the reconciliation of God and man. He *is* the reconciliation he enacts.

No theologian ever saw these two aspects of Christology, the being and the activity of Jesus Christ, in closer integration. They are but two differing descriptions, where we have no single description, of the one "self-enacted parable," to use Austin Farrer's eloquent phrase. Over and over, Barth's thought circles restlessly and celebratively about this wonder, from the first to the last of his theological reflections. It served as the *figura* for each and every one of the doctrinal *loci* in which he described the relation of God to his creatures. Likewise, in a slightly different way, each form of the divine-human relation was both itself and at the same time a figure to be fulfilled in the first and second advents of Jesus Christ. But the overwhelming conviction beyond all the others was that of the figural fulfillment of all created reality in the fit unity of God and man in Jesus Christ, uniting figuring and figured reality.

This was Barth's "given"—for his imagination, for worship and prayer, for rational theological reflection, for moral action, for life in church and world—in short, for faith. But, as I shall want to add in a moment, it was not necessarily the "given" for sensibility, elemental inward motion, or self-consciousness, if you will. Barth could not imagine or think God and man, indeed God and the whole creation, apart; and he would not think of their coinherence except as a parable of this self-enacted parable or figure.

Now one might say that surely this is a fairly standard affirmation for a Christian theologian. Quite right, and Barth stood largely within a classical Christian tradition. What was unusual about that fact in the modern context was that Barth saw this divine-human unity not only *actually* but *logically* grounded in God's self-enacted being. With that simple move Barth contravened the whole tendency of modern theology, at least since 1700 (barring a few rare spirits like Jonathan Edwards and, perhaps, F. D. Maurice). Barth assigned to a subordinate and ambiguous status the issue of the congruence between the divine-human unity in Jesus Christ and our experience in this present life. He covered the issue as a theologian—be it noted: As a theologian, though by no means necessarily as a practising Christian and as a pastor—with some hopefully enigmatic or enigmatically hopeful, but in any case ironic, remarks.

Whether Barth ever succeeded in persuading many people with his simple move and with his theological irony toward the things that were at the very core of liberal Christian preoccupation—the justification of the turn from unbelief to faith by people of "modern" sensibility—is doubtful. But what he suggested is worth hammering home again and again as a question, and more than a question, for all theologians. He seems to ask if we can proceed in any other way than he did, and also just what it means that most of the time we are unable to go with him. Perhaps picking up his huge tomes will force that double-barrelled question on us simply because, once one gets past the initial tedium and the curious repetitiveness of the material, Barth is remarkable reading, not only for his consistency but for his powers of description, his ability to "unpack," as we like to say today, his technical concepts. But there may be more substantive reasons for the question.

For one of the ways of putting what Barth said—there are others— is this: Barth said very simply and consistently that the possibility and even the necessity for God's assuming man unto himself by incarnating himself may be affirmed and explored *because he did so* and only for that reason. Of course, God is a transcendent God whom we know to be and to remain transcendent in his very union in flesh with man. Barth, thank goodness, remained a Reformed, a Calvinistic theologian to the end of his days and never gave way to the typically Lutheran temptation of putting second things (i.e., the mutual coinherence of the two united natures) first. Of course God is a transcendent God, but he has his own way of being transcendent; and that means that he is not transcendent in such a way that he cannot be related to his creatures. How do we know? Because he did and does relate himself to us by actually incarnating himself; and therefore it must be possible.

The ground of the actuality of the incarnation, of its ontological possibility, and of our being able to think about it, are one and the same. That God related himself to us means that it was possible, that he must be himself eternally in a way that is congruent with his relating himself to us contingently. For him to be in his unity is to be related to himself as one to another in love; to be, in other words, the Triune Godhead. And that is quite enough, and all we dare ask, to explain how God *could be* incarnately present, though it does not explain why he actually *was*. For the fact itself, one has no explanation. One simply celebrates it gratefully as the complete congruence or unity of that divine love with that active freedom. And again: How is it possible for these two perfections to be one? The possibility follows from the actuality, so that we must never define either divine love or divine freedom in such a way that the one contradicts the other.

Not only the *possibility* and the *actuality*, but also the *need* for incarnate reconciliation is simply to be affirmed as a reflexive consideration of the fact that it was actually so. For what do we really know of that need apart from or logically prior to that fact? Look at that huge mass or (to vary the figure) that cumbersome heavy artillery of theological reflection about "man" and "human existence," so characteristic of modern theology since 1700! What does it all amount to? And who is listening? Do we ever really know, no matter what anthropological model we employ, no matter to what sources of individual or cultural sensibility we appeal—do we ever really know or apprehend ourselves, our neighbors, or the process of history to be in real need of salvation? Isn't the natural evidence just as much in the opposite direction, except to the extent that we have already prejudiced it by a specific scheme for the analysis of what being human is like, or by appeal to a specific experience and sensibility on which we generalize recklessly and childishly?

Surely there are, to all appearances, good people mixed in with the evil. Indeed, it may well be that the whole conceptual framework for the discussion of the intelligibility of salvation—guilt, anxiety, despair, radical evil—is a figment of one kind of imagination. Do we really find a negative or positive preparation for the gospel when we examine ourselves, our neighbors, the course of culture, directly? Barth found many things there, but not a natural bent toward Jesus Christ, explicable apart from the fact itself of incarnate reconciliation.

And that leads me to suggest that in contrast to his *imagination* as a Christian and a theologian, in contrast to his wholly Christ-centered, or should I say (paraphrasing Novalis's famous remark about Spinoza) his God-in-Christ intoxicated imagination—in contrast to this, I say, Barth's *sensibility* as a Western human being in the twentieth century was, I believe, profoundly sceptical and secular, in a valueneutral, neither pejorative nor laudatory, sense of those terms. If you are interested in pursuing that aspect of him, read his comments on the existential religiosity of Karl Jaspers (vol. III/2 of the *Dogmatics*), or some of his most "situational" ethical comments, or his little chapters on solitude, doubt and temptation in the late small volume entitled *Evangelical Theology: An Introduction*.

Or again, read his completely secular appreciation of the completely secular, "fantastic" element in America, opening up to him an aspect of the human experience totally different from his own experience and sensibility, competing "to a certain extent" with divine providence. This vision no doubt conjured up for him a wholly different "image" of man than what he had experienced in himself and his neighbors, and even in the Nazis. In the few but lively words he devoted to these impressions, he sketched no great vision of a secular fulfillment, nor one of demonic or dehumanizing threat. He simply described something quite different from what he himself could experience, or anything the experience of which he could render in expression. Nonetheless, he saw it calmly and openly, in a slightly bemused and slightly amused but appreciative and even delighted manner.

It is not only the case, I believe, that Barth took pleasure in the vast variety of this indefinitely expansive human experience in this vast natural context—not only that he affirmed every part of it, at once in and for itself and for its potentiality as a *figura* of God's fulfilling work. Additionally, I believe, he looked with a long, cool scepticism at that scene and every part of it because he believed that none of it shows that figural potentiality by any inherent qualities or signs of its own—either positive or negative. I believe there was in Barth a self-conscious secularity of sensibility far, far beyond that shown by any of those modern Christian apologists who would make theological hay out of this very state of affairs. I suspect that much more consistently than any of them he knew the meaning of seeing no way from such a sensibility to faith in the Father of Jesus Christ. It is not at all inconceivable that Barth may have thought of his whole theological enterprise as theological witness in an era in which, for the time being—and a long time that may be—there is no discernible transition from secular, sceptical sensibility to a "Christian" sensibility or to Christian faith.

But there is of course a transition the other way, because God has reconciled man to himself. And, therefore, no matter how sceptical one's native tendency, one works with pleasure and hope on behalf of his fellow-men in the very contexts of secular life in which we are all set. One is grateful for the rise of black self-consciousness, one battles for nuclear disarmament, and one pleads with fellow-theologians to make their theology in this time of "nearly apocalyptic seriousness" a theology of (human) freedom. In sum, Barth may have explored at once calmly and passionately, at once positively and negatively, that secularity which from a theological stance he would have thought an "impossible possibility." He may have explored it far more searchingly than any of his opponents, as well as any of his own modifiers with their little apologetical nostrums, either in favor of or against the "secular situation."

Barth did indeed suggest a choice for the theologian, and I doubt that any theologian in our time has put the alternative so drastically. He put the choice not in the form of a challenge or a negative judgment but—*mirabile dictu*—in the form of an affirmation, the theological contents of which he developed in almost overpowering fashion and with extraordinary consistency. It abides at least as a question: If you cannot affirm Christian truth claims in their full integrity, dare you compromise or water down their meaning to accommodate your troubled sensibility? To do the job of theology properly today is first and foremost to avoid that temptation.

Now, Barth was the first to agree that being a Christian involves *doing* certain things (and therefore dogmatics must be ethics as well as ethics dogmatics, he said) and being *disposed* in certain ways, as well as *believing* and "confessing" certain things. And he would have been the first to insist that it is known only in heaven how these things are all rightly fitted together. But he would have urged, he did urge, that one's doing and being disposed do not logically modify the status of Christian affirmations as truth claims. So he stood, and will continue to stand, a rather isolated figure in modern theology. For it was precisely his denial that believing in the incarnate Reconciliation is in some unique sense *logically* dependent upon one's being disposed or behaving in a certain way that put him at odds with most modern theology.

Few theologians have denied that the *actuality*, the factual occurrence of incarnate Reconciliation, is based solely on the free grace of God and must, therefore, look like a completely contingent event—or perhaps like a non-event—from the human side. The contingency of the event entails that the actual occurrence of faith in it is likewise completely contingent, free and humanly inexplicable. But few, very few, would affirm that the *possibility* and especially the *need* for the event, and hence for faith in its saving power, are also to be explained solely from the event itself. Here it seemed to be Barth against the rest. Most theologians have spoken of a need endemic to the human situation as we experience and analyze it, and hence of Christian affirmation as logically dependent on decisions, dispositions and actions connected with that situation. They have spoken of an individual and collective insoluble contradiction that makes salvation necessary and hence a Savior intelligible, because he could be thought of as an answer to a genuine question.

Some theologians—one thinks of Schleiermacher and Tillich—undergird this argument from *need* with another from *possibility*. They argue that at a primordial, precognitive level we apprehend a relatedness to the divine ground built into our very being, an apprehension or awareness. This awareness makes possible a saving relation to God in our very disruption of the original relation. These two arguments from possibility and need, either singly or in combination, have been the linchpin of the systematic and apologetical enterprises of the modern era.

It was the energetic and logically consistent Christ-centeredness of his imagination and his thought that made Barth deny these arguments from need and possibility, and affirm instead those we mentioned earlier, based on the actuality of the occurrence of the incarnate Reconciliation. I doubt not that his deliberate secularity or scepticism was also at work in the denial of these arguments. They were for him at best dubious or philosophically privileged reports of the primordial and the existential human situations—even if he himself had been able individually to confirm them.

Instead, for him, not only the situation of sinning, but the doctrine of creation and of a primordial relationship of the creature to God are reflexive considerations of the fact that God was in Christ, reconciling the world to himself. The former situation is for him the anti-type of that fact, the latter relation its figure. The currently popular phrase "images of man" would have been congenial to Barth, though he might have preferred the word "parables." The phrase hints at a view he held very strongly, to the effect that we know "man" only by means of a reflected image, and not directly. For Barth this situation extends not only to that vague entity, man and his history in general, but to our neighbors—and even to our specific selves. Even our self-knowledge is not based on direct self-grasp. The knowledge of man, including ourselves, is mediated to us by the original of which we are the image: Jesus Christ. As a reflection of his relation to God we apprehend the primordial relationship with God in which we have been created good, a relationship that abides inalienably with us through all the distortions of the human condition. Likewise, the evil that we believe, do, and feel is unveiled to our self-apprehension not directly, but only as the refracted distortion of Jesus' free, obedient goodness in which God has overcome that evil.

So Barth turned his back on by far the largest part of the modern theological tradition with its anthropological starting point and logic. And yet it may turn out in historical hindsight that he was beholden to it, and that he took with him to the grave an era of Christ-centeredness in theology which began with the fight around 1700 against the Deists over revelation in history, and has been going on ever since. For the affirmation in most modern theologies of the systematic type has been that the uniqueness of Jesus Christ as Revealer and Savior is the chief, if not the sole content of Christian truth claims.

But even then, I believe it will be said that in Barth's theology this Christ-centeredness reached a well-nigh incredible consistency, because it was consistent not only in content but in method. It governed the whole of the procedure or procedures of theological reflection, not only the positive affirmations. If this way of doing theology is now coming to an end, what will come crashing down in the case of Barth is no mean "project of thought"—no mere Christocentric liberal whimper.

On the other hand, it may be that at least in the form which Barth gave it, this way of theologizing won't come crashing down, but that it will remain to haunt and comfort the rest of us with its iron and yet gay consistency, when we are less daring in our ways of doing theology. For what he was about was neither an anthropology in the guise of theology or Christology, nor yet a deductive Christological system. He was about the conceptual unfolding of a rich variety of beings and relations, all of them good and right, and all of them real in their own right, and all of them referring figurally to the incarnate, raised and ascended Lord who has promised to be with us to the end, and at the end. Has Christian theology succeeded in setting us another task instead of this?

Unlike Kierkegaard, Barth as a Christian man and as a pastor was no ironist because, as he liked to say, God's "no" to men was enfolded in his "yes" to them. And the one form of the imagination of which he really had little sympathy was the tragic—so closely linked to the sense of irony. "Titanism" he used to call it deprecatingly and wince whenever he saw it rearing its classical or romanticized head. But irony in theology is a slightly different matter. Where other Christ-centered theologians, liberal or conservative, are most eager and most nearly direct in an almost oppressive way, there Barth was most reticent, most dialectical or enigmatic. I think in this one respect one may rightly call his theologizing—in contrast to his other activities as a Christian— ironic. But again, even in this respect he was an ironist only under an enigmatic sign of great hope rather than tragedy. What we are speaking of is, of course, that dual journey in one—from unfolding the meaning of Christian assertions to claiming them as truth, from being a hearer to being a believer and a doer of the Word of God, mayhap even from secular (or even religious!) sensibility to Christian faith. That journey is a time for gentle irony in theological comment. For is it not right to begin to recede gradually into silence when one hears something that might be the sound of the wings of the Spirit of Life approaching?

At the end of his American lectures Barth said that even the best theology can be no more than the prayer *Veni Creator Spiritus,* prayed in the form of resolute work, clinging without scepticism but also without presumption to the promise that "not theology but 'the Spirit searches all things, even the deep things of God.'" And then he went on: "But one thing remains to be added. Allow me to say it a little enigmatically and cryptically with the words of . . . Stonewall Jackson, spoken at the hour of his death: 'Let us cross the river'—nobody knows whether he meant the Potomac or the Jordan—'and have a rest in the shade of the trees.'"[3] We are told in Holy Writ (Psalm 64:4) that there is a river, the streams whereof shall make glad the city of God, the holy place of the tabernacles of the most High. No doubt it is a figure of this river that we cross—in order to rest in the shade of the trees—in the hour of death, but equally in the midst of this life whenever we die to it, for life and death too are figures one of another. So we may cross that river anywhere at any time, for by prefiguration it is the same river—whether we do so by way of the Potomac near Washington, the Quinnipiac in New Haven, or the river Rhine at Basel on December 9, 1968.

Notes

Previously published in *Reflection,* vol. 66, no. 4 (1969), pp. 5–9.

1. Karl Barth, *Evangelical Theology: An Introduction* (New York: Holt, Rinehart and Winston, 1963), p. vi.

2. Erich Auerbach, *Scenes from the Drama of European Literature* (New York: Meridian Books, 1959), pp. 71, 73. For a dissenting view see Thomas M. Greene, "Dramas of Selfhood in the Comedy," in *From Time to Eternity: Essays on Dante's* Divine Comedy, ed. Thomas G. Bergin (New Haven: Yale University Press, 1967).

3. Barth, *Evangelical Theology,* pp. 58–59.

7

Barth and Schleiermacher: Divergence and Convergence

This essay was first presented in May 1986 at a conference held at Stony Point, New York, to celebrate the centenary of Karl Barth's birth. The first part, entitled "Divergence," had originally circulated as an independent piece prior to the conference, when the second part, entitled "Convergence," was added to comprise the essay in its final form. In the first part Frei examines Barth's critique of Schleiermacher as it appears in Barth's early Göttingen lectures and then in his essay from about ten years later in Protestant Theology in the Nineteenth Century *(Valley Forge: Judson Press, 1973). That critique is seen to focus on a discrepancy Barth perceived between Schleiermacher's intentions and the actual execution of his theology, for by intention Schleiermacher seemed to regard Jesus Christ as indispensable to the meaning of the Christian faith in a way that was undermined by philosophical commitments as Schleiermacher's theology unfolded. Without denying all truth to Barth's contention, Frei lays the groundwork in this section for the questions he will go on to raise about a possible "convergence" between the two theologians. For, Frei argues, Barth's own theology not only became more "practical" and more "ecclesial" in basic sensibility, but it also neglected, in these early critiques, similar features evident in Schleiermacher.*

The section on "Convergence" then seeks to exploit these insights. The "practical" and "ecclesial" aims of Schleiermacher's own theology are established, and Barth's final essay on Schleiermacher from 1968 is used to suggest that Barth may no longer have regarded Schleiermacher's work as being quite so philosophically overdetermined. At the same time, the developments in Barth's own theology, Frei suggests, allowed him to pose his final questions about Schleiermacher without making Christology into a special topic of critique. The issue resolves itself more broadly into how to relate theology and philosophy. Frei concludes by reflecting on the tradeoffs faced respectively by Barth's strategy of subordinating philosophy to theology, on the one hand, and Schleiermacher's strategy of correlating them, on the other. It is interesting to note that in his posthumous Types of Christian Theology, *Frei goes on to posit a further possible "convergence" between Barth and Schleiermacher with regard to the* sensus literalis *of Scripture and its bearing on the indispensable singularity of Jesus for the Christian faith.*

* * *

Divergence

When Karl Barth lectured on Friedrich Schleiermacher in Göttingen in the winter semester 1923–24,[1] he declared that he did not want to act the part of a theological historian. He eschewed, then and later, any lengthy account of Schleiermacher's development, and he referred only peripherally to his precursor's cultural context. Having been Schleiermacher's disciple once and rebelled against him, he wanted to keep coming to grips with him directly in his works. It was as though he were looking for a common context in which he and Schleiermacher both lived and in which they were both accountable for what they wrote. In 1923, the footprints of the second edition of the Romans commentary were still fresh in the sands of time, and the deliberate and significant change in title from the abortive *Christliche Dogmatik* to *Kirchliche Dogmatik* lay some years ahead. In one of the prefaces to the *Römerbrief*, Barth had poured out his wrath over those *wissenschaftliche* scholars who, once done with their spadework of philological, cultural, and historical commentary, called it quits and with obvious condescension turned the last volume of the series over to the practical theologians, the "Niebergalls" of this world. Just when *real* explication of the text should have begun! It was a denigration of both explicative and applicative labor in other words, of the very heart of conceptual exploration. Barth shared Hegel's contempt for those scholars who substituted historical explanation for *Anstrengung des Begriffs*. Schleiermacher was far too important to him for any other treatment than that curious combination of exposition and interpretation (some would say exegesis and eisegesis) of the text that one accords to an equal—a person with whom one shares a common platform, subject, and audience.

Schleiermacher as Apologist

Commentators have expressed surprise and disappointment that the Göttingen lectures were so thoroughly expository rather than interpretive, but with the twenty-twenty vision of hindsight we can say that that is just what one ought to have expected after the *Römerbrief* prefaces. In order to understand an author one must above all understand the author's text, and to understand the text is to think with the author, in agreement, disagreement, and constant reconceptualization. Understanding means using the text to treat the author as an equal. Historical understanding of the author, which can only be either propaedeutic to textual understanding or consequent upon it, achieves this equality only rarely and with great difficulty.

Barth's interpretation of Schleiermacher in the Göttingen lectures consists in shaping certain dominant themes, to the repetition of which we become accustomed; indeed, some of them, like the image of "peace" or the peaceful middle between extremes, or of "meditation," tend to become tiresome. But since, as John Updike has observed, martial images proliferate in the writings of our feisty author, the contrasting rhetoric of his nineteenth-century precursor and conversation partner might indeed have struck him profoundly. The theme of mysticism also tends to be repeated, especially in the wake of Emil Brunner's book on Schleiermacher, *Die Mystik und das Wort,* but right from the start Barth is hesitant about the appropriateness of that theme to Schleiermacher's thought. Much clearer and more continuous is the theme of Schleiermacher as Christian apologist, which is later heavily emphasized in Barth's long, sustained effort to come to grips with him in his essay on Schleiermacher in *Protestant Theology in the Nineteenth Century.*[2] In contrast to apologetics, "mysticism" seemed to Barth an inadequate denotative category for that transcendence of the subject-object duality which he thought Schleiermacher shared with his Idealist philosophical contemporaries but which, unlike them, he posited *theologically* rather than philosophically, setting it in the relation between the feeling of absolute dependence—not the intuitive or discursive intellect—on the one hand, and God as Spirit, on the other. The place of this notion in Schleiermacher's thought is central for Barth, especially in the long essay just referred to, not only in its own right—just where or how does the intercourse (*Verkehr*) between God and human beings, to use Wilhelm Herrmann's term, take place and does it involve a kind of coinherence of divine human apprehension?—but because it has immediate logical implications for other crucial topics, particularly faith and Christology. And so Barth will return to it but, as we shall note, rather differently and less programmatically, in his last comments on Schleiermacher some thirty-five years later. At any rate, "mysticism" is for Barth at best an awkward term for what is at stake in Schleiermacher's interpretation of the transcendence of the subject-object dialectic. If Schleiermacher is a "mystic"—at least in the way the word has usually been bandied about in Protestant polemics against other religions and parts of the Roman Catholic tradition—the place of Christology in his system becomes moot or at best secondary. Jesus Christ would be Redeemer only in a thoroughly instrumental and dispensable sense, an occasion for the realization of a divine-human communion in principle achievable without him. But Barth realized that Schleiermacher's whole system was directed toward arguing the indispensability of Jesus Christ to the meaning of Christian faith and that, successfully or otherwise, this is what he wanted to show to believers and unbelievers alike.

By contrast, then, to calling Schleiermacher a mystic, Barth has no problem in characterizing him as an apologetical theologian. His definition of apologetics in the large Schleiermacher essay has become famous:

> Apologetics is an attempt to show by means of thought and speech that the determining principles of philosophy and of historical and natural research at some given point in time certainly do not preclude, even if they do not require, the tenets of theology, which are founded upon revelation and upon faith respectively. A bold apologetics proves to a particular generation the intellectual necessity of the theological principles taken from the Bible or from church dogma or from both; a more cautious apologetics proves at least their intellectual possibility.[3]

The natural context of this definition is the relation of theology to other *Wissenschaften*, especially to philosophy as *Wissenschaft*. The crucial operative terms in the definition are *Denknotwendigkeit* and *Denkmöglichkeit*, precisely the terms that are at issue between Hegelian-Idealist theology and a Schleiermacherian-mediating theology. For the former there is no conceptual possibility of theology unless it implies conceptual necessity; for the latter the two are logically discontinuous and although theology is a philosophical, that is, conceptual, possibility, the compelling claim to truth and even to meaningfulness of its subject matter rests on other grounds than those of conceptual necessity. For himself, Barth describes those other grounds as "revelation," a concept that plays a dominant part in his thought throughout the twenties, climaxing in the program of an internal prolegomena to dogmatics in *Church Dogmatics* 1/1 and 1/2, in which he unfolds the concept of revelation descriptively rather than constructing an argument for its conceptual possibility (in contrast to the external prolegomena to Schleiermacher's *The Christian Faith*). The concern about the epistemic or epistemological status of dogmatic theology evinced by the use of concepts such as revelation or faith—the latter being seen in polar relation to the former—is stronger in the Barth of this period than it ever was in Schleiermacher. The communion of the Christian with God is, for Barth, the Christian's *knowledge* (however problematical) of God, and sometimes he faults Schleiermacher for two contrasting things at the same time: too close a relation between philosophy and theology, on the one hand, and the denial of the cognitive character of theological statements, on the other.

Schleiermacher was the mediating theologian par excellence, so that Barth's preoccupation with the theme of apologetics in Schleiermacher was appropriate. But what Schleiermacher's apologetical theology mediated between were a large number of different things, of which theology and philosophy, or theology and the more limited sciences—historical and physical—were only examples. There was, at least potentially, also a correlation between Christianity and the other religions, between Christian forms of living and other forms, between Christianity in its specific essence and culture as historically developing reality, and finally, between the church as a community and the civic community represented by the state, cultural associations, and the family. Clearly, whatever may be the case in some other writings, the Barthian Schleiermacher who dominates the essay in *Protestant Theology in the Nineteenth Century* is the apologist who mediates between *Wissenschaftslehre* (transcendental philosophy) and dogmatic theology, and the dominant note is that the test case for the success of this enterprise is Christology, which Barth takes to be the defining instance of the concept of revelation.

Barth's Reproach

We might put Barth's question to Schleiermacher like this: Are statements about the uniqueness and absoluteness of Jesus as the revelation of God intelligible and plausible in a broader, trans-Christian conceptual, philosophical-cultural context? Early on in the essay Barth indicates the answer:

> Christology is the great disturbing element in Schleiermacher's *Glaubenslehre*. . . . Jesus of Nazarerh fits desperately badly into this theology of the historical "composite life" of humanity, a "composite life" which is really . . . self-sufficient. . . . But nevertheless he is in fact there.[4]

And then, toward the end, we listen to the same strain when he says that the Reformation correlation between Word of God or Jesus Christ, and faith becomes equated with the correlation between history and experience as the two foci of an ellipse for Schleiermacher. This is a favorite Barthian (if not exactly Ritschlian) metaphor for the reproach that divine grace or prevenience and human possibility are simply synergistically related in this theology, nullifying the central thrust of the Reformation, for which not only can "Word of God" and "faith" not be exchanged for any other terms but their "correlation" takes place only in the absolute priority of Word to faith. This is again a way of criticizing Schleiermacher's theology for its dual and interconnected Christological and epistemic deficiency.

Only at the end, and as a brief afterthought, does Barth take note of the basic *soteriological* rather than epistemic arrangement of Schleiermacher's whole Christological enterprise, namely, the organization of the whole of *The Christian Faith* into the division between consciousness of sin and consciousness of grace, and the location of the christological topics under the latter. Even then he does so in effect only to illustrate the previous point—that in this case too Schleiermacher moves toward a synergism or relativization in which there is no untranscendable "juxtaposition [*Gegenüberstellung:* the translation "opposition" is wrong] between God and man, between Christ and the Christian."[5] And the viewpoint from which this antisynergistic polemic is launched is, as I said, the epistemological one—a revelation Christology and revelation trinitarianism that is logically prior to soteriological considerations.

In short, the agenda of this large Schleiermacher essay appears to parallel that of *Church Dogmatics* I/1. Barth asks whether Schleiermacher's theology presupposes the deity of the Logos (the content of revelation) as seriously as the Reformers presupposed that of the Holy Spirit.[6] He doubts it; he suggests that the seriousness of the Reformers' mutual juxtaposition (*Gegenüberstellung*) of the Second and Third Persons of the Trinity prevented either or both from being regarded as—or collapsed into—a mode or predicate (as Barth liked to say) of human cognition: both are equally "moments of the divine revelation."[7] There are no adequate safeguards of this sort in Schleiermacher's theology, and that is of course the basic threat not only to his pneumatology but to his Christology as well.

Barth wanted to bring together four questions or critiques of Schleiermacher: (1) On the assumption that Schleiermacher's mediating theology is basically one of religious consciousness and therefore at least potentially a theology of the Spirit, he asks whether it really is a theology of the Holy Spirit or instead one of relational or even purely monistic spirituality. Is the latter, he asks, what the feeling of absolute dependence is really about. (2) He asks whether this theology can be a theology of the Holy Spirit short of a far stronger correlation between pneumatology and Christology than Schleiermacher's mediating procedure can provide, and he implies that the answer must be negative. That is, for Barth the correlation between Christ and the Spirit present now in and to faith, or between the Second and Third Persons of the Trinity, must be absolutely prior to and something much more than the communal spirit—identical with the church—that provides the continuity between the Redeemer or history and present experience. (3) He asks whether Schleiermacher's apologetical or correlationist motif will allow for a strong enough doctrine of *revelation*, in which God and creatures are untranscendably and therefore unconfusedly juxtaposed to each other, even in faith. (4) He asks whether Schleiermacher's apologetical or correlationist motif will allow for a strong enough doctrine of *prevenient grace* to assure that faith is the work of divine forgiveness and not merely a cooperative enterprise between grace and repentant faith.

Barth was looking for ways to show that the correlation of distinctive Christian concepts with concepts derived from general human experience inevitably leads in the direction of the reduction of Christian concepts. Mediating theology is an unstable compromise between a Christocentric theology properly at risk because stripped of all external foundational support, on the one hand, and a theology that has put itself at the mercy of consistent conceptual "demythologization," on the other. Mediating or apologetical theology has a superior standpoint from which to mediate between these two extremes on even and harmonious terms—Schleiermacher's "peaceful center"—but of course Barth thought that it was a place that did not, or should not, really exist. Right theology is a *theologia viatorum* that has no secure earthly resting place, and that includes the lack of a secure philosophical, experiential, or cultural home.

In the process, Barth conflated the two issues expressed in the third and fourth questions (about adequate doctrines of revelation and prevenient grace), arguing that the issues were in effect two aspects of one and the same more basic problem, that of the untranscendable objectivity of the divine-human juxtaposition in Christian faith. But they were not two aspects of that issue, certainly not historically and probably not logically. They may well, of course, have been aspects of some other, more basic problem, but that would have meant that Schleiermacher's *basic* correlation was not the theological one between revelation and the universal character of the feeling of absolute dependence. Barth did not consider that possibility in this essay.

In fact, the first of the two issues (that of the third question) is about the communication of divine truth through a privileged historical event that is its indispensable channel. Is such a thing either conceivable or, if conceivable, likely? It is the problem of Lessing's ugly ditch, of accidental truths of history being able or unable to furnish proof for eternal truths of reason by means of miracle, proph-

ecy, and inspiration or—in Schleiermacher's case—to furnish meaningfulness, though not proof, for them by means of religious experience. This is the problem of the conceivability of revelation.

The second problem (that of the fourth question) is whether the
experience of sin, or something like it, is a universal phenomenon
that is at least *to some extent,* even if not wholly, intelligible apart from
the understanding of particular historical redemption in Christ. Here
the meaningfulness of the concept of Christ is (again, to some extent
at least) logically dependent on the meaningfulness of sin as a universal rather than a specifically Christian concept. This is the problem of the universal meaningfulness of redemption or reconciliation
through a particular, historical Savior. The most powerful modern
endeavor to combine the topics of revelation and reconciliation systematically and conceptually was mounted in the theologies of the
German classical period, Hegel's and Schleiermacher's at the forefront.
But apart from such systematic combinations, revelation and reconciliation are at least logically two different conceptual issues, and in
each case "correlation" with nontheological conceptions can be carried out differently.

Christian Theology as Practice

We cannot pursue these topics here, but as Barth's *Dogmatics* developed past the prolegomena, it is clear that the concept of revelation
tended to recede in significance and the doctrine of reconciliation
became more important. In the process, the doctrines of the person
and work of Christ, Christology and soteriology, moved closer to each
other, the bond between them being a concept of personhood as self-
enacted agency or performative project rather than the epistemic
notion of revelation as existentially imparted and appropriated knowledge or understanding. In that sense and that alone, one can say that
Barth became a "narrative" theologian: Jesus was what he did and
underwent, and not simply his understanding or self-understanding.
He was an agent in a narrative plot, in his particular narratable plot,
that is, the restoration of the broken covenant which is also the realization of the aim of divine creation. It is more accurate to say that
the meaning of the theological doctrines or conceptual redescriptions
is the *story* of which they are (partial) redescriptions, rather than conversely, that the meaning of the story is the doctrines. The unity of
Christology and soteriology is their unity in the narrative rather than
a *conceptual* unity in which the two concepts "person" and "work"
become perfectly integrated. As for our *appropriation* of person and
work, it receives no systematic but only a dogmatic correlation in
Barth's later work. Its logical possibility in a church-dogmatic context
is based strictly on the actual, once-for-all accomplishment of Christ's

work on our behalf, and not even partially on a native, inherent capacity—or for that matter incapacity—of ours for responding. Schleiermacher would not have found it a very congenial view.

These developments in Barth's theology would surely serve, however, to circumvent his earlier endeavor to see the problems of revelationally founded Christology and of soteriology in Schleiermacher as together *simply* aspects of the more basic, in fact the *most* basic, issue of the "untranscendable over-againstness" of God and humankind, and thus to see the relation between the problems solely in epistemic terms—even if the knowledge is "practical" rather than "theoretical." Not that this issue would be eliminated, but it would now be relativized and come up—together with the character of Schleiermacher's theology as one of the Spirit—as *one* question rather than as *the* test case for judging the adequacy of Schleiermacher's theology.

The recession of the restrictively epistemic character of Barth's earlier views makes him more relaxed about the practical character of Christian theology. The tension between the "indirect objectivity" or constative quality of Christian statements, and their appropriative, that is, illocutionary and perlocutionary performative character—the latter the emphasis of pietists and existentialists—becomes not solved but simply relaxed in Barth's later work. The affirmation of the practical aspect and aim of theology had always been there for him anyway: right from the beginning he knew that theology was there to serve preaching and the Christian life in Christian as well as civil community. But later on, the emphasis was less problematical: in a proper theological hermeneutics, explication, reflective understanding, and application simply go together. Likewise, for any proper theology, faith is a coherence of knowledge with acknowledgment and obedience. More than that cannot and need not be said.

In Barth's 1923–24 lectures, Schleiermacher's *Brief Outline of the Study of Theology* had received extensive treatment.[8] Never again; and Barth neglected two important aspects of it thereafter in his treatment of Schleiermacher in the late 1920s and 1930s: (1) To a somewhat lesser degree, he neglected the strong emphasis on the *ecclesiastical aim* of theological training and its influence on Schleiermacher's theology. He repeated it often but drew relatively few material consequences from it for his evaluation of Schleiermacher's theology. (2) To a greater extent, he neglected Schleiermacher's cognate emphasis on the *practical* character and aim of theology. And yet his own theology became not only more "practical" in basic sensibility, as we have mentioned, but increasingly *kirchlich* rather than simply *christlich*. Not only was that in a subtle manner contextually, psychologically, and existentially important but, I believe, it made an increasingly important conceptual difference in his writing as he grew older: Concepts are social skills, theological concepts are ecclesiastical and ecclesiological skills. In turn,

I believe, this development made a basic difference for his treatment of fundamental and broad methodological issues such as those concerning the relation between philosophy and theology when he finally looked at Schleiermacher for the last time shortly before his death. It allowed him, without receding for a moment from his own Christological concentration in theology, not to make Christology the immediate and explicit touchstone for agreement or disagreement with Schleiermacher's mediating theology. Instead, he could take a fresh look at the conceptual differences that Schleiermacher's ecclesiastical aim and practical intentions might have made in his theology and in the way he correlated philosophy and theology.

Convergence

The subtitle of this part of the essay might well be "Journey to Dullsville," for unlike the first section, this part involves one of those minute clarifying operations that could perhaps pay off handsomely, but only if one could push it considerably further than I can on the present occasion. The line along which the convergent movement either takes place or turns out to be a mirage continues to be that which traces the character of theology and its relation to other disciplines, particularly philosophy. But the focus of that relation will no longer be confined so explicitly to Christology and revelation. The question I want to ask is, What would have to be the character of theology for there to be such a convergence—no more, and certainly not agreement— between these two theologians? My claims, you will note, are not only modest, they are entirely in the subjunctive mood. Still, there might be important consequences, if only time, patience, and skill were available in equal measure. I will now spend more time on Schleiermacher, but I will again begin with Barth and end with him.

A Hypothesis

We must now look at Barth's "Concluding Unscientific Postscript on Schleiermacher,"[9] in which he recounts three stages of his relation to his theological forebear. First, he was Schleiermacher's disciple during his youthful liberal days. Then he distanced himself from Schleiermacher in his dialectical and postdialectical days, with greater acerbity at first than later on. This was the period of Barth's Schleiermacher lectures and essays, of which we have taken note. But now Barth, in his last year, distances himself from, without abandoning, his earlier self-distancing from Schleiermacher's theological outlook.[10] Barth now raises five questions, each with first a positive and then a negative edge: (1) Is Schleiermacher's enterprise intrinsically concerned with theology and accidentally with philosophy, or vice versa? And note that Barth speaks of intrinsic or authentic Christian theology as the kind that is "oriented toward worship, preaching, instruction, and pastoral care."[11] (2) Is Schleiermacher talking about a religious (my term, not Barth's) relationship to an untranscendable *other* toward whom "adoration, gratitude, repentance, and supplication are concretely possible and even imperative"? Or is he talking about a relation that is essentially one of *unity* between human consciousness and that which transcends it? (3) For Schleiermacher, are human beings primarily related to a *particular* and concrete reality, or is the reverse the case? (4) "Is the spirit which moves feeling, speaking, and thinking persons an absolutely *particular* and specific Spirit" to be distinguished from all others and called "Holy"? Or is that spirit a universally effective spiritual power that is basically diffuse? (5) And finally (and admirably put), are these the right questions for further conversation about Schleiermacher's intentions? (Note the absence of Christology as a *special* topic.)

Even if we respond yes to the last query, the others are put in that shorthand or summary fashion which comes from a tradition's longstanding use of the same technical philosophical and theological language applied to the same technical issues. Let me reword them a little, just to make them a little more accessible. They concern respectively (*a*) the relation of theology, the enterprise of a specific religious community, to philosophy, the self-grounded and coherent set of formal rules and universal criteria for intelligibility, meaningfulness, and truth for all fields of reflection, and perhaps (debatably!) the material science informative of the structures of reality; (*b*) the "objective" God of the "classical" tradition vs. the God of the transcendence of the "subject-object schema"; (*c*) the place of the "scandal of particularity" in Christian theology (presumably Christology and reconciliation in particular) vs. the hermeneutical priority of the "meaning context" requisite for the epistemological and religious significance of Christology, and so on; and (*d*) the especially German and Idealistic inquiry into the apparently disjunctive alternative of the unity of the Holy Spirit either with the "objectivity" of divine grace or else with the creative spontaneity of universal human subjectivity or "spirit"—the inquiry into which of these two is the source of the possibility of "spiritual" community between the divine and the human. The parallels between these questions and the topics covered in the large, earlier Schleiermacher essay are striking. But so is their open-endedness and less integrated or systematic character.

We will have to enter into this conversation on its own terms. If, in answer to the fifth question, we say that Barth's questions point at least in the right direction, part of what we are buying is (*a*) the common *philosophical* heritage between the two theologians which permits them common ground for agreement and disagreement about philosophy, and *(b)* the possibility that there is more than one way of relating that philosophical heritage with the theological heritage, if in fact the two disciplines are not identical. About *(a)* there can be little doubt, even if Barth's philosophical sounds are a bit like Hegel's, while Schleiermacher makes noises more reminiscent of Schelling. About *(b)* there is at the very least a lively possibility that Schleiermacher, like Barth, thinks that philosophy and theology are generically different enterprises. Given the rather vague area of agreement between the two theologians, a genuine convergence of their views would entail for Schleiermacher a vigorous emphasis on the radical difference rather than the compatibility between the two disciplines; for Barth, conversely, it would mean stressing strongly that radical difference means incomparability rather than incompatibility. Let us explore this two-sided possibility, all the while bearing in mind the hypothetical character of this enterprise, and therefore the prejudicial, highly selective character of my choice of texts, especially from Schleiermacher. In effect, I am confining myself to Barth's first question, viewing it as a central topic between the two theologies that may be disentangled, without at the same time arguing the question of priority between Christology and soteriology, or the relation of both to the character of revelation or our knowledge of God—important as all these issues are for discussion between the two men.

Theology as a Christian Skill

In his important book *Theologia*,[12] Edward Farley traces the history not only of theological education but of the concept of theology itself. We learn that from the High Middle Ages until the beginnings of the Enlightenment a distinction was made between theology as a cognitive state or *habitus*, usually though not always of practical kind, a "state or disposition of the soul which has the character of knowledge,"[13] and theology as a science or discipline. Farley goes on to say that, especially from the days of Pietism and the Enlightenment on, the notion of theology, particularly as a technical discipline, has become determined by the disposition of clergy education into a set of distinct "sciences" (I suppose one might say "skills") for study, destroying a previous unity and forcing to the fore the question of their interrelation.[14] From being a unitary discipline, second-order theology went to being an aggregate of specialties, while first-order theology changed from "sapiential habitus" to practical know-how. This new outlook grew out of several changes, prominent among them the Pietist treatment of theology (*Gottesgelahrtheit*) as a means to an end, namely, the exercise of the Christian life or Christian piety (*Gottseligkeit*). The climax of this development, both in theological method and ministerial education—characterized by a series of writings called "theological encyclopedia"—is Schleiermacher's *Brief Outline of the Study of Theology* (finished in 1810),[15] written about the same time as his essay *Gelegentliche Gedanken über Universitäten in deutschem Sinn* (1808; written in connection with the founding of the University of Berlin and in response to essays on the relation of the faculties in universities and on the method of academic study by Kant, Fichte, and Schelling).[16] Farley draws attention to both of Schleiermacher's essays. Schleiermacher, according to Farley, sees theology as a means to an end of professional education for the ministry. Theology is a practical or "positive" skill rather than a pure science. Like law and medicine—and the faculties in which they are taught—theology provides the cognitive skills for a social practice: the governance of a religious community. "Theology is unified by the social situation of clerical praxis external to the university and the faculty of theology."[17] But Schleiermacher also proposes a second and "material" rather than "teleological" unity for the three theological disciplines—practical, philosophical, and historical theology—in which he appeals to the distinctive "essence" of Christianity. This appeal involves the conception that Christianity belongs to a religious and religious-communal genre that must be distinguishable from other areas of culture and their study, and the affirmation that the student is to develop internal or participative (my term) access to Christianity's historical shape and, along that route, also to its reality and truth as a universal reality—faith—in one particular cultural form.[18]

The question I want to focus on is to what extent the first or "clerical paradigm" for theology, as Farley calls it, provides not only the *aim* (as Farley seems to think) but part of the very *essence* of theology, as well as of its pedagogic structure, for Schleiermacher. Is it not only in aim but in procedure "oriented toward worship, preaching, instruction, and pastoral care," as Barth asked in his first question? An answer satisfying Barth would obviously have to include the "practical" aspect of theology, on which Schleiermacher lays such strong stress in the third part of the *Brief Outline*. But more than that, the "philosophical" and "historical" aspects would also have to indicate signs of strong ties to the practical aspect and aim of theology—and so would "dogmatic," as part of historical theology. That, in turn, would mean (negatively) that in two senses the philosophical aspect of theology *cannot* unequivocally set the criteria for the meaningfulness, meaning, and truth of theological statements: (1) Any purely formal, universal canon of reason which adjudicates the coherence, consistency, and intelligibility of the "method" governing a particular field of study cannot do so in this case. (2) There cannot be a priority to theology of any specific (material) philosophical scheme—whether of a rationalist, transcendent (a priori), empiricist (a posteriori), or transcendental kind—that would assert that theological descriptions and claims must be subsumed under it. In short, neither formally nor materially can philosophy be a foundational discipline for theology.

We know from Schleiermacher's constantly reiterated assertions that he denied that theology is an aspect of philosophy in the *material* sense, that its content—for example, its notion of God—is identical with philosophical "ideas." The consistency of this disavowal might perhaps best be tested by an intensive investigation of that most difficult of his unfinished works, the *Dialektik*. But certainly he reiterates it constantly in his theological works, while at the same time affirming the compatibility, indeed the convergence, of the two disciplines. By consensus, the hard question is the relation of his theology to philosophy in the more *formal* sense, that is, to philosophy as universal W*issenschaftslehre*. Here the *Gelegentliche Gedanken über Universitäten in deutschem Sinn* (rather similar to the *Dialektik* but with a different immediate purpose in mind) are very useful. In this essay he clearly associates *Wissenschaft* with transcendental philosophy qua foundational, formal structure for knowledge rather than qua compelling ontological system. The business of *Wissenschaft* is not only to constitute the basic character of the "academy of the sciences" but to provide the idea, if not the reality, of the university. The business of the university is to teach youths to see everything from the point of view of "science"—"to see everything particular not for itself but in its nearest scientific relations and insert it into a wide common frame, in steady relation to the unity and total comprehensiveness [*Allheit*] of knowledge [*Erkenntnis*], so that they may learn in all thinking to become conscious of the basic laws of *Wissenschaft*."[19] But this cannot be done by "mere wraithlike transcendental philosophy," but requires the association of philosophy with real knowledge (*reales Wissen*) "so that from the start the supposed opposition between reason [*Vernunft*] and experience . . . can be annihilated" and the "large realms of nature and history be opened up."[20]

There is for Schleiermacher a *parallel* between the relation of formal *Wissenschaftslehre* and individual empirical fields of study, on the one hand, and religion in general and positive, cultural forms of religion, on the other. In both arenas the status of what is general is transcendental, the formal condition of a possibility inhering solely in the actuality of what is positive, empirical, or particular. But there is also an important *difference*, so that the parallel is at best imperfect. For the three faculties of law, theology, and medicine are not part of the "idea" of a university founded on a *wissenschaftliche* basis. Their subjects are therefore not related to "science" qua formal philosophical structure in the way that a particular content is related to formal, general possibility. These three faculties have their original *raison d'être* prior to or outside the university understood as a scientific construct. They are *Specialschulen* "that the state has either founded or at least, because they relate to its essential needs, taken under early and privileged protection. . . . The positive faculties originated individually through the need of founding with sureness an indispensable practice (*Praxis*) through theory, through a tradition of *Kenntnisse*."[21] In the context, it appears to me at least likely that *Kenntnisse* here means something like the "abilities" or "cognitive skills" requisite for carrying out the given practical work, and that the awkward expression "through theory . . . " means that becoming acquainted through well-accustomed use with the *tradition* of these *Kenntnisse* is pretty much what "theory" amounts to in the "positive" areas governed by these three faculties. "Theory" here does not function foundationally in a strong sense but functions more nearly as a set of grammatical remarks in the use of this particular language (to appropriate the terms of the later Wittgenstein and his little flock).

"The theological faculty was shaped in the church in order to preserve the wisdom of the fathers, in order to distinguish truth from error—as already in the past—and not allow it to be lost to the future, in order to provide a historical basis, a sure and certain direction, and a common spirit for the further development of doctrine and of the church."[22] So far, then, this "positive" enterprise is neither transcendental philosophy nor specific method based on a universal, philosophical foundation but the acquisition and impartation of a developing tradition that is in a broad, nonscientific sense historical (*geschichtlich* rather than *historisch*, to make use of that unpleasant but at times helpful distinction which became onerous only when it was elevated to rigid and absolute status). One could say that theology is part of the heritable social currency of a specific religious community, the Christian church. It is its self-critical inquiry into the use of its language for purposes of applying it and handing it on for use by the same developing and changing community in the future. It presupposes connection to another, more elemental use of the same communal language, that is, the constant transition from the Christian religious affections to their kerygmatic, poetic, rhetorical, and finally their descriptively didactic linguistic shape.[23]

The Functions of Philosophy

From what I have said it should be evident that were there to be a convergence between Schleiermacher's theology and Barth's views underlying his questions of 1968, it would depend on our being able to take Schleiermacher's "teleological" and practical outlook on theology and ministerial pedagogy as more than a final cause or *telos*—that in addition we would have to be able to see the outlook as part of the material cause, the very substance, of his procedure. This is the possibility I have been suggesting. The governing principle is that theology as a practical skill is not simply the application of logically prior philosophical and historical theological insight to logically subsequent and practical matters of church leadership, such as the cure of souls.[24] Theology is a practical discipline as a whole and not merely a theoretical or scientific enterprise—either of a transcendental or of an empirical character—with an as it were external aim. (This *may* be the bearing of *Brief Outline*, §§257–63.) This does not, of course, question the fact that it is *also* a scientific enterprise.[25]

Now Farley, we recall, also spoke of a "material unity" in Schleiermacher's theology provided by the "idea" or "essence" of Christianity. Something like this is indeed the case, even if "material" may be a bit misleading, and the "essence" of Christianity may be one of several contexts in which this second outlook surfaces. Let us recall the important additions Schleiermacher made in the second edition of *The Christian Faith*, additions completely in tune with the *Brief Outline*. He had suggested that dogmatic theology—itself part of historical theology—is founded not on "general principles" but solely in association with the concepts of church and Christian church. The particular character of the Christian church can "neither be comprehended and deduced by purely scientific methods nor be grasped by mere empirical methods."[26] So far this is what we would expect. How do we then grasp the concepts of church and Christian church? By "propositions (*Lehnsätze*) borrowed from" ethics, philosophy of religion, and apologetics. These headings are new and intended for clarification.[27] We are moving in concentric circles toward the essence of Christianity with the help of a group of narrowing specifications, all of them properly *wissenschaftlich* and applicable to empirical, cultural phenomena or data. "Ethics" is the broadest category (its counterpart is "physics," the study of nature) and designates the systematic study of culture and/or history. I think we may safely say that it is Schleiermacher's equivalent of social science, and embraces what came to be the university disciplines of sociology and cultural anthropology, but of course, since he was a German Idealist, in *geisteswissenschaftliche* manner. The "conception of the church" is properly speaking sociology or anthropology of religion and has for its subject matter the distinctive structure of religious communities. Given his orientation toward a view of human being as basically self-conscious (*Geist*), that structure will not be described in socioscientific terms (which were not then developed, anyway) of social structures or institutions but in terms of what Schleiermacher thought to be the basic, preconceptual, prelinguistic awareness that all people hold in common and that is therefore the bond of communal existence. He calls it "feeling" or "immediate self-consciousness."

While "immediate self-consciousness" in relation to the other human capacities of knowing and willing is part of an elaborate anthropology, its own content is not. That content consists simply of "affective receptivity," or the "feeling of dependence," and "spontaneous activity," or the "feeling of freedom," and Schleiermacher says that "to these propositions assent can be unconditionally demanded." How so? we ask, and his reply is, "No one will deny them who is capable of a little introspection and can find interest in the real subject of our present inquiries."[28] No phenomenological reduction, no elaborate and philosophically founded technical phenomenology, but *a common-sense instrument ("a little introspection") for bringing together a* wissenschaftlich *pursuit, the description or analysis of religious community as a cultural phenomenon, on the one hand, and the Christian-religious conceptual skill of orienting oneself within the church, on the other.* What enables them to come together in self-consciousness cannot be shown straightforwardly by a methodological procedure. For on the one hand, the scientific aspect of the inquiry proceeds on principles that are "borrowed" and thus cannot be applied as though they were on their own terrain: as soon as they *are* applied in strict rather than "borrowed" fashion, it is no longer theology that is being done.[29] But on the other hand, the feeling of absolute dependence is the—empirical? quasi-empirical? transcendental? all of the above?—common basic descriptive content of self individually as well as in community and does allow a family resemblance (even if it is not systematically specifiable) between "scientific" and Christian-participative, practical description of the same community, the church, and of its life and language. In other words, even though "borrowed," the "propositions of ethics" are not inapplicable or inappropriate. And then, in narrowing concentric circles, neither are the further, increasingly focused discriminations of propositions borrowed from the philosophy of religion, rendering for us a scheme for comparing actually existing religious outlooks and traditions, or finally the narrowest and most central discriminations of apologetics, in which "science" and the participative self-description of Christian cognitive skills join most closely. Propositions borrowed from apologetics set forth the specific essence of Christianity, that is, the coherence of redemption, on the one hand, with the specific person of Jesus, on the other. From cultural community we move to religious-cultural and then to specifically Christian community in a journey of reflection that is participative but also quasi-scientific. *If* this hypothetical description of a single procedure in which two logically disparate but not contradictory capacities—positive skill (together with its "grammar") and *wissenschaftliche* understanding—are focused on or correlated by means of the one common phenomenon of immediate self-consciousness is indeed Schleiermacher's path, three consequences are entailed: (1) There is no formal, transcendental scheme under which the two can be unified, the cognitive skills involved in Christian-pious membership in the Christian community—especially its leadership on the one hand, and the scientific understanding, in which a particular empirical religious content is made intelligible by a method derived from general principles, on the other. *Their unity is a matter of application alone, of direct correlation that allows no further or all-embracing justification of its possibility or intelligibility.* (2) Hence, the introduction to *The Christian Faith* is in fact not an actual theological or dogmatic exercise (and it certainly is not "philosophy") but a pre-liminary orientation or location,[30] quasi-external and quasi-internal, of the character of theology as scientific discipline and ecclesiastical skill. The introduction functions as an invitation to the cultured reader to exercise Christian understanding, by moving the reader toward it through a sort of indirect communication or maieutic guidance (description by means of concentric, increasingly focused *borrowed* propositions), so that there may be an ability to follow and perhaps even to carry out that skill in the form of a dogmatic system. (3) Hence the system itself has no further or actual systematic principle apart from the preliminary, quasi-scientific yet common-sensical one of the introduction: the feeling of absolute dependence. Beyond that, the persuasiveness, coherence, and completeness of the system consist solely in its actual performance, in the convincing aptness and com-pleteness of its formal organization—perhaps rather like an aesthetic whole. (That formal organization in turn must therefore always be subject to revision.)[31]

In sum, the relation between theology and philosophy as a mate-rial system of true ideas virtually does not exist for this hypothetical Schleiermacher as a teacher in the church, except as a purely formal appropriation of the language of various philosophical systems for dogmatic purposes.[32] The relation between the notion of theology as Christian conceptual skill and the notion of it as science in the sense of the specific application of a system of formal, general principles (*Wissenschaftslehre*) is one of direct—that is, not further or transcenden-tally founded—correlation between independent equals. The correla-tion takes place by "borrowing" the general principles and applying them to immediate self-consciousness, which not only is the center of selfhood but also as a concept comes closest to specifying the focus or continuing center of the Christian community.

The Integrity of Theology

This hypothetical Schleiermacher and Barth are agreed that theology is the critical self-examination by the church of its own specific lan-guage under a norm furnished within that pious linguistic commu-nity.[33] There would be a real convergence between them here, be-cause the implication for both is the irreducible specificity of this communal language, which is not even (except in a "borrowed" sense) an instance of a general class called religious-communal language. For Barth the question would be whether the *correlation* of this language on a level of equality with the scientific understanding of religious-communal language as a general class does not already serve to give away the independence and practical aim of the church's critical self-description of its language. The focal, though not the only, problem would be that the feeling of absolute dependence might well, on the correlationist assumption, become a far stronger or more comprehensive integrating factor between the two kinds of skill or procedure than my hypothetical Schleiermacher has suggested and that in consequence it would also become a far stronger systematic focus for interpreting *dogmatic* as distinct from prolegomenal statements. Barth in 1968 seemed to think that something like this was the risk though not the certain consequence of Schleiermacher's policy of correlation. He had already posed this very issue of the independence of theology from the "sciences" with which it may be correlated, or one strongly resembling it, in his Göttingen lectures in connection with the convergence of Schleiermacher's *Brief Outline*, Schleiermacher's critique of Schelling's "Über die Methode des akademischen Studiums," and Schleiermacher's essay on the nature of the university. Is it possible, Barth had asked, that Schleiermacher maintained that so far as science or speculative philosophy go, theology is actually poised in mid-air?[34] In that case "correlation" would obviously not be nearly as nefarious as if it were a stronger systematic and integrating principle. But then Barth expresses his skepticism that this is Schleiermacher's real intention and backs off,[35] never (to the best of my knowledge) to pose the issues between Schleiermacher and himself primarily in these terms again. But in 1968, the possibility appeared on the horizon once more.

As we all know, Barth decided that the formal structure of an independent *Wissenschaftslehre* (to say nothing of a strong transcendental version of it) is not even in "borrowed" fashion a criterion for the meaning of dogmatic language. Not that dogmatics can do without such a structure, but it is subordinate to, rather than an independent correlate of, the rules governing or implied by the church's use of language. Even less than for Schleiermacher, formal reason is simply not a single, demonstrably self-identical transcendental reality or potency for Barth which could by virtue of its apodictic and universal status provide the rules for every language game. And thus, dogmatic prolegomena are an internal part of dogmatics, formal rules of dogmatic reasoning adduced from the dogmatic use itself.[36] Subordination, however, is not necessarily denial. Even if he does not give them transcendental, that is, independent a priori status, Barth never denies that such categories or criteria as coherence, and distinctions such as that between meaning and reference, and even the law of contradiction, are indispensable formal tools for the theologian. But in application they are fragmentary and incomplete this side of the grave or eschaton. We simply do not know, for example, *how* the principle of noncontradiction applies to the doctrine of the incarnation, but we believe that since it does for God (who has neither created an irrational universe nor redeemed it irrationally), we need not resort to evasive substitute and general categories such as "paradox."

Surprisingly, Barth's subordination of *Wissenschaftslehre* to the rules inherent in critical Christian self-description allows him much greater, freedom than Schleiermacher to use what he wishes from a variety of *material* philosophical systems or conceptual schemes—for example, medieval realism or Hegelian Idealism.[37] Not being a correlationist, especially not of the transcendental Idealistic kind, Barth does not have to use, as Schleiermacher does, anthropology (whether of immediate self-consciousness or any other kind) as the focus for integrating two independent types of conceptual skills or understandings. So although he agrees with Schleiermacher that no material philosophical system has an intrinsic relation to dogmatics and that any such scheme ought always to be used formally in theology, still he acknowledges that many schemes may be at least as fit, unsystematically, to serve the purpose of dogmatic articulation as non- or pretheological anthropology is. In fact, such schemes are indispensable tools that may be, if we are careful, firmly governed by dogmatic reflection.

Now, my hypothetical Schleiermacher might want to ask some questions of his own about a possible convergence between himself and Barth. There are obvious and not very telling remarks, such as those about Barth's "revelation positivism," his "Christomonism," his "exclusivism," his "obscure conceptuality," or his "objectification" of theology, that I suspect Schleiermacher would leave to others. The maximization of the difference between *Wissenschaftslehre* and theology Barth and Schleiermacher might well (on this account of a possible Schleiermacher) have in common. But Schleiermacher might want to ask Barth whether, despite himself, he has not turned maximum difference into incompatibility through the instrument of the subordination of *Wissenschaftslehre* to Christian-communal critical self-description of the community's language. Without the constant, continuing *practice* of correlation (although surely it must be without a comprehensive principle of correlation), do not all criteria for intelligibility except the minimal, formal rules of grammar and syntax in fact go out the window for Christian theology? Do not principles like that of noncontradiction become not eschatological but Pickwickian if they have no clear theology-independent status in their application to theology? Does not Christian theology threaten to turn into the in-group talk of one isolated community among others, with no ground rules for mutual discourse among them all?

Finally, what about the sympathetic observer to this possible convergence between the two men on the relation between Christian
theology and philosophy? Perhaps one's final comment has to be that
on this topic or issue any theologian of integrity has to cut his or her
philosophical losses, and it is perhaps simply a matter of how it is done.
One way results in one kind of loss, the other in another. You simply
have to make your choice about what is most important to you in
this respect and what is less important and therefore can be allowed
to remain more problematical. *Correlating,* for example, the moral life
of the church and the problematic requirements of culture, or the Jesus
of historical-critical, *wissenschaftlich* reconstruction and the Lord and
Savior of the sinful people of God, or the conceptually objectified
dogmatic articulation of Christian faith and the general principles of
religious-language use, will give you one kind of result, *subordinating*
one to the other a different kind. Cutting one's philosophical losses is
an occupation that is theologically disastrous only if it means *either* a
complete elimination of philosophy as an issue and a means for reflection in Christian theology *or* a pathetic obeisance to philosophy as the
master key to certainty about all reason and certainty and therefore
to the shape or possibility of Christian theology.

Notes

Previously published in *Barth and Schleiermacher: Beyond the Impasse?*
ed. James O. Duke and Robert F. Streetman (Philadelphia: Fortress Press,
1988), pp. 65–87. Copyright © 1988 Fortress Press. Used by permission of
Augsburg Fortress.

1. Karl Barth, *Die Theologie Schleiermachers,* ed. Dietrich Ritschl (Zurich:
Theologischer Verlag, 1978).

2. Karl Barth, Die *protestantische Theologie im 19. Fahrhundert: Ihre Vor-
geschichte und Geschichte,* 2d, rev. ed. (Zurich: Evangelischer Verlag, 1952).
English translation of essay is in *Protestant Thought: From Rousseau to Ritschl,*
trans. Brian Cozens (New York: Harper Bros., 1959), 306–54.

3. Ibid. (English trans.), 320 ff.

4. Ibid., 313.

5. Ibid., 354.

6. Ibid., 343.

7. Ibid.

8. In fact, Barth's painstakingly thorough examination of this brief work,
together with Schleiermacher's nearly contemporary essay on the concept
of a university (we shall tackle its significance for the theological approach
of the two men later), is most remarkable. He unerringly poses at least the
possibility that Christian theology may be without *wissenschaftlich* foundation
for Schleiermacher. That is surely different from the then-customary view
of Schleiermacher, including Barth's own! But nothing really comes of it,

either then or in the large essay in *Protestant Theology in the Nineteenth Century*.

9. *Schleiermacher-Auswahl*, ed. Heinz Bolli, afterword by Karl Barth (Munich: Siebenstern Taschenbuch Verlag, 1968), 293 ff.

10. Dietrich Ritschl's contrary judgment in his edition of Barth's 1923–24 Schleiermacher lectures in Göttingen, that the shift was one of tone only (*Die Theologie Schleiermachers*, viii), is unpersuasive in the absence of substantiating argument.

11. *Schleiermacher-Auswahl*, 307.

12. Edward Farley, *Theologia: The Fragmentation and Unity of Theological Education* (Philadelphia: Fortress Press, 1983).

13. Ibid., 35.

14. Ibid., 49–50.

15. Friedrich Schleiermacher, *Brief Outline on the Study of Theology*, trans. Terrence N. Tice (Richmond: John Knox Press, 1966).

16. Friedrich Schleiermacher, "Gelegentliche Gedanken über Universitäten im deutschen Sinn," *Sämmtliche Werke*, vol. 3/1 (Berlin: G. Reimer, 1846), 535–644.

17. Farley, *Theologia*, 84.

18. Ibid., 92–93.

19. Schleiermacher, *Gelegentliche Gedanken*, 558.

20. Ibid., 572–73.

21. Ibid., 581.

22. Ibid., 582.

23. Friedrich Schleiermacher, *The Christian Faith*, trans. H. R. Mackintosh and J. S. Stewart (Edinburgh: T. & T. Clark, 1948), §§15, 16.

24. Schleiermacher, *Brief Outline*, §263.

25. The most powerful contrary argument, claiming historical *Wissenschaft* to be the constitutive character of theology for Schleiermacher and therefore straightforwardly to govern theology's practical aspect for him can be found in the excellent chap. on Schleiermacher in B. A. Gerrish's *Tradition and the Modern World* (Chicago: University of Chicago Press, 1983). See chap. 1, esp. pp. 39 ff. For perceptive discussions of Schleiermacher's views which are closer to this essay, see S. W. Sykes, "Theological Study: The Nineteenth Century and After," in *The Philosophical Frontiers of Christian Theology: Essays Presented to D. M. Mackinnon*, ed. Brian Hebblethwaite and Stewart Sutherland (Cambridge: Cambridge University Press, 1982), 95–118, esp. 103–8; and idem, *The Identity of Christianity* (Philadelphia: Fortress Press, 1984), chap. 4, esp. 87–88.

26. Schleiermacher, *The Christian Faith*, §1.2.

27. Friedrich Schleiermacher, *On the Glaubenslehre: Two Letters to Dr. Lücke*, ed. James A. Massey, trans. James Duke and Francis S. Fiorenza (Chico, Calif: Scholars Press, 1981), 80.

28. Schleiermacher, *The Christian Faith*, §4, p. 13.

29. Cf. Schleiermacher, *Brief Outline*, §6.

30. Schleiermacher, *On the Glaubenskhre,* 2d letter, pp. 56, 76 ff.

31. Ibid., 69–70.

32. Ibid., 62 ff.

33. Karl Barth, *Kirchliche Dogmatik* I/1:1 ff.

34. Barth, *Die Theologie Schleiermachers,* 256.

35. Ibid., 263–64, 274, 283, 292–93, 308 ff.

36. Barth, *Kirchliche Dogmatik* I/1:5 ff, 24 ff.

37. Ibid., I/2:816–25.

8

Of the Resurrection
of Christ

In 1987 Frei was asked to contribute to a volume of essays by American writers on the historic "Thirty-nine Articles of the Church of England," edited by John F. Woolverton and A. Katherine Grieb (forthcoming from the Church Hymnal Corporation). Along with two other brief essays, on those Articles concerning Christ's descent into hell and the work of the Holy Spirit respectively, Frei wrote the commentary on the Article pertaining to Christ's resurrection. This commentary is interesting for a number of reasons, not least for the light it sheds on the views of Frei himself, who often wrote on this theme though never more straightforwardly than here. He distinguishes his own position from three others in contemporary theology.

First, there is the well-known Bultmannian view that the resurrection accounts pertain not to the ultimate destiny of Jesus but only to "the rise of faith in the disciples." Then there is the peculiarly "historicist" view, which, in contrast to more decidedly skeptical versions of historicism, contends that the weight of the available evidence points heavily in the direction of Christ's resurrection as a verifiable fact. Some such view is held by figures as diverse as Pannenberg, von Campenhausen, and various evangelical-conservative apologists. Finally, there is the view that conceives the reality of Christ's resurrection as something that can be reconstructed "behind the texts" by means of modern historical criticism and philosophical speculation. Although Frei's sketch of this option remains somewhat elusive, one may perhaps think of New Testament

scholars like Jeremias, on the one hand, and philosophical theologians
like Tillich, on the other.

Frei's own more nearly Barthian view—with its stress on the mysterious conjunction of theological transcendence and concrete reality with
respect to the risen Christ—stands in clear contrast to these other proposals. It sees the first option as doing more justice to the elements of
ineffability than to the evident truth-claims of the resurrection accounts,
whereas the complaint against the second view is essentially the reverse,
namely, that it stresses the truth-claims at the expense of their attendant
mysteries. The third view, like the first, is seen as opening up too wide a
gap between the reality of Christ's resurrection and the texts that depict
it. Frei's alternative to these proposals attempts to take the relevant New
Testament texts seriously, without taking them either literally (in some
misplaced "historicist" sense) or else merely symbolically (in some "existentialist" sense that effectively turns language about the resurrection of
Jesus into little more than a manner of speaking). Frei's own view seems
to be that the reality of Christ's resurrection stands in some close, if not
fully specifiable, analogy to the New Testament texts that attest it, and
that we finally do not have epistemic access to that reality apart from its
textual depiction.

* * *

Christ did truly rise again from death, and took again his body, with
flesh, bones, and all things appertaining to the perfection of man's
nature; wherewith he ascended into heaven, and there sitteth, until he
return to judge all men at the last day.[1]

The resurrection of Jesus from death on the cross has always been
central to Christian faith. It has been at once glorious and disconcerting to Christians right from the beginning of the formation of the
Christian community (as reflected, for example, in Saint Paul's
Corinthian correspondence): glorious because it is the heart of the
good news of salvation, disconcerting because it is utterly mystifying
to our ordinary understanding and belief. That Jesus was raised from
the dead is the virtually unanimous testimony of the New Testament,
although modern commentators have disagreed about the historical
and theological import of that testimony. We may distinguish four
modern views about the nature of the resurrection, each of which
entails a specific outlook on the relationship of the New Testament
texts to the reality of the resurrection. In the first view, the statements
of the New Testament that Jesus was raised from the dead are simply
a mythological way of saying that the cross of Christ came to be
accepted for its saving efficacy by the earliest Christian community.
The miracle of the resurrection—whatever the fate of Jesus—was
something that happened to the faith of the disciples and other fol-

lowers of Jesus, not to Jesus himself. At most, in this view, one can say that we do not know what happened historically in the original events called "resurrection," but it is in any case not theologically significant. The important thing is that where there had been despair among Jesus' followers, now there was faith. This is the meaning of "resurrection." To be sure, it was taken by them as well as later Christians to be part of the miraculous grace of God, and they believed that this miraculous effect could not have taken place without the prior, greater miracle that Jesus himself was raised from the dead. But at this point a "modern" believer has to affirm that the history of Jesus ends with the crucifixion, and the reality of the resurrection is the faith of those who have confessed him as Lord. This, of course, runs counter to the interpretation of the New Testament texts by the vast majority of "premodern" Christian readers, all of whom, according to the demythologizing version, would have to be consigned by definition to the "mythical" state of mind, because they read the resurrection narratives as applying to Jesus and go on furthermore to affirm that application as the truth. In the demythologizing view, the real textual subject matter of the New Testament narratives is the birth of faith after Jesus' death, and not the historical Jesus himself; and the extratextual *reality* of the resurrection is the re-presentation of Jesus wherever the life of faith is truly proclaimed and accepted.

Passionately opposed to this view are those who believe that the New Testament accounts are an absolutely accurate record of the things that actually happened when Jesus was raised from the dead. They take accounts such as those of the empty tomb (Matt. 28:1–8; Mark 16:1–8; Luke 24:1–10), the resurrection appearances of Jesus in the Gospels, and Paul's account of the resurrection appearances (1 Cor. 15:3–8) to contain no contradictions among themselves and to constitute reliable evidence in favor of an earthly event, Jesus' resurrection. It has the straightforward character of a fact to which historical evidence is pertinent. In this view, the subject matter of the texts and the reality to which they refer are to be taken equally literally; indeed, they are one and the same.

Between these two poles, those who read the New Testament accounts literally and those who demythologize them, there are two other kinds of readers. First, there are those who affirm that the primary subject of the resurrection was Jesus, but that the New Testament accounts of that event are not to be taken literally. There were "resurrection appearances" of Jesus, but they were of a broadly spiritual rather than physically miraculous sort, so that the truth or falsehood of reports such as the empty tomb and the physical details of the resurrection are not of primary importance. Text and reality are not that closely related; the reality is more important than the text and to be reconstructed from the text through strict historical research together with philosophical speculation.

Finally, others read the accounts as meaning what they say, so that their subject is indeed the bodily resurrected Jesus. They also believe that a miracle—the miracle of the resurrection in particular—is a real event; however, it is one to which human depiction and conception are inadequate, even though the literal description is the best that can be offered, not to be supplanted or replaced by any other and therefore itself not simply metaphorical in character. In this view, text and reality are adequate, indeed, indispensable to each other but not identical. Inadequate by itself, the literal account of the text is adequate to the reality of the events by divine grace. The text is not a photographic depiction of reality, for not only are the accounts fragmentary and confusing, but they depict a series of miraculous events that are in the nature of the case unique, incomparable, and impenetrable—in short, the abiding mystery of the union of the divine with the historical, for our salvation from sin and death.

In this view the text taken literally is understood primarily as the adequate testimony to, rather than an accurate report of, the reality. Narratives such as the empty tomb and accounts of the resurrection appearances are understood to be the indispensable means for grasping, even though not explaining, the mystery of Christ's resurrection as a real event. This, and not their credibility as evidence for the factuality of the event, is their primary function as texts. The very notion of "evidence" applies to this event only to the extent that it is a human historical event like any other; it does *not* apply to the event as one *both* identical with and yet at one and the same time utterly *different from* any other. In other words, to take the account of the empty tomb (for example) to have primarily the status of a factual report used as evidence is from this point of view to mistake its textual function. It is to turn it from a witness of faith into a report, from testimony to the truth of the mystery that unites the divine and the human into a report of a simply and solely natural-type event that is supposed to demonstrate its divine character by running counter to customary natural experience. This is the miracle of Christ's resurrection as conceived—whether positively or (more usually) negatively—by the eighteenth-century Enlightenment rather than the Christian tradition.

This is not to deny the possibility, in this point of view, that the story of the empty tomb may have the tentative secondary role of rendering historical evidence, but the argument in its favor is at best likely to be as good as, but no better than, the contrary position, namely, that the textual account is not likely to have been derived from genuinely early or reliable accounts. Faith in the resurrection of Jesus Christ cannot be articulated except by way of the resurrection narratives; but though indispensable, they are not the sufficient condition of the faith that Jesus himself (not merely faith in him) is the subject of the resurrection. That Jesus, and not merely faith in him, is raised from the dead is the mysterious gift of the one God who accomplished both and linked them together. Seeking to understand the primary and secondary, major and minor, functions of texts (such as that of the story of the empty tomb) in this larger context of faith, we can perhaps do no better than to endorse the cautious words of a recent writer: "[The empty tomb story] functions as a negative condition which contributes to the overall shape and character of the resurrection."[2]

The mystery to which the New Testament accounts testify—or which they render for us as texts inadequate yet adequate—is the continuity of the identity of Jesus through the real, complete disruption of death. He is the same before and after death. We know nothing of a reversal of the physical conditions of full death once it has set in; moreover, we also know nothing of a human identity that is not physical. The New Testament accounts do not invite us to speculate on a specific solution to the quandary of a live physical presence after death, nor do they answer the question of how the person raised can be one with the One who raised him from the dead. The point of the stories is simply to bear witness to the fact that Jesus, raised from the dead, was the same person, the same identity as before. That is the central Christian affirmation, vigorously reaffirmed both in the Creeds and in this article with its stress on the physical nature of the risen Jesus—a physicality that is indispensable if he is to be efficacious in our behalf. The great Patristic saying, "What he did not assume [i.e., anything less than full humanity], that he could not save" is as true of him in the resurrection as in his life before death. That, stated straightforwardly, is what affirmation that the resurrection happened in the first place to Jesus, not to the Christian community, is all about. It is Jesus Christ who remains capable of saving us in our mortal condition, who continues to be efficacious on our behalf. In his full and constant identity as Jesus of Nazareth, he is God's Word in our midst. He remains himself. This message is far more important than any theories we may form about the "nature of the resurrection" and its relation to the New Testament texts. The only reason for preferring the last among the four views set forth above on this question is that it articulates more fully than the others at once the *truth* claim and the *mystery* of this message.

Even more startling than the continuity of the identity of Jesus through death and resurrection is the affirmation associated with it in Christian faith: his identity as this singular, continuing individual,

Jesus of Nazareth, includes humankind in its singularity. He is the representative and inclusive person. That, together with his efficacy to save, is what the New Testament tells us about him: the Word of God is the man whose very identity it is to be for others, and as this single individual to live, die, and be raised on their behalf. To be "the first born among many brethren" (and sisters) is his vocation and his very being. And these "many," these "others" are all humankind (Rom. 8:29; 11:32).

In the fourth view stated earlier, the position of the first is both embraced and reversed. For both there is a vital connection, though not identity, between the texts and the reality of the resurrection. For both the miracle of the resurrection is the miraculous rise of faith out of unfaith—now and in the future, just as it took place at the beginning according to the texts' testimony. That rise, so the fourth view holds, is not accounted for by adopting some one hypothesis rather than another about a causal event in the reconstruction of a temporal sequence; rather, it is accounted for by the miraculous inclusion of us all vicariously in the singular identity of Jesus, the fact that it was his very identity, his being, to give himself efficaciously on our behalf. He enacted his identity on the cross and it was confirmed in his resurrection. He was and is what he did for us. Because we are comprehended in his self-identifying action ("we were there") and his resurrection includes us, he is the ground of our faith and the source of its arising in us through the New Testament message, as it did in the early Christian community (cf. Rom. 10:13–17; Eph. 2:4–6) In the first view, the "representation" of Jesus is a function and part of the message that now as then miraculously evokes faith out of unfaith; and so Jesus and faith, as well as reality and text, belong together as the miracle of resurrection. In the fourth view, the message and miracle of faith are accounted for by the very character, and are therefore a function of, Jesus' being and his resurrection from the dead; and so Jesus and faith, as well as reality and text, belong together as the miracle of resurrection.

Having affirmed the Creed on Christ's bodily resurrection, the fourth article goes on to assert that Christ's solidarity with humankind ended neither with his death nor his resurrection. Having assumed our nature (i.e., having identified himself fully with us), this identification remains. In one respect the fourth article simply follows the historic creeds, affirming the eternal identity of Christ and God ("He ascended into heaven. . . ."). But in another respect, the article goes beyond the Creeds, adding a strong element that echoes certain sixteenth-century Lutheran affirmations: Christ bore the physical human nature ("wherewith he ascended . . . ") with him into eternity. His full self-identification with us is perpetual and not temporary. It is well to understand this powerful assertion religiously rather than metaphysically, for metaphysical schemes, like myths, change but the Word of God abides. In his eternal rule Jesus Christ maintains that solidarity with us that he established in the days of his flesh. That is the point of this matter, and it entails the consequence (in the Creed as in this article) that we are judged and are to be judged by none other than the one who is our saving representative. This is comfort that pierces to the heart (Heb. 4:12–13): our common Judge is no ruthless stranger appearing suddenly out of an eternal nowhere but the one who bore the universal burden on our behalf, both when we were victimized and when we were victimizers. Compared to that universal Judge and the scope and depth of his juridical work, how feeble is the pretense to righteousness, and how hypocritical the pride, of individuals, nations, races, classes, interest groups and the like.

Notes

Previously published in *Anglican and Episcopal History*, vol. 53, no. 2 (June 1989), pp. 139–45.

1. Article IV of "The Thirty-nine Articles of the Church of England." See Philip Schaff, *The Creeds of Christendom*, vol. 3 (New York: Harper & Row, 1931), p. 489.

2. David Fergusson, "Interpreting the Resurrection," *Scottish Journal of Theology*, vol. 38, 303.

9

Response to "Narrative Theology: An Evangelical Appraisal"

In November 1985, Carl F. H. Henry gave a series of three lectures at Yale. One of them offered Henry's critique of what he called "narrative theology," considering principally the work of Frei and Gabriel Fackre. Frei responded to that lecture, and both Henry's lecture and a transcript of Frei's response were later published in the Spring 1987 issue of the Trinity Journal.

Frei further discussed Henry's work in Types of Christian Theology *(New Haven: Yale University Press, 1992), where he classified it in the unlikely company of David Tracy and other theologians who, Frei argued, approached specifically Christian doctrines and beliefs in a way that seemed overly determined by general philosophical considerations. This essay likewise contends that Henry's thought is too influenced by a particular set of philosophical commitments. In the course of the argument, Frei's own position regarding the place of historical claims in Christian theology emerges with particular clarity.*

* * *

I have no coherent paper to offer; only a series of marginal comments on the things that Dr. Henry has said. I want first of all to say that as I reflect on matters that concern us all, many things are needed in the Christian church. Sound theology is not the first of them, by any means, but it sure would help a little now and then. We all try, from time to time, to contribute towards that end. My own vision of what might be propitious for our day, split as we are, not so much into denominations as into schools of thought, is that we need a kind of generous orthodoxy which would have in it an element of liberalism —a voice like the *Christian Century*—and an element of evangelical-ism—the voice of *Christianity Today*. I don't know if there is a voice between those two, as a matter of fact. If there is, I would like to pur-sue it. But I have conceded to Dr. Henry that I'm not sure that there *is* a voice between liberalism and evangelicalism. I am not well prac-ticed in discussion with evangelical orthodoxy, but this is a great opportunity for me because I think no one has done as much in our generation in America towards making that conversation possible as one between friends in the faith rather than enemies as Dr. Henry, and therefore it is a great privilege for me to make a very quick response.

Not all of Scripture is narrative, obviously. There are narrative accounts which the traditions have focused around the covenant that God made with his people, but that by itself does not make for a narrative theology. There is a liberal sense of using the term, narra-tive theology, which generally says that to be human is above all to have a story. I am not sure that that's above all what it is to be human. There are a great many other things involved in being human. But even if it were, the Bible has a very *particular* story to tell. That doesn't mean all elements in the Bible are narrative. It only means, so far as I can see, that something like John 1:14—"And the word was made flesh and dwelt among us, full of grace and truth"—is something that we don't understand except as a sequence enacted in the life, death and resurrection of Jesus. The Christian tradition by and large took verses like that to be the center of its story and took them to refer to the real world. That's a big remark, "refer to the real world." Let's put it this way. When I wrote *The Eclipse of Biblical Narrative*, I had liberals much more than conservatives in mind. And what I had in mind was the fact that if something didn't seem to suit the world view of the day, then liberals quickly reinterpreted it, or as we say today, "revised" it. And my sense of the matter though I'm not antiliberal, was that you can revise the text to suit yourself only just so far. There really is an analogy between the Bible and a novel writer who says something like this: I mean what I say whether or not anything took place. I mean what I say. It's as simple as that: the text means what it says. Now that doesn't mean that there aren't metaphors there. It doesn't mean that I take every account literally. But it does mean that I cannot take the biblical story, the gospel story especially, in separa-tion from its being the identification, the literal identification of some-one identified as Jesus of Nazareth. It's not about something else, not about somebody else. And it's not about nobody in particular, nor is it a story or an allegory about a mode-of-being in the world or something of that sort, although it may include that kind of dimension. That does not mean that I don't believe that we refer *by means* of that story. We do refer by means of that story and I would say that we refer in a double sense. There is often a historical reference and often there is textual reference; that is, the text is witness to the Word of God, whether it is historical or not. And when I say witness to the Word of God, I'm not at all sure that I can make the distinction between "witness" to the Word of God, and Word of God written. That is to say, the text is sufficient for our reference, both when it refers historically and when it refers to its divine original only by itself, textually.

I believe that what we think and how we refer is not language-neutral. We are, and are able to think, only by way of the language in which we think. Our referencing, especially in cases where empirical objects are not involved, like God (who, Saint Thomas tells us, is beyond genus and species) is language-bound. God is perhaps like us, but we also know that He is very much unlike us. Our referencing then and there is simply not ordinary referencing. The one thing I dislike about the term "supernatural" is that it seems to be a gigantic, enormously portentous way of saying "natural." It is the same as referencing naturally except much more so. But there is not only a *via eminentiae* in Christian language, there is also *via negativa*. Because we have both, we have not so much *doctrines* of analogies as that when we talk about God we do in fact analogize. But we analogize more on the basis of our *literal* reading of the gospel story than on the basis of something more nearly metaphorical. We start from the text: that is the language pattern, the meaning-and-reference pattern to which we are bound, and which is sufficient for us. We cannot and do not need to "transcend" it into "limit" language and "limit" experience. The opposite is the case, for example, in many of the parables: Ordinary language and ordinary work or political or household experience is sufficient for the utterly odd, the disproportionate, the "transcendent," the Kingdom of God, to be rendered verbally and proclaimed.

But of course it remains true that there is a great deal of God and of his ways that we do not know. It is enough to have the reference of Christ crucified and risen. I have a much harder time than Dr. Henry thinking in clear and distinct ideas. I'm sure you have already realized that. That's the difference between his remarks and mine. He is clearer than I am. If by a miracle of divine grace I should get to heaven, I am going to listen in on a conversation that I am going to request among Wilfred Sellars, Alvin Plantinga, Willard Quine, John Stuart Mill, Immanuel Kant, and Aristotle. I am going to listen in, and when they agree on what they mean by logic, and when they agree on the transcendental categories that get them started on their way to formal certainty and clarity, and on their epistemologies or lack of them, then I'll have a starting point for a natural theology (independent of theology as the right conceptual redescription of the biblical narrative) or for an appropriate theological "prolegomenon."

But until then, that's my problem. I indeed can't do without some philosophical equivalent to natural theology, some philosophical equivalent to epistemology, let's say, but I have to piece it together eclectically and provisionally. I proceed on the conviction that there is genuine continuity in the language of the Christian church as it readapts itself in every age to the paradigmatic language of Scripture, particularly to the story of the gospel and to reading the OT as the "figure" leading toward fulfillment in that story. I have to go on the conviction that there is more continuity in the language of the church and the Scripture than there is in the philosophical languages and their use of "knowledge," "God," and so on, and so on. And again, let me simply refer here to what I said earlier. For example, using the term "God" Christianly is in some sense referential. But that doesn't mean that I have a theory of reference to be able to tell you *how* it refers. It is also true in some sense other than a referential one: It is true by being true to the way it works in one's life, and by holding the world, including the political, economic and social world, to account by the gauge of its truthfulness.

God is both one who exists truly as no other being exists and Holy Spirit. That is to say, the word "God" is used both descriptively and cognitively, but also obediently or trustingly, and it is very difficult to make one a function of the other. That is why pietist and orthodox folk can quarrel all the time, and it doesn't seem to me that in the logic of the Christian faith there can be any final adjudication of that quarrel; you have both uses together. We have such things as the doctrine of the Trinity, to try to reexpress that sort of togetherness.

So "reference," again, is a difficult thing to get hold of even though one wants to refer. Unlike Dr. Henry, I think "reference"—to say nothing of "truth"—in Christian usage is not a simple, single or philosophically univocal category. (Problems of formal certainty and clarity again!) I did not mean to deny reference at all, as Dr. Henry worries I do, whether or not I intend it. I don't think any of us do want to, but that may be a clue to the difficult path between liberalism and conservatism for which I'm searching. The truth to which we refer we cannot state apart from the biblical language which we employ to do so. And belief in the divine authority of Scripture is for me simply that we do not need more. The narrative description there is adequate. "God was in Christ reconciling the world to himself" is an adequate statement for what we refer to, though we cannot say univocally how we refer to it.

Of course I believe in the "historical reality" of Christ's death and resurrection, if those are the categories which we employ. But they weren't always the categories employed by the church. There was a time when the church didn't talk about "the Jesus of history" and "the Christ of faith." There was a time when we didn't talk, as many people have talked for nearly two hundred years now, about Jesus Christ being "a particular historical event." And it may well be that even scholars won't be using those particular terms so casually and in so self-evident a fashion for much longer. In other words, while I believe that those terms may be apt, I do not believe, as Dr. Henry apparently does, that they are as theory-free, as neutral as he seems to think they are. I do not think that the concept "fact" is theory-neutral. I do not think that the concept "probability" is theory-neutral. I do not think that we will talk theologically in those terms, perhaps, in another two generations. We didn't talk that way three hundred years ago. One talked in that day and time much more nearly about one person in two natures, undivided, but also unconfused. And that was just as adequate and just as inadequate a way of talking. If I am asked to use the language of factuality, then I would say, yes, in those terms, I have to speak of an empty tomb. In those terms I have to speak of the literal resurrection. But I think those terms are not privileged, theory-neutral, trans-cultural, an ingredient in the structure of the human mind and of reality always and everywhere for me, as I think they are for Dr. Henry. Now that may mean indeed, you see, that I am looking for a way that doesn't exist between evangelicalism on the one hand and liberalism on the other hand. If that's the case, well, so be it. But it may also be that I am looking for a way that looks for a relation between Christian theology and philosophy that disagrees with a view of certainty and knowledge which liberals and evangelicals hold in common.

I am uneasy about the way contemporary historians investigate all history, not just the way they investigate the Bible. I no longer know how it is to be done, and I find that there are many historians who no longer know how to do history. It is one of the things that seems to be up for grabs in this generation, when so much is up for grabs. Even if I say that history is first of all the facts—and I do have a healthy respect for evidence—I come across something else. Is Jesus Christ (and here I come across the problem of miracle) a "fact" like other historical facts? Should I really say that the eternal Word made flesh, that is, made fact indeed, is a fact like any other? I can talk about "Jesus" that way, but can I talk about the eternal Word made flesh in him that way? I don't think so, just as I don't think that I can say "God created the world" and mean by that a factual referent like any other. Austin Farrer once said that people seem to think that if they could find an analogy to the notion of creation, they would secure that notion. He said that on the contrary, if there is an analogy to it, then the concept is lost. And that is in a different way true of Jesus Christ too. I have to qualify my language. Once again, yes, "Jesus" refers, as does any ordinary name, but "Jesus Christ" in scriptural witness does not refer ordinarily; or rather, it refers ordinarily only by the miracle of grace. And that means that I do not know the manner in which it refers, only that the ordinary language in which it is cast will miraculously suffice. It is historical reference (to use our cultural category) but it is not historical reference in the ordinary way: nor of course is it metaphor.

These have been very unsystematic remarks, but maybe they will help start a kind of conversation that Dr. Henry has so helpfully begun for us.

Note

Previously published in *Trinity Journal,* vol. 8, new series (Spring 1987), pp. 21–24.

10

H. Richard Niebuhr on History, Church, and Nation

Frei wrote this essay for presentation at a conference in honor of H. Richard Niebuhr held at Harvard in September 1988 and jointly sponsored by the Harvard and Yale Divinity schools. The occasion celebrated the posthumous publication of Niebuhr's Faith on Earth *(New Haven: Yale University Press, 1989). The conference papers, including Gordon Kaufman's response to Frei, appeared in* The Legacy of H. Richard Niebuhr, *edited by Ronald F. Thiemann (Minneapolis: Fortress Press, 1991). Frei's paper had to be delivered in his absence, for he was stricken just prior to the conference by an illness that proved to be fatal.*

Niebuhr was Frei's most important teacher, and this essay represents a lifetime of engagement with him. Frei here reflects on what he learned from Niebuhr and Barth. He contrasts Niebuhr's "radical monotheism" (which has notably influenced the theology of another speaker at the conference, James Gustafson) with Niebuhr's "Christ-centered and church-centered 'henotheism'" (with which Frei found himself more sympathetic). Among other things, this essay is valuable for understanding Frei because of the way it addresses political themes. An interest in progressive politics was an important part of his life, but something he wrote about only rarely.

Many of those often placed in the same theological camp as Frei seem to propose that the Christian community focus on its own internal identity, arguing that it serves the larger society best when it witnesses to the possibility of a different kind of community formed by a different language. Stanley Hauerwas maintains such a stance most forcefully, but it also sometimes appears in the works of George Lindbeck. Frei favored a more direct involvement, though always critical and ironic, and this essay hints at ideas he might have developed.

* * *

A distant but very distinct fragment of a layer of memory remains from the days of World War II at Yale Divinity School. H. Richard Niebuhr, introduced by Ralph Gabriel, gave a lecture on post-war aims. (There were many lectures of this sort in those bleak days, when no decisive turn had come yet in the war's fortunes.) Apparently no manuscript or notes of his talk are extant, but the heart of what he said was powerful: Our innocence was gone, that innocence so much associated with our previous, semi-detached place among the great powers with whom we associated. We were now a worldwide empire. We could either exercise our position with restraint, or recklessly, with a heavy hand that could not rest until it had encircled the globe. That and that alone was now our difficult choice.

Like Britain in the tension between Gladstone's and Disraeli's foreign policy, we inched forward as nations usually do when their sense of insecurity increases proportionally to the growth of their power. We can recall a whole host of balkanized local area quarrels submerged and weirdly caught up in the threat of global Soviet aggression. We can recall the bitter pill that Dean Acheson had to swallow when he declared Korea outside the immediate interest-sphere of the United States, and therefore was thought to have encouraged North Korea to attack her neighbor to the south. The very notion of the "containment" of Soviet expansion proposed by George Kennan, chief of the State Department's defense planning board, never very popular in government circles even in its heyday, was abandoned under John Foster Dulles.

By a series of steps about which Reinhold Niebuhr would no doubt have invoked the word "ironic"—he was himself, to some extent, affiliated with Kennan's policy (Richard Fox, *Reinhold Niebuhr* [New York: Pantheon Books, 1985], 238)—we were clearly on our way to answering H. Richard Niebuhr's war-time query at least in one respect: if self-restraint meant global self-limitation, it was becoming more and more difficult. Increasingly the spirit, if not the flesh, of American foreign policy was embodied in the heady rhetoric of John F. Kennedy's inaugural address. Americans were ready to go anywhere and pay any price to sacrifice for freedom, even if the burgeoning consumer culture—to say nothing of the Vietnam war—questioned that flamboyant and heroic rhetoric.

In *The Rise and Fall of the Great Powers* (1987), the sales of which testify to the timeliness of the debate which it and other works like it have started, Paul M. Kennedy summarizes the situation of the early 1970s with a quotation from Ronald Steel's *Pax Americana* (1967):

> The U.S. had more than 100,000 soldiers in 30 countries, was a member of four regional defense alliances and an active participant in a fifth, had mutual defense treaties with 42 nations, was a member of 53 international organizations, and was furnishing military or economic aid to nearly 100 nations across the face of the globe. (389–90)

Has our time come to fade gradually, though perhaps not as dramatically and quickly as Great Britain earlier in this century, from the global scene? Is our strategic situation perhaps as perilous as our heavily dependent economic situation—a debtor to nations overseas, especially to East Asian investors? Will our national role, even apart from our defense budget capacities, be limited by the power of new and rising demographic epicenters?

Let me be sure to state my argument carefully. I am not necessarily arguing that we were totally unrestrained in our policy as a new empire, only that we could not find any restraints less than those encircling the whole globe. In that sense, at least, Niebuhr's visionary plea received grim but clear answer.

From there I want to go on to state another tentative proposal, and tentative is all it ought to be. You will remember the early Reagan administration argument for drastically higher defense expenditures. The economic productivity of the Soviet Union was clearly shrinking, but that is precisely what made its empire so dangerous and so likely to be dangerously aggressive. *Mutatis mutandis,* if we are now decreasingly competitive, our industrial base inefficient in comparison with others, our indebtedness nearly out of control, and our military and non-military budgets dangerously imbalanced—though not as dangerously as those of the Soviet Union—why shouldn't the United States, precisely at this point and no matter how well-intentioned, be most dangerous to the balance of the world's precarious equation of power, even with recent improvements in Soviet-U.S. relations? Unless, that is, there is some privileged virtue to the species *homo americanus* (or *femina americana),* a speculative matter about which theologians may well have some built-in skepticism.

Given our open society, we do not have the luxury—as the Soviet Union, for instance, has—of foreign policy reversal without the danger of domestic face-saving embarrassment. The reversal of Soviet Afghanistan policy, difficult as it was, seems to have been child's play compared to the agony and bitter conflict of the U.S. reversal on Vietnam. The magic appeal to our "credibility" in foreign eyes, which Henry Kissinger invokes so ardently—credibility apparently as much for domestic appeal as for foreign policy reasons—might well make the Soviet Union at some crucial points a less adventure-some and dangerous nation than our own, a more open and electoral one.

I am not saying that these reflections are certain dogmatic pro-posals. I am simply saying that, given H. Richard Niebuhr's far-sighted remarks in 1943, he might well have taken the present time to be one in which the two terms, "responsible" and "restrained," were not only far more imperative but also far more difficult to achieve than we have witnessed in the development of U.S. foreign policy. In fact, the partnership between responsibility and restraint is so precarious as to be virtually unachievable without heavy countervailing foreign pressure on our own policy. A carefully modulated foreign policy for which a world of genuinely independent power structures exists, so that neither global policy integration nor a sense of our unlimited policy initiative will allow us to say that China or Iran are ours to "lose," is a hard thing to achieve for an empire which graduated to global power status only about fifty-five years ago.

To talk with confidence of the nation's duty was somewhat unusual for Niebuhr who, in striking contrast to his fellow clergymen, was quite restrained and circumspect in the agenda he set for the country as a whole. The nation was *the* crucial collective historical agent of the day. But at least Niebuhr had to share with his colleagues a certain kind of confidence in two respects, of which we are no longer sure.

First, the deadly serious and immensely learned search for a proper hermeneutic in our own day is a sign that on the foreign exchange markets, not only has the value of one kind of linguistic coinage gone up against others, but the mechanisms for exchange have become far more complicated. H. Richard Niebuhr and his contemporaries were more fortunate. The *lingua franca* between the mainline churches and responsible establishment leaders had not yet been broken (except for writers and readers of the *Partisan Review*). What we later came to call "civil religion" was an inheritance, still in place, of Puritan and evan-gelical traditions, in which the outlines and images of popular bibli-cal history were still adequate to provide the mythology for the sig-nificant occurrences and turns of American history. This *lingua franca* was embraced by people like Walter Lippmann, who were pleading for a "public philosophy" in which people were public citizens rather than private believers, and as such were part of the linguistic com-pact. (In 1966, the acerbic, iconoclastic critic Edmund Wilson gave us in *Patriotic Gore* one long, grumbling and reluctant acknowledgment of this linguistic state of affairs.) It was a time when even rivals like Marxists were globally interpreted by American Christians not for their critique of ideology, but for their view of human nature, their practical vision of human agency, and the likelihood of achieving a just society under their scheme. The age of unbroken ideologies, each a means of support for interpreting the others in the same sweeping ways, was still in full hue and cry. The myth of the "American century" and of the "American way of life" was rife.

Second, the hermeneutical plan onto which this biblical or biblically derived *lingua franca* was projected was human history, the future projections of which, to put the matter cautiously, were not totally veiled from human insight, so that the history of human affairs was not a mere trackless wilderness without any pattern whatsoever. We did not then look, as members of the *Annales* school do today, for the eventless or synchronic sequence of ordinary life in a stable society, in order to discover a meaningful basis for the pattern of difference and sameness in everyday life between then and now, to find out how it felt to be alive within a community of that time, compared to one here and now. They do so with the conviction that to look for anything more from history, such as a pattern of unique, unrepeatable events, is useless.

H. Richard Niebuhr shared the confidence in the diachronic, unbroken thrust from eventful past into eventful future, and the belief that this vision was part of the business of the interpreter of history. History, including American civil and religious history, as the course of human events, gave him the impetus for appropriating the patterns of language and interpretation which he chose in the late 1930s. It made available to him the partially but certainly not wholly revealed pattern in which the interpreter himself is directly involved in an intricate web that makes him both agent and analyst. Niebuhr wrote at the outset of *The Kingdom of God in America:*

> All attempts to interpret the past are indirect attempts to understand the present and its future. Men try to remember the road they have traveled in order that they may gain some knowledge of the direction in which it is leading, for their stories are begun without present knowledge of the end. (1)

And again:

> The confused events of the past revealed a pattern to scribes and rabbis as well as to prophets and poets, and with that pattern in mind they made their choices in an ever critical present. In somewhat the same spirit we ask today whether there is in the history of American Christianity a pattern which may perform a similar function for us. (2)

On that rare occasion during the war, to which I referred at the beginning, the Christian interpreter of history, the ethicist, and the theologian were all united in seeing the Christian as citizen in the public

arena where all citizens meet, and where the citizen of a nation
becomes a citizen, not merely of his own country, but of a global
domain.

When H. Richard Niebuhr turned from *The Social Sources of Denomi-
nationalism* (1929) to the appropriation of a tradition in *Kingdom of God*
(1937), he was deliberately moving from social to narrative or intellectual history. It was a move toward what we would call a "hermeneutical retrieval" or, in less grandiose terms, an affirmation that
the language we use for our deepest religious convictions in our day
is continuous with that of earlier ages, and that the earlier language
is indispensable for us. Collective concepts available for these purposes—phrases such as "kingdom of God"—enter into a common time
and linguistic frame of which we are all members, in other words,
into a common "tradition." *Kingdom of God* is testimony to the compelling force of the bedrock, to the unavoidable and linguistically
unsubstitutable language of tradition.

With that persuasion went another larger, and perhaps more
dubious one: that the compelling force and connection of collective
ideas runs through time for all those who inherit and loyally recreate
and transform them. The history of ideas is not a self-engendered
mystery with special, inherent explanatory powers (except in a limited way, explaining the relation between concepts). It is, rather, the
retrospective understanding of a public tradition's moral and verbal
coinage, and of our willingness to assume responsibility for it by
entering into its usage. (This was in some ways a very un-Troeltschian
affirmation, from a disciple of Troeltsch.) Niebuhr deliberately reversed
the very route that most historians have traveled in recent years by
moving from social to narrative or intellectual history. This reversal
was also the adopted American son's ritual self-appropriation, so much
more popular in America in that day than in ours, when the stories
of our "foreign" traditions were incorporated into common, American ancestral lore. Today, in painful reversal, our stories are more apt
to be those of alienation rather than appropriation of the common
lore.

These grafts, however, were not entirely *de novo* for Niebuhr. Not
only the content but also the method of this retelling took the form
of the story. In method, it was at least in part an acknowledgment of
the pilgrim or narrative shape embodied, perhaps more than in other
sub-forms of Christianity, in the Calvinist tradition. Within English-
speaking countries, it was also an acknowledgment of those characteristic Calvinist devices such as the allegory of the *Pilgrim's Progress*.
The story told was that of God's active universal governance of all that
he had made, and of his own unlimited, gracious, prevenient initiative toward all creatures.

In his interpretation of history Niebuhr was, despite his own denial, a man of powerful metaphysical vision. This vision, however, was not a shape to be separated out from the narrative shape in which we experience and retell the appropriation of any tradition. There is no identifiable metaphysical residue left over from the story of which it is a part. The two—the time-filled story, and its mysterious, over-arching metaphysical or reality affirmation—are given together. Story images and general concepts are united but *never* convertible into each other. On the one hand there is a God, and furthermore, as Niebuhr once put it in a striking remark, "God is not simply up in heaven but in time itself" ("The Grace of Doing Nothing," in the *Christian Century*, 49 [1932], 380). In a series of late, tantalizing and undeveloped remarks, especially in *Radical Monotheism and Western Culture* (1960), Niebuhr indicated that the structure or principle of "being" and of the highest "being" are neither to be equated, nor are they to be disasso-ciated—parallel to principles he had maintained in his value theory (*Radical Monotheism*, e.g., pp. 33, 38, 43, 46–47). This kind of repeti-tive, general (ontological) structure cannot in principle be anything more than a weak, retrospective, transcendental reading of the neces-sary ground for contingent, cumulative (ontic) relation of the respond-ing creature with God. There is here, as in much of Niebuhr, a meta-physical vision for the fullness of divine initiative in relation to the created order, but its descriptive force is rendered solely by the given, specific "life story" of any creature or traditional group.

On the other hand we, the creatures responding to God, live wholly in time, and it is there that we encounter him: "What is past is not gone; it abides in us as our memory; what is future is not non-existent but present in us as our potentiality. . . . Time in our history is not another dimension of the external space world in which we live, but a dimension of our life and of our community's being. We are not in this time, but it is in us" (*The Meaning of Revelation* [1941], 69; see also all of chapter 2, "The Story of Our Life"). Our time-filled, inescapably time-structured existence allows us neither to reduce the images of special occasions to general concepts nor to reduce concepts to images. Yet we cannot disassociate them; we can only tell the story of our communities as part of a fragmentary yet not wholly unknown, a hidden but genuinely universal narrative, a narrative the account of which is not only sequentially but synchronically unfinished.

Our story, our inquiry as observers into patterns which we as agents may act out, goes on, here in time, on the plane where God and humans meet. It is an inquiry into not only the church's but also our country's future, an inquiry into the polarity between the two, but always under the limited contingent conditions of response for our time to the creating, judging and redeeming work of God.

We know there are other contingent encounters than those of our story, so that each of them and the images through which we tell them cannot be reduced to those of other stories. Hence the unapologetic confessionalism of our understanding of the mediation of our understanding of God through Jesus Christ, our Christian "special occasion" of revelation. But hence, equally, the profound insistence that all attempts to universalize this story are unwarranted attempts to substitute our own religion for the full glory, the infinite, mysterious, unapproachable richness of the universal God who is active in and near to all things. It would be a characteristically Christian attempt to substitute our religious henotheism for the radical monotheism called for by loyalty to Jesus Christ.

By combining these motifs—the distinctive story of our specific confession within specific traditions, and its subordination to the sole glory and the universal, transcendent governance of the one God—Niebuhr entered the lists of the Reformed tradition, indeed the Reformed tradition as shaped, to his mind, in the early, perduring American Reformed tradition. He did this with a power and consistency that nobody in his generation in America could match, for his was an original refashioning and not a warmed over, traditional evangelical reaffirmation of that most mysterious word and experience of Christian confession. It was testimony to the experience of the sheer contingency of one's own life and of life among contingent creatures, and at the same time, it was effective witness to the sheer grace of God's glory. This was a refashioning message not addressed primarily to those evangelical conservatives who might receive it naturally—at least doctrinally, if not morally—but to those for whom this extraordinary claim and the very notions of a divine interruption of the human initiative and the throwing back of human questions as a divinely authorized force, were an absurd puzzle and an offense. In short, it was a message of unflinching, Reformed offense in the midst of a puzzled, liberal or post-liberal audience, including those Christian "existentialists" for whom "faith" is the highest existential act and creative force to which human beings must always be radically obedient. Hence Niebuhr's relative isolation among American theologians, but hence also the strength in his day, and yes, in our day, too, of the original shape of his theology.

In the quest to understand contingent existence as the manifestation of divine glory as sheer grace, Niebuhr was infinitely more than the ordinary, standard neo-orthodox, anti-liberal theologians, who in so many ways were really liberal theologians under the skin. "We have," he once said in a sardonic side comment on us all, "in our wisdom substituted for the holy God a kind, heavenly father" ("The Anachronism of Jonathan Edwards" [Address delivered at Jonathan Edwards's church on the occasion of the bicentennial of his death,

Northampton, Mass. March 1958], p. 13). He was an original voice restating the Puritan heart of the matter for our day. In this service he found Jonathan Edwards, more than any other precursor, to be his mentor. Edwards had tirelessly expressed the same convictions in aesthetic, moral, biblical, historical and metaphysical coinage.

Niebuhr's only qualification of Edwards was that the sole mediation of that divine grace to us through Jesus Christ must be subordinated to the insistence that God alone is the universal source of all being and action. Niebuhr's view of Edwards was, perhaps, at least partially refracted through the later vision of Schleiermacher. But these two predecessors did, for all their differences, share a Reformed tradition. Refracted or not, it was Edwards, even if this subordination of Christology to theology did make for some genuine problems.

One must go on to ask whether even those problems weren't perhaps inherent in the American Puritan version of the Calvinist *soli Deo gloria*, or perhaps in Calvin himself. (Besides, to lean the other way and embrace the two, theology and Christology, as coequals, makes for other kinds of problems. That seems to be the nature of theology.)

In a passionate defense of Edwards, Niebuhr put the matter of the sheer grace of God's glory like this:

> What Edwards knew, what he believed in his heart and with his mind, was that man was made to stand in the presence of eternal, unending absolute glory, to participate in the celebration of cosmic deliverance from everything putrid, destructive, defiling, to rejoice in the service of the stupendous artist who flung universes of stars on his canvas, sculptured the forms of angelic powers, etched with loving care miniature worlds within worlds. In the light of that destiny, in view of that origin, because of the greatness of that calling, it depressed him, angered him that men should throw away their heritage and be content with the mediocrity of an existence without greater hope than the hope for comfort and for recognition by transient fellow-men. Man who had been made to be great in the service of greatness, had made himself small by refusing the loving service of the only Great One; and in his smallness he had become very wicked, covetous, of the pleasures that would soon be taken from him. *But in the end, man could not make himself small, Edwards knew, for the way of man is not in himself.* (Ibid., pp. 8–9)

To understand how this holy, mysterious power can be a universal, liberating source far, far beyond the scope of our selfish love to turn away from its narrow, parochial exclusiveness, Niebuhr reflected on the impact of this sheer grace on the inhibiting, selfish flow of our own contingent love:

> There is only one way out of the dilemma of human love. What if men could see that the universal, the eternal, the fountain and center of all being is their true good? What if they could learn to love their neigh-

> bors not insofar as these are persons, lives, minds, but because they are
> creatures of God and sacred by relation to the ultimate Being who is
> also man's true good? That is precisely the possibility that has been
> opened in Jesus Christ. In him the intention of the universe, to speak
> anthropomorphically, has become apparent; in his fate, even more than
> in his teaching, it has been made manifest that God is love. Through his
> life, death and resurrection, it has become possible to love the "Enemy"
> who seemed to destroy all his creatures but now is shown to be seeking
> their redemption. (*Kingdom of God*, 115–16)

This eloquent passage shows the way in which the language and
pattern of Niebuhr's thought reacted strongly to Jonathan Edwards,
his own precursor, just as is meet and right in as strong a reader as
Niebuhr was.

In the radical realism of this Reformed, Puritan *soli Deo gloria*,
Niebuhr gave no quarter. It was, from beginning to end, the governing motif, the driving force of his theology. More than anything else
this was the motif under which he read divine governance—and also
divine judgment and crucifixion—in Scripture. It was also the prime
universal principle under which he applied the images of biblical
eschatology to an ever-present, merciful and objective, divine, universal, causal action. "Radical monotheism," as he came to call it,

> dethrones all absolutes short of the principle of Being itself. At the same
> time it reverses every relative existent. Its two great mottoes are: "I am
> the Lord thy God; Thou shalt have no other gods before me" and "what-
> ever is, is good." (*Radical Monotheism*, 37)

It was an echo of Jonathan Edwards's "consent of being to being."
To conceive of a more radically realistic theology than the yoking of
these two affirmations would be difficult. In a way, one could say that
Niebuhr risked almost everything not on methodological boldness, but
rather on a somber, sober, even agonizing theodicy, as his great fond-
ness for Spinoza's universalism, the wholly disinterested intellectual
love of God, suggests. The images of creation, judgment and crucifixion, and redemption echo each other in a tightly linked continuum,
where the hint of one divine action always carries, by dint of a mysterious, yet fit transcendent governance and initiative which we cannot fully grasp, the overtones of the other two.

Niebuhr thought hard upon the rift in our finite historical experience between the lack of power of the good, and the lack of goodness of temporal power. He saw in our natural experience the seem-
ing two faces of God, as life-giver and as slayer. In this case, too, he
refused to stay content within dualism and restrict God's action either
to a thin, evanescently spiritual gruel within human spirituality, or
else to turn it into a cruel, hard-nosed, objective, punitive, divine
expedition on sinful humanity. It was a difficult row to hoe in

between. Increasingly, especially in his reflection on World War II, the images of universal divine authority, of crucifixion, of divine-human sacrifice above all, and then, of the Calvinist understanding of penitence as the life-long act of the Christian person, moved together for him, into a mysterious pattern of coherence of Christian moral images in the moral life as told in the Christian story. (See Niebuhr's essays on the war in the *Christian Century*, May 13 and August 5, 1942, and April 28, 1943.) No set of events, including war, could conceivably echo a real absence of God from his world.

One needs to add that Niebuhr is quite unlike some present-day theologians for whom certain dogmatized categories or hypostatizations of creed and temporal history—"hope," "revolution," "resurrection," and so on—serve as an apologetic argument for the justification of divine goodness. Cognately, Niebuhr is equally unwilling to develop speculatively into a theodicy the parallel argument of divine fellow-suffering, whether through a process theory of divine passibility, or through some sort of equivalent inner-trinitarian speculation. In the face of all these temptations, Niebuhr remained unalterably agnostic. The price to pay for affirming the overwhelming, life-giving divine goodness is that of the sheer disinterested service of the only real God, and the condition of that service is one of total, life-long revolution in us—a repentance the initiator of which is not woman or man but God himself. Niebuhr would not go beyond these austere assertions, beyond the affirmation that through this quest for total revolution a mysterious sacrifice, in which a temporary design of fitness between God and man is woven together into one story of redemption, becomes manifest (at least for Christians). At that point he stopped exactly where his adopted Puritan ancestors and their ancestors would have stopped.

If Niebuhr was at once bold and agnostic regarding theodicy, he was far more cautious in adopting a methodology for articulating the principle of divine sovereignty, including that of theodicy. One sees a certain, tension—yet it is rather more like a welcome disproportion—between his primary radically realist assertion of God's sovereign initiative, and the coordinate (or should one say subordinate) assertion of the religious or "faith" method under which to make this assertion. (The classic expressions of that ambivalence are contained in the magnificent supplementary essay, "Faith in Gods and in God," in *Radical Monotheism;* in "The Deity of God," the concluding chapter in *The Meaning of Revelation;* and in *Faith on Earth.*)

Wherever Niebuhr has been treated either as a systematic theologian or put in the line-up of Protestant-liberal-neo-orthodox theologians, this theme has been developed, and I will not dwell on it. The common heritage of neo-orthodox and liberal theologians—from their Protestant origins, as they saw it, including their common rejections of classical theodicy as a valid problem—is that it is not God "in himself," but only "God revealed," or rather our relation with God, that is the object of our communion with God. "Faith" not only removes into a special, self-based kind of insight, but gradually, by a kind of merciless Kantian or perhaps Fichtean logic, is deconstructed into a totally originative human construction, in which the moment of divine revelation is no more than a self-positing move of the constructive intellectual capacity, in which the mind imagines or sets over against itself a transcendent "other" for its own regulating and constructing purposes.

A certain degree of caution is necessary before including Niebuhr in this line-up. Our reading of Niebuhr is onesided, if not wrong, for example, if we take the section in *Meaning of Revelation* on "History as Lived and as Seen," or on "internal" and "external" description, as methodologically nothing more than a Kantian dualism, an internal, traditional or self-participative perspective on the same historic scene which is described objectively under "external" causal categories. Actually, Niebuhr is usually restless with full, residual dualisms, moral as well as epistemological. Beyond that, in his interpretation of history, Niebuhr distinguished carefully between history as interpretation of the pattern or course of human events, and history as the story of the constructive reenactment of human understanding. The priority, especially if we take *Kingdom of God* seriously, belongs to the former, and the "internal" method certainly looks as if it were appropriate for this task.

Niebuhr's interpretation of history is a case of the disproportion or disequilibrium in which one has to choose between the priority of a radical realism on the one hand and a secondary, qualifying, critical, idealistic perspective on the other hand. This is not the case in his development of faith's self-understanding. As an interpreter of history, especially of our own traditions, Niebuhr asked himself—and us—to think more boldly, more realistically, than he did in the carefully, systematically balanced, critical-idealist analysis (or phenomenology) of faith, with its matching of phenomenal object to phenomenal reflection.

Of a piece with this disequilibrium in the interpretation of history, and probably more basic, is Niebuhr's developing anthropology in his final lectures on *The Responsible Self* (1963). It is almost startling to see the late, emerging consistency with perennial themes he had been pursuing ever since the 1930s. In his introduction to *The Responsible Self*, James Gustafson has rightly written that an imperative like, "Responsibility affirms—God is acting in all actions upon you. So respond to all actions upon you as to respond to his action" (*The Responsible Self*, 25, cf. 126), was "for most of H. Richard Niebuhr's students . . . the most memorable theme in his course of lectures on

Christian ethics" (ibid.). One remembers from the course the sharp, almost colloquial question, preceding every moral response to God as Creator, Judge and Redeemer: "What is going on here?" The response was always carefully calibrated so that it was an answer not simply to a divine prevenient action, but to divine prevenience as refracted through our own interpretation of it. (For a suggestion of the intricacy of this relation, see the first two pages of Niebuhr's "Reflection on the Christian Theory of History," an undated paper among the H. Richard Niebuhr Papers, Yale Divinity School. See also *The Responsible Self*, 61–62.)

Niebuhr wanted to integrate the notion of the human being as a dual function-in-one, agent and interpreter. The two were one complex for him. Furthermore, in both aspects, separately and together, the person was basically a "dialogic" or "alternative" being, responding to a previous "alteraction." This anthropology takes (1) the image of man-the-maker with his freedom appearing "in this context as the necessity of self-determination by final causes" (*The Responsible Self*, 51) and (2) the image of man-the-citizen, living under law, asking for "what is possible to us in the situation in which we find ourselves . . . and not much more" (ibid, 52). In a very clear fit, it subordinates them both to the image of respondent to prior universal action on man—all in a way which these images would not fit if subordinated to a prior theology of radical and active divine prevenience. It is the doctrine of the human person—and of specific human communities— natural to a theology of radical monotheism. but it is a deliberate subordination, a kind of ruled priority in the explanatory use of Christian language, rather than a proposal for a systematic principle that would embrace both divine and human actions under one comprehensive heading.

There is no causal law and no law of theological perspective that would allow "response" to become part of a matched pattern of the interaction-in-one of divine and human agencies. (The center of the "disequilibrium" lies in the question whether "interpretation" is to be understood finally as a wholly autonomous response or whether, like agency, it is under the mysterious pattern of the divine Spirit as universal underlying prime cause. The issue is one completely natural to a theology whose greater impetus comes from the Augustinian, Reformation, and American Puritan traditions.)

One result of the priority of divine over human agencies, signalled by Niebuhr's choice of the "dialogic" or "responding" image over the other two, is the reaffirmation of some profound convictions that went back over the decades. The shock of recognition of what is to come is almost startling when one goes back to the early discussion between H. Richard Niebuhr and Reinhold Niebuhr in the pages of *The Christian Century* in 1932, and realizes how ill-matched they were. What must have been distressing to H. Richard Niebuhr was that, despite doubtless many years of discussion, his central concern, his most powerful persuasion of the prevenient initiatory action of God in time and in human events, was brushed aside by his brother simply as a casual *theologoumenon*.

Even then H. Richard Niebuhr said that God was a tangible, if mysteriously active structure and being, not a "third force" alongside of human beings and nature, but the "Other who is encountered in all human and natural challenges" ("Reinhold Niebuhr's Interpretation of History," 4, an unpublished paper delivered in 1949, also among the H. Richard Niebuhr Papers at Yale Divinity School). This is a reality on which all Christian assertions, both theological and moral, depend. Instead, Reinhold Neibuhr converted the dispute into that of an ethical imperative under a practical injunction—from a question of an ethics dependent on active, divine governance in history into an ethics under an absolute, fixed standard with one divine, efficacious aim in sight. His brother's claim, Reinhold Niebuhr said, was that "of dissociating a rigorous gospel ethic of disinterestedness and love from the sentimental dilutions of that ethic which are current in liberal Christianity" (*Christian Century*, 49 [1932], 415). It is no exaggeration to say that Reinhold Niebuhr took what, for H. Richard Niebuhr, was central and motivating for Christian ethics, and turned it into a background belief whose sole utility was that of conceptually safeguarding the imperative of "disinterested" and "sacrificial" love from the sentimental simplification that liberal Christian moralists proposed as substitutes for the ambiguities of rational public policy.

What was important here for H. Richard Niebuhr, first of all, was that there was no sense of an aim in human history, understood as the course of human events. Furthermore, there was little sense of history as "remembrance of things past." In an incisive but profoundly generous critique of his brother's interpretation of history, written about two decades after this *Christian Century* discussion, H. Richard Niebuhr said of Reinhold's view of history as the process of later human reflection on past events: "Memory interests him primarily as an aspect of man's freedom" ("Reinhold Niebuhr's Interpretation of History," 2). What Reinhold Niebuhr interpreted as history

> is not the "course of human events" nor yet the activity of the rememberer but the conception of social process as this is present in the mind of an ethical agent. Hence his questions about an interpretation of history are always questions about its ethical results insofar as it modifies conduct and somewhat, too, about its ethical origins, insofar as it has its sources in human faith or pride. (Ibid., 3)

This is Marx's or Comte's rather than Toynbee's or Collingwood's way of coming at history. What is at stake here, not to put too fine a point on it, is H. Richard Niebuhr's Augustinian view of human freedom as always governed by some compelling motive force, and Reinhold Niebuhr's modern view of human freedom, where even the knowledge of ourselves as limited and not disinterested is simply a function of our own originating exercise of agential freedom. "Man's freedom," said H. Richard Niebuhr of his brother's view, "is not only the freedom of the knower, it is also the freedom of the doer, though I am not quite sure how the transition is made from the freedom man has as one who knows to the freedom which he has as one who can change the course of natural events" (ibid., 5).

But for H. Richard Niebuhr we are not utterly originating, and in that sense we are only categorically "free," both as knowers and as rememberers or doers, and in the subtle unity of the two. This strictly contingent independence holds true even in the self-criticism in which we supposedly adopt a divine, impartial, transcendent perspective upon ourselves. "Realized eschatology is realized theology," H. Richard Niebuhr said (*Responsible Self*, 167), making human, historic action contingent, qualified and limited, an initiative for the short or medium rather than long range, not only tactically but in principle.

On the other hand, Reinhold Niebuhr, *mutatis mutandis*, held the reverse coin of this persuasion. Whereas for H. Richard Niebuhr the theological assertion subordinated the ethical to an eschatological imperative, for Reinhold Niebuhr the opposite was the case. The ethical imperative totally subjected all eschatological perspectives to its own action frame. This is the very opposite of what H. Richard Niebuhr understood as "radical monotheism." An uninterrupted moral and self-starting initiative on the part of individual persons and especially of human collectivities was the explanatory framework for translating theological terms into the coinage of public moral action. We may not want to go quite as far as Reinhold Niebuhr's biographer, who summed up the 1930s discussion between the brothers as follows:

> In his undemonstrative, soft-spoken way . . . Helmut pointed out what Reinhold's other critics had not yet seen. Despite his fulminations against sentimental liberalism, against complacent faith in the redemptive character of human goodwill, Reinhold remained a thoroughgoing liberal. His God did not act in history. His faith was built not upon abandoning himself to God's will but upon the old liberal dream of transforming human society. (Fox, *Reinhold Niebuhr*, 134)

But surely it is not exaggerated to say that, for H. Richard Niebuhr, theological and anthropological statements were more tensely and uneasily yoked. His effort at interpreting a Christian linguistic world so that it would be accessible to modern American audiences had to be more fragmented, qualified, partial and nuanced than his brother's. Both of these immigrant sons dedicated themselves to this interpretive task with a devotion and a searching quality that no other of their generation in America's mainline Protestantism could match. But for the one the liberal tradition, in rebellion as well as agreement, was the means of access to the modern, educated American mind, whereas for the other, even with all the phenomenological analyses of faith, it was finally more than anything else the highly risky and often rather lonely confidence that the Puritan-Protestant tradition provided the chief clue to the long-range continuity between Christian and American identities.

H. Richard Niebuhr's task, more than Reinhold's, was a lonely, difficult one. For when he looked around to see who was taking seriously the interpretation of his own *soli Deo gloria*—his persuasion of God's initiative not only in theological conception and judgment but in moral action—he immediately came upon Karl Barth, and what was then termed Barth's theological "actualism" or "occasionalism."

Niebuhr was deeply sympathetic even to Barth's radical assertion of the overarching efficacy of divine, predestinating grace. But increasingly what he could not swallow was the startlingly consistent Barthian identity of universal divine action with divine action in Christ alone. There were, for H. Richard Niebuhr, other mysterious forms of the *logos asarkos*, not only in the world's religions but in its philosophies, too. Between his brother's liberalism and Barth's consistent Christocentric prevenience, Niebuhr's radically monotheistic affirmations had to wind their own unique way.

Barth once said, in characteristically biblical as well as Hegelian terms, that all we have to apply for theological interpretations are our own concepts, but that they themselves must die and rise again before they can be applied to their subject matter. Here Niebuhr said *no*. This was a miracle not at our disposal. As a result, his "faith method" stayed in place as a singular, religiously interpretive tool and a precondition for the knowledge of God, making him finally—despite all disagreements about the meaning of "radical obedience"—more sympathetic to Bultmann than to Barth. Niebuhr also insisted increasingly that Christian ethics are sufficiently part of a larger conceptual totality to allow comparison.

Barth, despite his denial that "Christology is anthropology," had understood all human beings in the light of this one man, Jesus Christ, as portrayed in the Gospels. The general concept of "man" had to die and rise through its appropriation and transformation in this unique Christological image. Niebuhr, in his quest for both a universal form of theology and, in *The Responsible Self,* for a fitting, universal anthropology of the person as a responding creature, said no to this. The brief, brilliant, and tantalizing comment on "symbolic form" for Christians in the Earl Lectures was an answer to Barth. We are, in effect, dealing not with one symbol and image, as Barth proposed—though

Niebuhr is like Barth in saying that we are dealing not with images that are simply allegories for general concepts—but with two that become interlocked. It is the interlocking synecdoches of Jesus Christ, first as a unique, non-generalizable instance of the image "responding person," and second as one who in his response is both prophet, priest and king, that together become the image of mediation between God and human beings in history. It is a set of images leading to an ethos that is not unique to Niebuhr, but bears resemblance, for example, to Jewish and Stoic ethics.

Niebuhr trod a delicate path between image- or story-shaped and universal ethics, and between universal and particular story-shaped theology. Unlike Barth, he refused to make a decision between a narrative and, shall we say, a trans-narrative, universal understanding of God's acts in history.

We can observe a parallel ambiguity in Niebuhr's subtle, rich and varied phenomenology of faith, with its universal characteristics fully affirmed and yet finally brought up short with the confession that the story of that faith's loyalty and trust to the loyal and trustworthy, transcendent source cannot be separated out from this particular history or narrative as it has been transmitted to us both through our tradition and our own personal placement within it. It is a dual line often repeated in his works. Indeed, in *Faith on Earth* the strong association of faith with christological images drawn from the biblical narrative may well be puzzling to non-Christian readers.

In this unique, profound path between Reinhold Niebuhr's type of undisrupted, liberal human initiative and Barth's consistently Christocentric divine prevenience, I am left with an uneasy but hopeful sense. In the interpretation of history which is, even more than the analysis of faith, the very heart of Niebuhr's theology, the divine governance of the course of human events and our symbolic and interpretive reenactment of the past are not evenly yoked. Critical realism and critical idealism vie for priority. But, in contrast to *Meaning of Revelation, Kingdom of God* gives us a clue to priorities.

The narrative, interpretive retelling through such images as the Kingdom of God provides a kind of bridge between these two parts of historical interpretation. Not that such images or even collective concepts have, as they do for the ordinary run of intellectual historians, a mysterious, explanatory power to substitute for social or causal explanation, but they are indispensible ways of understanding a tradition so that we can act within it for a common future. The kingdom of God was one of a number of mediating, interpretive principles drawn from tradition's usage that bridged the gap between the reality of divine agency in history, as course of human events, and the symbolic part played by our own faith's constructive act. The priority belonged to the radical realism of divine action, so that the critical-idealist method tended to become a qualifying safeguard of human limitation, the *nescio,* or "we don't know how our understanding fits our faith's claims," that has always, even before Kant, accompanied every Christian confession of universal divine causation.

In the choice of this priority and the consequent anthropology exemplified by the synecdoche of "responding person," the pressure is toward the denial that divine universal initiative and human interpretive construction are epistemologically equally matched. Neither as interpreter or metaphysical constructor of what has been in the past, nor as agent in present social process, am I totally free or purely originating. Once again, at least if we follow *Kingdom of God,* in both respects we are responding rather than initiating persons. Furthermore, the response is not simply temporally posterior to the reading of history as the divinely originated course of human events. It is located, instead, in a logically different plane to that of the divine initiation. God's objective action is a primary cause acting in, with, and through its secondary causal agencies. The classic disequilibrium of the Protestant tradition, expressed in its understanding of the Holy Spirit's activity, is always present in the background of Niebuhr's theory of history, no matter how carefully balanced the method of "faith" sounds. "Faith" is not finally a creative cause matched evenly against divine causation; it is, simply, a gift of God in repentance.

I want to conclude with a brief postscript on the Niebuhr lecture with which I began. It was a prescient lecture, given by a man deeply concerned with his nation's approaching role in history. But it was also the reflection of a man deeply persuaded that you and I do not finally govern the course of human events: God does. There is a powerful final sentence, of which Niebuhr would have approved, in a book he didn't much like, Austin Farrer's *Finite and Infinite* (1943), written at the time of the German conquest of France: ". . . rational theology knows only that whether Paris stands or falls, whether men die or live, God is God, and so long as any spiritual creature survives, God is to be adored." Niebuhr, who rejected the distinction between rational and revealed theologies, would have added that not only "rational" but "revelational" theology, too, must make room for this confession.

The advice is tough, sober and stern; Reinhold Niebuhr would have thought it the poison of the theological paralysis of social action. One can understand why the anthropological theology of a Reinhold Niebuhr could be pulled in a liberal and neo-conservative direction. On the one hand, there was the appeal to restraint contained in emphases on ambiguity and self-criticism; on the other hand, there was not only the inevitability or realism of collective self-interest, but above all the rejection of denying the uninterrupted freedom of initiatory human action.

It is a different story with H. Richard Niebuhr's short-range historical action, in principle limited by divine governance, in which our "alterations" are limited in, with, and through agencies other than our own, and they by ours. It is a different matter also when the chief created agencies under God's governance are not simply the political collectivities of nations and empires, but when divine action is located in the uneasy, at first sign almost ludicrously ill-balanced "polarity" (as James Gustafson has rightly said, a favorite word of Niebuhr) between the nation, or other assorted social collectivities, and the church. "Radical monotheism" insisted on this polarity because the universality of one sort of group is always henotheistic (we might as well say idolatrous, including, of course, the church). "The task of the present generation," Niebuhr could say at about the same time he was working on *Kingdom of God*, "appears to lie in the liberation of the church from its bondage to a corrupt civilization" *(The Church Against the World* [1935],124). But twenty years later, under different circumstances, he could speak equally well (with recent, rather distasteful ecumenical discussions in mind) of Christ-centered and church-centered "henotheism," and say that "history is reinterpreted so that the story of the mighty deeds of God in creation, judgment, and redemption is replaced by church history or 'holy history'" *(Radical Monotheism*, 58–59). It is virtually impossible to think of H. Richard Niebuhr's theology and ethics leading to neo-conservatism.

Why be a poet, Hölderlin asked, in these non-lyrical times? Why, we might ask of H. Richard Niebuhr, be a theologian in our utterly untheological times? I think he would have made short shrift of that question. He would have asserted, I believe, that our responsibility to affirm the glory of the Lord, and his glory alone, has not been altered one whit, and that this remains our duty in propitious or unpropitious times. In the name of the Puritan heritage itself, he would have rejected the notion of a special covenant between God and the American nation. A sobering call to take our place in an increasingly pluralistic world with a humanitarianism modified by Christian hope, and to restrain the global anxieties unleashed by global power would, I think, have appealed to him.

We have a more modest mission to play without losing the distinct role the Christian tradition has contributed to the best of American ideals. We are not a specially chosen nation, but we might, under appropriate circumstances, be an internationally useful people. If the Puritan ideal of America as a city set upon a hill now recedes, Niebuhr would have been confident that other aspects of the same tradition could have handled the now less ardent dreams. I am sure he would have rejected the kind of special-election-in-disguise claim that Puritans resorted to in their times, the so-called "jeremiad," which has so fascinated commentators from Perry Miller to Sacvan Bercovitch.

We theologians could have expected from Niebuhr an unsentimental call to do our duty, no matter whether we were finally of weighty cultural influence or not. To remain in our particular station in America, as testifiers to that almost lost Puritan heritage of the universal governance of God in the Reformed tradition, which can only be articulated in the polarity of the church and nation, with responsibility to the interaction of the two, even if it becomes culturally and linguistically more difficult than it was in the past—that is our heritage.

To be sure, with his carefully modulated pluralism, Niebuhr would have said that other people have other stories, and even Christians in other lands may have other responsibilities to their civilizations and, through them, to their God. Some may have more conservative responsibilities, for instance, in Poland; others may have to urge the "preferential option for the poor" in a systematic way. But for us in the right now increasingly residual "mainstream" American Protestant heritage, the imperatives of our Puritan ancestors still hold us to the dual responsibility to church and nation under mysterious, divine prevenience, even if that language is restricted right now to an increasingly smaller circle.

In the service of this heritage, Niebuhr might have asked us at least to consider the possibility that the more modest scope of a renewed Puritanism might have a natural parallel—the possibility of a new, far more limited role for the American nation. He might well have suggested that this modest scope might actually be more liberating than the careening, constantly burgeoning anxiety of power, and that this possibility might be a positive alternative for a public theological posture between those two notorious collective mood swings— national self-hatred and national self-glorification—those twin evils which afflict American Christian moralists so much in our day. There is a great deal of unadvertised, unglorified reconciliation to be done "in church and civil state."

Niebuhr might well have approved Karl Barth's insistence that there is no natural line of affinity from liberal politics to the witness of the church. (One remembers Niebuhr's wartime remark that many liberals have never forgiven God for making a nationalist U-boat captain, Martin Niemöller, witness to him.) But he might equally well have agreed with Barth that with caution, care, forethought and luck, there might just be an affinity the other way around: that a gospel of the universal, present, governing glory of God might have more to do with a carefully circumscribed progressive politics than with either a theology of revolution or some other political theology, which some fellow-Christians have proposed to us (thus far with little effect, it must be admitted, or else with the battlements of neo-conservatism). One step at a time, no more than that for the task of public theology; but always with the protest against national self-aggrandizement and idolatry in mind. It is a slim line, but a goodly cause.

In H. Richard Niebuhr we had a teacher who represented, more than anyone else in the mainline Protestant church tradition and its educational institutions in this country, a fiercely radical monotheism which was at the same time an equally positive affirmation of God's active lordship in our midst. Niebuhr believed it to be a faithful tradition for Christians on these shores to hold. None was greater than he in upholding this simple, yet complex theological mission. It is a distinctive vocation that must not be lost.

Note

Previously published in *The Legacy of H. Richard Niebuhr*, ed. Ronald F. Thiemann, copyright © 1991 The President and Fellows of Harvard College, by permission of Augsburg Fortress.

Afterword: Hans Frei as Theologian

George Hunsinger

In December of 1967 Hans Frei was invited to deliver a lecture at the Harvard Divinity School. As the title of his lecture suggests—"Remarks in Connection with a Theological Proposal"—he was apparently being asked to elucidate and expand upon material he had already set forth elsewhere. A long essay had appeared three years earlier in the *Christian Scholar*, called "Theological Reflections on the Gospel Accounts of Jesus' Death and Resurrection."[1] Then only a year later an even longer version of the same argument came out in *Crossroads*, an adult education magazine of the Presbyterian Church, U.S.A., under the title, "The Mystery of the Presence of Jesus Christ."[2] It was this longer version which was eventually published in 1975 in book form as *The Identity of Jesus Christ*.[3] Regardless of whether Frei's audience at Harvard would have been familiar with his theological proposal in both its published forms or, as may well have been the case, only with the briefer *Christian Scholar* version of it, Frei himself would in all likelihood have had both versions in mind as he prepared his remarks. The Harvard lecture, therefore, although never published until now, would seem to offer Hans Frei's most sustained written reflections on the principal work whereby he is known to us not as an intellectual historian or as a commentator on the theology of others, but as a theologian himself.

Although I propose to draw upon the Harvard lecture in order to set the stage for an analysis of *The Identity of Jesus Christ*, this procedure is not without its dangers. Few theological writers, it would seem, have ever been so beset by the agony of setting pen to paper as was Hans Frei. The tortured syntax so often evident in his prose seemed to be matched only by the profundity of insight which that very syntax seemed at once to promise and yet also so vexingly to withhold. Although the sources of this particular brand of writer's ailment were undoubtedly complex, I myself have wondered whether it did not arise in part from the special brilliance of his own unique sensibility. It was almost as though his mind were an extraordinarily sensitive photographic plate, taking in a mass of data all at once, yet with a fine-grained reception of detail. Regardless of the subject matter he was discussing, it was as though he possessed a strong, immediate intuition of various complex interrelations between the whole and the parts, as well as among the various parts themselves. The agony seemed to arise from trying to describe some particular part without losing its concrete and complex embeddedness in the matrix of the whole, with all the subtle interrelations and contrasts which that embeddedness seemed to entail. The painful fits and starts by which the argument in *The Identity of Jesus Christ* so continually arrests itself, and finally almost thwarts itself, are only the most extreme example of the phenomenon I am trying to decipher. To some extent the same crabbed and cryptic prose, the same allusiveness and elusiveness, the same vexatious mixture of the subtle, the obscure, and the profound, also mark the Harvard lecture which I want to use to illumine the book. The first danger, then, is that I may simply have embarked upon the ill-fated task of trying to interpret the obscure by the obscure. What my result gains in clarity it may lose in accuracy, subtlety and depth. A second and not unrelated danger is that Frei may perhaps have said some things in his unpublished lecture to which he would not necessarily have wanted to be held later on, at least not without qualification. Nonetheless, with these caveats in mind, I think the Harvard lecture can help us interpret *The Identity of Jesus Christ* in at least three ways.

Part I. Polemic

First of all, the lecture can help to bring Frei's polemical objectives more clearly into focus. With a directness which surpasses even Frei's masterpiece, *The Eclipse of Biblical Narrative*,[4] the lecture makes it clear that Frei has nothing less far-reaching in view than to break with the entire modern liberal tradition in theology, while still remaining within the purview of that tradition to the extent that he does not wish merely to relapse into the pitfalls of the older orthodoxy. He wishes to accept and yet subvert the liberal tradition by simultaneously correcting and outbidding it. "The conviction underlying these pages," he says in his opening words, "is that the story of modern Christian theology, beginning with the end of the seventeenth century, is increasingly, indeed almost exclusively that of anthropological and Christological apologetics, that the new interest in hermeneutics by and large serves the same aim, and that this development has now just about run its course, that whether it has or not, it is time to search for alternatives" (p. 27). Modern theology, as Frei describes it, has been one long set of variations on a single, recurring theme. While the content has varied only within definite limits, the aim and the method have remained essentially the same. The aim has been almost wholly apologetic, the method has been to combine some independent version of historicity and rationality with divine revelation, and the content has been some Christologically focused version of anthropology, regardless of the different ways in which that anthropology has been conceived.

"I am saying," Frei states, "that we have lived for almost three hundred years in an era in which an anthropologically oriented theological apologetic has tried to demonstrate that the notion of a unique divine revelation in Jesus Christ is one whose meaning and possibility are reflected in general human experience. . . . To say it another way: Theology has to validate the *possibility*, and hence the meaning of Christian claims concerning the shape of human existence and divine relation to it, even though the actual *occurrence*, and hence the *verification* of the claim is a matter of divine, self-authenticating action and revelation" (pp. 29–30). The apologetic aim of modern theology, Frei suggests, is evident in its persistent attempt to find the condition for the possibility of divine revelation in some general aspect of human experience. Although the source of revelation may be transcendent, the condition for its possibility is immanent. Although its truth may be self-authenticating, its meaning pertains to the shape of human existence as it can be known and understood apart from faith. Although the actuality of revelation is a matter of faith, its possibility is demonstrably there for all to see.[5]

The method of modern theology corresponds to this apologetic aim. It has essentially been a method of correlating the past with the present in the sense that past event is correlated with present meaningfulness. More specifically, Jesus (as the actualization of genuine human selfhood there and then) is correlated with faith and revelation (as the continuation of such actualization here and now). In the modern period, says Frei, "systematic theology is precisely the enterprise of indicating that history and faith hold together. Notions of progressive revelation, tradition and tradition history, the Church, all may help the task, as do more nearly methodological devices such as resort to paradox or, in the early nineteenth century as again today, ontologies, to span the hiatus between temporal positivity of the past, and moral or self-conscious presence, that is, contemporary faith" (p. 29). For example, to take only one typical instance among innumerable variations, Jesus as reconstructed by historical-critical methods may be correlated with faith as the particular actualization of a rationally validated human potentiality, and thus with revelation as the mysterious or transcendent source of that actualization.

The key move behind this apologetic aim and correlationist method, as Frei sees it, is allowing the criteria of meaningfulness to be determined on rational grounds independently of biblical narrative. This move ensures that an independently validated anthropology, whatever it may be, will set the terms for the significance of Jesus Christ. In one way or another, his significance will simply be that of having actualized or confirmed a potentiality that can be discerned and validated by reason alone. Regardless of how Christological the focus may seem to be, the content will always be some independently determined conception of human existence. "And it doesn't matter," says Frei, "if human existence was conceived in rational-moral fashion, as in the Enlightenment; in aesthetic fashion, as by Schleiermacher; in phenomenological-ontological fashion, as by the contemporary hermeneutical school and its nineteenth century forerunners; in existentialist-phenomenological fashion, as by Bultmann, Ogden, and Buri; in universal historical terms, as by Pannenberg; in dialectical-historical fashion, as by Moltmann; in various personalistic mixtures of these categories, as by Brunner and Althaus; or in a mixed historical, ontological, and evolutionary vision, as by Karl Rahner" (p. 30).[6] In each and every case the criterion of meaningfulness is thought to be determined by the putative effectiveness of Jesus Christ for shaping human life in the present. The consequences are twofold. First, interpretations of the New Testament story about Jesus become increasingly arbitrary. "The story seems to mean whatever you want," Frei says, "depending on what 'perspective' or 'modern view of man' you happen to come from as you read the story and want to find substantiated there" (p. 40). Second, Christology comes to play an increasingly "peripheral role" (p. 27). Christology becomes a mere cipher for some independent version of anthropology. It is the doctrine of human nature, history and existence, not the doctrine of Jesus Christ, which serves as "the integrating, organizing, or enabling principle around which to gather at least the meaning, and often to evaluate the truth of theological assertions" (p. 28). In short, Christology becomes the mere form to which anthropology provides the real content.

Frei's polemical objective provides a foil for setting off his own constructive proposal. The aim, the method, and the content of Christian theology, as he conceives it, are all radically different from those he finds in modern liberal theology. Before turning to this directly, however, some further elaboration is in order. For the question that most immediately presents itself is how the polemical objective in the Harvard lecture relates to that in Frei's book, *The Identity of Jesus Christ.*

The lecture enables us to see more clearly that modern liberal theology is also the real, or at least the ultimate, opponent in the book. Recall how the polemic in the book unfolds. The entire middle section of the argument, Part 3, is entitled "Distortions of Christ's Identity" (IJC54–84). In this section two targets are lined up: the Christ figure of myth and the Christ figure of the modern novel. As Frei's argument proceeds, it becomes clear that each of these has a more directly theological counterpart. Mythic Christ figures, especially in their Gnostic forms,[7] are explicitly correlated on at least one occasion with modern liberal theology (IJC 98–101), and this correlation is often implicit elsewhere (e.g., IJC xi–xii, 86–87, 89–90). Literary Christ figures, on the other hand, are essentially failed attempts to carry through Frei's own project. By unsuccessfully depicting the savior figure as a specific human being, they offer no real alternative to the universal figure of Gnostic myth (IJC 82). But this is precisely the alternative Frei himself seeks to provide, and he seeks to do so because he thinks that the Christ of myth and the Christ of liberalism (at least in some of its most characteristic forms) are theologically inadequate for roughly the same reasons.

Two strategies are employed to display the secret convergence of the mythic and the liberal Christ figures. The first strategy is one of internal critique. Frei argues that, taken on their own terms, the christological premises of ancient myth and liberal modernity are equally and comparably self-defeating. What they have in common is a Christ figure which does little more than provide symbolic form, however powerfully, for an essentially anthropological content. In both cases the symbolic figure functions to express, focus, and evoke a certain kind of elemental and universal experience, whether participation in the vitalities of human life or deliverance from its painful alienations. It is this kind of experience which confers meaningfulness on the symbol. Yet when such experience is equated with the presence of Jesus Christ so that it defines his identity for the believer— as occurs in any number of ways in modern theology—then certain consequences follow. According to Frei, not only does Jesus Christ become "diffused into humanity by becoming one with it" so that he loses all self-focus and singularity, but we human beings are also finally left by the same token with "our own ultimate lack of abiding presence and identity" (IJC 86). Just as Christ's identity disappears into his presence and finally dissolves into his absence, so also does our own identity disappear and dissolve with him in much the same way.[8]

What we have just seen Frei argue about liberalism is directly parallel to what he also argues about myth. As in liberalism so in myth, "the unity of presence and identity . . . lies in the acceptance of the common loss of both" (IJC 61). The polemical force, therefore, is really the reverse. As in myth so also in liberalism, the attempt to move from presence to identity finally results in dissolution, not only for the Christ figure but also for ourselves. As in myth, therefore, so also in liberalism, the premises are self-defeating. The promise of self-focus or deliverance ends, in each case, in dissolution.

Frei employs a second strategy to disclose inadequacies shared by the mythic and the liberal Christ figures. This time, however, the critique is much more nearly external than internal. That is, this time Frei attempts to show that even if these Christ figures were not fatally inadequate on their own terms, they would still be inadequate for a certain hermeneutical task to which they are often applied or from which they are supposedly extracted. Namely, as is argued at length, they would still fail in the task of interpreting and understanding the gospel narratives about Jesus. Frei's external critique is thus simply the negative consequence of his own constructive proposal. As indicated by the subtitle of his book, that proposal has to do with "the hermeneutical bases of dogmatic theology." It thus makes sense to present the external critique along with the proposal itself. What needs to be kept especially in mind, however, is that Frei intends his own proposal to overcome precisely those inadequacies which he uncovers, on both internal and external grounds, in the Christ figures of myth and modernity.

Part II. Method

In the Harvard lecture Frei describes his departure from liberalism as one which renounces apologetics and yet proceeds to argue on purely formal grounds. Whether this self-description is really accurate is a matter I will take up later. Yet the two are closely connected in his own mind. To renounce apologetics is to renounce the project of explaining how Christian truth can be possible, and this renunciation in turn leads to the pursuit of a purely formal kind of description. "Here," says Frei, "I agree with Karl Barth . . . I believe that it is not the business of Christian theology to argue the *possibility* of Christian truth any more than the instantiation or *actuality* of that truth. The possibility follows logically as well as existentially from its actuality" (p. 30). In other words, the meaningfulness of Christian belief is not something independent of its truth, but can only be known and understood on the basis of that truth. The business of Christian theology is thus descriptive rather than explanatory. Its job is simply to describe the structure and content of belief, not to argue that some anthropological condition supposedly makes belief meaningful (and thus not to explain belief in terms of some independent anthropological theory).

"Hence," Frei continues, "I should want to draw a sharp distinction between the logical structure as well as the content of Christian belief, which it is the business of theologians to describe but not to explain or argue, and the totally different logic of *how one comes* to believe, or the possibility of believing immanent in human existence, on which the theologian has relatively little to say, and on which he should in any case not base the structure of his theology. Yet doing so has been the preoccupation of theologians for nearly three hundred years" (p. 30; cf. IJC xii).[9]

Yet if the structure of Christian theology should not be based on independent anthropological considerations, then just what should it be based on? "My simple answer," Frei told his Harvard audience, "is that for a beginning let's start with the synoptic Gospels, or at least one of them, because their peculiar structure as narratives, or at least as partial narratives, makes some hermeneutical moves possible which we don't have available elsewhere in the New Testament. And having started there, I would propose to go on to say, let's see how much more of the New Testament can be coordinated by means of this series of hermeneutical moves" (p. 32). This remark places Frei's project in a wider scope than he ever quite indicated elsewhere. Although unfortunately he never pursued the task, in principle he clearly thought it was necessary to coordinate his narrative analysis of the Gospels with the rest of the New Testament if theology itself were really to be served. Only this wider coordination, and not narrative analysis alone, would provide an adequate hermeneutical basis on which the structure of theology could be built and by which it could be sustained.

This remark also indicates that Frei sees something about the Gospels—their peculiar structure as narratives, insofar as they are narratives—which affords a certain advantage in the task of interpretation. As stated in the lecture with exceptional clarity, this advantage is the enticing possibility of an interpretation which is at once formal and descriptive and yet also unimpeachably normative. Frei opts for an interpretive procedure which he wants to be as formal and unencumbered by prior commitments about meaningfulness as possible. "My plea here is—the more formal, the less loaded we can make the notion of understanding, the better. And that, in turn, involves a search, in deliberate opposition to most of what I find in contemporary theology, for categories of understanding detached from the perspectives we bring to our understanding, including our commitments of faith" (p. 31). In other words, the formalist turn in Frei's hermeneutical procedure, whatever else it may entail, signals a methodological break with liberalism.[10]

This method promises to yield great results. It promises to ratify Frei's break with liberalism by wresting a meaning that is really constant and normative (rather than arbitrary and ever-changing), from

a procedure which is authoritative just because it is so irreproach-
ably formal. "My proposal . . . is that in regard to aesthetic or quasi-
aesthetic texts, particularly narratives—and the Gospels are such in
part—'normative' interpretation may be possible. That is to say, the
meaning of the text remains the same, no matter what the perspective of succeeding generations of interpreters may be. In other words,
the constancy of meaning of the text is the text and not the similarity of its *effect* on the life-perspectives of succeeding generations"
(p. 32). Note that normative interpretation as so conceived has nothing to do with prior determinations about meaningfulness. Indeed,
such determinations would actually run counter to the possibility of
normative interpretation insofar as they are, in the final analysis,
unstable, arbitrary, and transient. Instead, normative interpretation
is, according to Frei, "a matter of the structure of the narrative itself,"
that is, of demonstrating that "the text *as given* has a genuine structure" (p. 33). The meaning of a narrative cannot be found apart from
"the formal structure of the narrative itself" (p. 34), and a normative
interpretation is thus one by which that formal structure is laid bare.
The meaning of a narrative text has simply nothing to do with "its
perennially similar affective impact" (p. 34) or with any such anthropological possibility conceptually independent of the text. The narrative text as such has no meaning other than itself.

When we leave the Harvard lecture at this point and turn back
to the argument of the book we do not find that the connection
between formal description and normative result is quite so explicitly
drawn, yet otherwise the account Frei gives of his procedure remains
essentially the same. In the book the gospel narratives are said to
converge with the genre of realistic narrative, and to that extent their
significance is to be sought "in the narrative structure itself" (IJC 47).
Just because the meaning of such narrative is embedded in its formal
structures, it is not remotely located but "directly accessible" (IJC xv).
Of realistic narratives it can therefore be said that "they literally mean
what they say." There is no discrepancy "between the representation
or depiction and what they are *actually* about" (IJC xiv). The appropriate method of interpretation is simply "to observe the story itself—
its structure, the shape of its movement, and its crucial transitions"
(IJC 87). "And therefore the theoretical devices we use to make our
readings more alert, appropriate, and intelligent ought to be designed
to leave the story as unencumbered as possible" (IJC xv). With
polemical allusion to liberalism, he thereby sums up: "The aim of an
exegesis which simply looks for the sense of a story (but does not
identify sense with religious significance for the reader) is in the final
analysis that of reading the story itself" (IJC xv).

If a narrative's meaning is inextricably connected with its formal
structure, then a wide range of alternatives can be ruled out. It fol-

lows, for example, that the meaning of a narrative is not to be found in the author's intention,[11] nor in some philosophical or theological anthropology, nor yet in the text's religious or moral impact (cf. p. 34). Most interestingly, it follows that regardless of the history-like shape of the text, its meaning is not to be found in its factual historicity. Frei applies this distinction between meaning as formal narrative-structure and meaning as factual historicity to the Gospels with good effect. What historical narrative has in common with realistic fiction is "the close interaction of character and incident" and "the nonsymbolic quality of the relation between the story and what the story is about" (IJC xiv). These are also formal features, Frei urges, shared by the gospel narratives. In such cases, he argues, not excluding the Gospels, "the meaning of these texts would remain the same . . . whether or not they are historical" (IJC 132). Actually the gospel narratives in their *formal* aspect resemble historical narratives in some ways and fictional narratives in others. Yet in the Gospels the conjunction of history-like and fiction-like qualities is such as to serve a definite and important purpose. Together they conspire to describe and affirm the identity of a particular, concrete individual. They are the formal means by which the identity of Jesus is depicted in his role as the savior of the world. "The narration is at once intensely serious and historical in intent and fictional in form, the common strand between them being the identification of the individual in his circumstances" (IJC 145).[12] The meaning of the gospel narratives—their depiction of Jesus' identity—is thus fully embedded in the formal structuring of the narratives themselves. To suppose that the meaning of these narratives resides in their factual historicity would be to commit a category mistake. The question of factual historicity, although directly posed by the narratives themselves, is simply *not* a question of their meaning. It is the question of their truth.[13]

Frei drives home the point that in the gospel narratives the formal structures are designed to depict the identity of a specific person. "If we regard the gospel narrative simply as such, that is, as a story (whether fictional or real)," then we find that what its formal structure sets forth is "the individual, specific, and unsubstitutable identity of Jesus" (IJC 49). Again, what the gospel story does is to present "Jesus' identity as that of a singular, unsubstitutable person" (IJC 52). "The New Testament story," Frei elaborates, "deals simply and exclusively with the story of Jesus of Nazareth, whether it is fictional or real, and not with anybody else or with every man under the cover of Jesus' name" (IJC 56). The latter point, of course, is directed against readings which view Jesus simply as a religious symbol—in other words, against the views of myth and modernity. To view Jesus as merely a symbol would be to divest him of the very characteristics with which he is depicted by the gospel narratives, namely, self-

focused identity and unsubstitutability. The genre of the gospel narrative is therefore precisely the opposite of that of myth. "Unlike what
one finds in so many Christ figures Jesus has, in his story, a clearly
personal center, a self-focused identity" (IJC 108). "Unsubstitutable
identity," Frei adds, "is simply not the stuff of mythological tales" (IJC
136). Yet "it is simply the unsubstitutable person about whom the story
is told—his unsubstitutable deeds, words, and sufferings" (IJC 59). Just
as the mythic or symbolic views of Jesus would effectively divest him
of his personal specificity, so "the gospel story's indissoluble connection with an unsubstitutable identity in effect divests the savior story
of its mythical quality." The mythic elements are supplanted by precisely those features which are realistic. "The gospel story is a demythologization of the savior myth because the savior figure in the gospel
story is fully identified with Jesus of Nazareth. The early Christians
would substitute no other name" (IJC 59).

The technical aspects of Frei's method may be noted in this context. In order to elucidate those formal structures by which the meaning of the gospel narratives is determined and by which the specific
identity of Jesus is thus depicted, Frei has recourse to two different
conceptions of identity description. The one he calls "intention-action
description" and the other "self-manifestation description" (e.g., IJC
127). These interpretive devices are meant to be as formal in status
as possible. Frei has little or no interest in them for their own sakes.
He is not interested, for example, in how the two kinds of description
might cohere at the theoretical level. He simply wants to employ them
to illumine how the narratives work to convey their sense. Thus he
simply applied them simultaneously, or rather in an alternating way.
"As long as two alternative descriptions do not conflict there is really
no need that one maintain a connection between them" (p. 62;
cf. IJC 127f). It would perhaps not be too far amiss to suggest that
Frei uses the intention-action scheme primarily to elucidate Jesus'
death on the cross, and the self-manifestation scheme primarily to elucidate his resurrection from the dead. For it is the narrative sequence
which culminates in the crucifixion wherein Jesus' saving intention
is seen to be most fully enacted. And it is the sequence of his resurrection appearances wherein his self-manifestation seems to cast a retrospective light over the whole stretch of previous narrative, offering
a sense of his continuous identity through all the various transitions
in the story (IJC 127; cf. 121–22). Frei thus sums up his use of these
schemes as follows. "This, then, is the identity of Jesus Christ. He is
the man from Nazareth who redeemed men by his helplessness, in
perfect obedience enacting their good in their behalf" (the intention-
action description). "As that same one, he was raised from the dead
and manifested to be the redeemer" (the self-manifestation description) (IJC 149). Together these descriptive devices illumine how the

gospel narratives are structured, especially in their culminating portions, to depict the identity of Jesus Christ. This depiction is what they mean.

Given this account of Frei's hermeneutical method, we are now finally in a position to appreciate his polemic when it assumes the mode of an external critique. Frei's internal critique, it will be recalled, was that the mythic and the modernist Christ figures are self-defeating on their own premises. His external critique is that these same Christ figures are either useless or misleading for interpreting gospel narratives. To adopt an interpretive strategy less formal than that used by Frei would obviously, he says, "endanger the integrity of the story. This would be especially true if we were to go 'back' of what is given in the story and infer the character of Jesus, his policy for action, and his significance for mankind by means of preconceptions of human nature, human existence, or the human condition derived from elsewhere, especially from our psychological or cultural experience" (IJC 137–38). In effect, this kind of strategy ends up "supplying the material content to the gospel story rather than deriving that content from the story itself" (IJC 101). The story is finally taken over by the categories of interpretation. It is made forcibly to conform to some anthropological notion whose status is "independent of, prior to, and only tenuously connected with the story" (IJC 90). The story is interpreted symbolically rather than realistically, as merely illuminating or illustrating this or that aspect of our common existence (IJC 89). This strategy of interpretation, says Frei, is "useless . . . for describing the exegesis of a realistic narrative qua realistic narrative" (IJC xvii).

Having strikingly exposed the descriptive inadequacy of the typical modernist interpretive procedure, Frei then administers his *coup de grâce*. If the significance of the gospel story is determined by its formal structure and not by prior determinations of meaningfulness, then what are the real options confronted by the modern interpreter? "The realistic or history-like quality of the narrative, whether historical or not, prevents the person who regards the account as implausible from regarding it as mere myth. Rather, it is to him a kind of hyperfiction claiming to be self-warranting fact" (IJC 143). In other words, if one chooses to regard the gospel accounts as fictional or factually false, the formal structure of the accounts itself prevents one from resorting to the strategy of symbolic interpretation. One can in that case read the gospel narrative only as "a piece of hyperfiction," bereft of contemporary religious significance (IJC 146; cf. 50–51).[14]

I am not sure that this external critique can be regarded as entirely successful. Frei wants to show that "the story as story—not necessarily as history—should be taken in its own right and not symbolically and that, if it is read for its own sake, it suggests that Jesus' identity is self-focused and unsubstitutably his own" (IJC 102). Yet Frei's lib-

eral opponent might retort, "Very well, but just why should the story
be taken in its own right and read for its own sake?"[15] The liberal
tradition, in fact, has a well-entrenched polemic of its own directed
against taking the gospel narratives literally. It might be possible to
adapt this polemic to take into account more directly precisely those
formal features to which Frei would grant privileged status. To be sure,
Frei's external critique might force the liberal interpreter to concede
that modernist interpretations do run remarkably against the grain
insofar as the Gospels display realistic narrative features. But if in the
final analysis Frei's own position should still not seem plausible, is the
liberal interpreter really forced by Frei's merely formal argument into
abandoning symbolic interpretation and into conceding that all one
has left is a piece of religiously useless hyperfiction? Frei certainly does
not make things any easier for the liberal interpreter, especially since
liberal interpretations seem to gain much of their power from telling
us what the texts "really" mean. To what extent, if any, can meaning
as religious significance be maintained with respect to the gospel narratives if it flies in the face of their meaning as formally structured?
Moreover, as Frei also wants to ask, to what extent can such against-
the-grain interpretations still reasonably continue to present themselves as Christian? Nonetheless, without trying to resolve these matters, I simply want to suggest that, taken by itself, Frei's external
critique may not finally be a substantive success even if it is a formal
success. The liberal interpreter might perhaps be able to concede Frei's
formal point while still managing to wriggle out of the forced option—
either realistic identity-depiction or else religiously useless hyperfiction—posed by Frei's attempted *coup de grâce*. I do think, however,
that Frei has significantly shifted the burden of proof as to whether a
merely symbolic interpretation is really possible for the church.

Part III. Content

What the Harvard lecture has to offer on the question of theological
content is minimal but nonetheless significant. It helps us to see the
connection in Frei's own mind between his interpretive method and
the theological content it yields. Of his interpretive method, Frei writes:
"My suggestion is that when we apply this proposal to the exegesis of
the Gospels, what we find to be the meaning of the Gospels is what
one might term a 'high Christology,' and I would propose *that* as the
basic datum for a start toward an answer to the question, 'what is
the essence of Christianity?'" (p. 32). The very large claims Frei is
making here for his interpretive method ought not to pass unre-
marked. Although Frei regards it as merely descriptive and formal, his
method is offered not only as exposing the dubiousness of his major
theological competitor (namely, modern liberalism), but also as estab-

lishing the viability of his own substantive alternative (namely, a high Christology).

There are at least two issues here. If some of Frei's statements about the status of his method are taken at face value, then despite his disclaimers he is really engaged in a kind of apologetic enterprise after all. Certainly, it is not the apologetic enterprise against which he polemicizes, the type which engages in prior determinations of meaningfulness as a stratagem of interpretation.[16] Yet when apologetics is seen more generically, its occurrence need not be limited to that type alone. Apologetics can also encompass the project of ad hoc clarification.[17] It can take the form of a challenge or a rebuttal in which an opposing view is shown to be untenable because it rests on a conceptual confusion. Ad hoc apologetics in this sense is thus essentially a matter of clarifying the meaning rather than demonstrating the truth of a particular claim or set of claims. Frei seems to become this kind of apologist when he resorts to a single descriptive procedure designed at once to disarm his opponent while yet also vindicating his alternative. For he seems to be suggesting on strictly technical grounds that liberalism rests on a deep and fateful confusion with respect to the genre of the synoptic gospel narratives.

Moreover, if Frei is read this way, then he also seems to have committed himself to a hermeneutical strategy within the bounds of dogmatic theology. Thus it is perhaps somewhat misleading when he remarks that "I am not going to write an outline of dogmatic or systematic theology that takes for its presupposition faith in the presence of Jesus Christ" (IJC 1). Certainly as far as it goes there is nothing wrong with this disclaimer. Frei's argument does not presuppose that Jesus Christ is present to faith. Therefore, the work of dogmatic theology per se is not undertaken. Yet the domain of dogmatic theology is not for that reason left behind. Frei's argument does presuppose the *truth-claim* that Jesus Christ is present to faith, since it is just this truth-claim whose meaning Frei proposes to clarify. These observations suggest that Frei's method and its results can be construed in what are called "coherentist" terms. He would then be regarded as conducting a series of formal hermeneutical clarifications within a larger network of Christian belief and practice. Some implications of this way of locating Frei's argumentation will be examined later on.[18]

The next question I want to pose, however, is whether Frei really offers us a high Christology in his book. To answer this question I want to look first at what Frei says about the work of Jesus Christ and only then turn to what he says about Christ's person. Does Frei's book offer a high doctrine of the work of Jesus Christ and an equally high doctrine of Christ's person as well?

The "pattern of exchange" is the chief category which Frei uses to organize his remarks about the work of Jesus Christ. This pattern is said to unite the "unsubstitutable individuality" of the savior with the "universal saving scope" of his significance, and it culminates in the story of his death upon the cross (IJC 74). The pattern of exchange also somehow unites "the unique purity" of Jesus (IJC 58), who "incurs no guilt of his own from which he would have to be redeemed" (IJC 57), with his "radical identification with sinners" (IJC 58). In this radical identification Jesus deliberately and vicariously adopts the guilt of others. He becomes helpless and powerless with them to the point of dying with them and like them. He becomes as needy as they are, in love for them and obedience to God, in order to enact their salvation. What Frei finds in the gospel narratives is thus a guiltless Jesus who enters fully into the situation of the guilty, so fully that like them he needs to be redeemed himself. In obedience to God, Jesus exchanges his purity for their guilt, dying on their behalf for the good of all (IJC 83).

No doubt can exist about Frei's intentions. He intends to offer a high doctrine of Jesus' obedience, passion and death. He proposes to interpret the gospel narratives in a way that is consistent with classical vicarious atonement passages like Isa. 53 and 2 Cor. 5:21 (IJC 58, 69, 111). Yet much in Frei's account remains murky at best. The sin from which the human race is said to need redemption and its connection with death is never clearly defined. Nor does Frei ever explain what he means by the word "vicarious," which is especially puzzling in light of his apparent rejection of the notion (or at least one notion) of "penal substitution," with which the term "vicarious" is often synonymous (IJC 31). Most seriously of all, it never really becomes clear, it seems to me, how the significance of Jesus' work can be conceived as cosmic in scope. It never becomes clear how his work can have universal efficacy or saving power.

I am suggesting that Frei is more convincing about Jesus' powerlessness than he is about Jesus' power. "About the coexistence of his power and powerlessness, we shall not say much, important though it is. Were it not there at all, it would be difficult to see wherein the actual saving efficacy of his helplessness lies" (IJC 112). Even so, in Frei's book the difficulty of seeing this is never really overcome. In some respects it is actually heightened by certain other aspects of his interpretation. Note, for example, that the pattern of exchange as Frei presents it is essentially unidirectional.[19] Although Jesus is repeatedly said to exchange his purity for the guilt of others, nothing is said about an exchange in the opposite direction whereby his purity would at the same time become theirs before God. Yet without such a movement in the opposite direction, how can Jesus' self-sacrificing purity have the kind of cosmic scope that Frei ascribes to it? That is, how can it have universal meaning and saving power, not symbolically but realistically, and therefore as a finished, unrepeatable, and vicarious work? Is there perhaps something about the logic of Frei's interpretation which prevents him from including such a movement in the opposite direction? Indeed, could it be that what he says, or does not say, about the person of Jesus Christ actually makes it difficult to ascribe saving efficacy and universal significance, in realistic terms, to Christ's work?

Perhaps in part under the pressure of the running polemic against gnosticism, Frei's account of the person of Jesus Christ is skewed in a certain direction. All the weight seems to fall on Jesus as a specific and unsubstitutable human being. The identity of Jesus as disclosed by the New Testament is said again and again to be a "human identity" (IJC 46). The humanness of this identity is stressed at every possible juncture in Frei's argument. Whether the theme is Jesus' obedience, his death, or his resurrection, it is humanness of which Frei speaks. The intention-action scheme is used to accentuate Jesus "as obedient man" (IJC 108) and finally as the "crucified human savior" (IJC 118) who enacted God's saving intention. Similarly, the self-manifestation scheme is used to elucidate how the resurrection narratives are structured to disclose Jesus "as a full human being in manifest identity, rather than as a mythical savior" (IJC 136). Frei leaves no doubt that as obedient, crucified and risen, Jesus Christ has a fully human identity.[20]

Does Jesus also have an identity which is fully divine? Frei is very reticent on this point. Given the restricted hermeneutical base from which he chooses to work—namely, from within the New Testament only the synoptic Gospels, from within those Gospels only the narrative portions, and from within those narratives primarily the climactic sequences—and given the level of generality at which he works—no detailed exegesis of any passage is offered—Frei does nonetheless point toward the possibility of a fully divine identity for Jesus as well. He sees this possibility as more nearly a dogmatic than a hermeneutical conclusion (IJC 125). Hermeneutically, however, the results Frei actually gleans from applying his method of formal description all seem to point toward a relatively low Christology when it comes to Christ's person, despite what he said in his Harvard lecture (i.e., about an exegetically based and narrative-oriented "high Christology" as the essence of Christianity). In his book, the resultant Christology is low in this regard for the following reasons. The union between God and Jesus as it emerges from the intention-action description is much more nearly moral than personal, it seems to increase as Jesus moves toward his death, and it does not seem to be fully actualized until after Jesus' resurrection (IJC 116, 125, 154). Up until the resurrection, at the very least, what Frei seems to depict are two different ascriptive subjects, God and Jesus, who are united in nothing but a common intention. The Christology of Frei's book is thus constantly skirting along the

edge of those problems which have typically beset the more Antiochan
forms of Christology, namely, Nestorianism and adoptionism. It skirts
along the edge of Nestorianism insofar as God never seems in any sense
to be the ascriptive subject of Jesus' intentions and actions, to say
nothing of Jesus' passion and death, as would be the case if the union
were personal rather than moral. And it skirts the edge of adoptionism
insofar as the self-focused presence of God does not seem fully to
coincide with that of Jesus until after the resurrection. Although Frei
does finally speak of "the New Testament's complex rather than simple
identification of God and Jesus" (IJC 164; italics added), throughout the
book Frei is simply more convincing about their differentiation than
he is about their union to the point of identification—if, that is, what
he intends to depict is a high Christology.[21]

A higher profile for Christ's divinity is what Frei needs, it seems
to me, if what he says about the nature of Christ's saving work is
finally to be conceptually sustained. In the kind of Christology to
which Frei actually leans—in the Harvard lecture he explicitly associates himself with Anselm, Calvin, and Barth in this regard (p. 43)—
the universal significance and saving efficacy of Jesus' work are
regarded as inconceivable apart from his full divinity. It is Jesus' full
divinity as well as his full humanity which is logically indispensable
to his work of bearing and bearing away the sin of the world. It is his
full divinity as well as his full humanity which is indispensable to
conceiving of his work as finished, unrepeatable, and vicarious. And
it is his full divinity as well as his full humanity which is indispensable to conceiving the pattern of exchange in terms that are bidirec-
tional rather than unidirectional so that Jesus not only exchanges his
purity for the guilt of sinners, but sinners also exchange their guilt
for his purity as well. No merely human Jesus, regardless of how
obedient, self-sacrificing and pure, is thought to be sufficient for the
possibility of carrying out this work of salvation, This work is only
conceivable if Jesus was at once fully human and yet also fully divine.
Frei himself, I think, was not inclined to disagree. Yet the argumentation of his book on this point is simply less than satisfying. We are
left with a relatively low depiction of Christ's person and a relatively
high depiction of Christ's work. This incongruity raises further questions about the status of Frei's method.

In the opening pages of the book, Frei describes his method as
being neither apologetic nor dogmatic. He intends by his own account
to engage in conceptual and literary analysis (IJC 1–6). He apparently
conceives of this analysis as purely formal or descriptive and to that
extent as normative. However, if we regard Frei's argumentation as a
kind of ad hoc apologetics, and therefore as embedded within a larger
network of Christian belief and practice, as previously suggested, then
at least three conclusions would seem to follow.

First, as already noted, it would seem that Frei's analysis is best regarded as falling within the scope of dogmatic theology rather than outside it. Frei would not be supplying dogmatic theology with an independent literary or conceptual basis, but would instead be clarifying the place of certain literary and logical considerations within a larger if mostly tacit dogmatic framework. Second, it would seem that insofar as this larger framework remains suppressed from view, Frei's argumentation is fragmentary and abstracted as it stands. It leaves too many logical and substantive connections implicit to be fully satisfactory as a dogmatic exercise, even within the limits that Frei sets for himself.[22] Finally, the incongruity between the relatively low depiction of Christ's person and the relatively high depiction of Christ's work can perhaps be understood as a consequence of Frei's methodological parsimony and reticence. Frei needs a larger set of concepts and a wider hermeneutical base to sustain what he says about Christ's saving work. Yet he is prevented from openly acquiring them insofar as he strives for deliberate methodological austerity and independence of dogmatic theology.

Consider, for example, a remark from the *Christian Scholar* article. There Frei also speaks of the significance of Jesus' powerlessness and helplessness as the savior. Yet he goes on to include a set of statements which unfortunately have no parallel in the book. With respect to the savior's powerlessness, Frei writes:

> The theme on which we are touching now is dangerous and has sometimes been driven to the point of a literalistic, simple-minded, speculative, and rather incredible heresy (i.e., that in the incarnation the Word of God divested himself deliberately and self-consciously of *omnipotence* over the world). But a heresy is often a sign that orthodoxy has sacrificed the elements of *mystery*, and along with it tentativeness or open-endedness, to an oversimplified consistency. Jesus' followers in the early church did not doubt *that the work of saving men was the work of omnipotence.* But it is equally true and far more easily forgotten that they believed this power to be *miraculously* congruent with Jesus' all too human helplessness and lack of power in the face of the terrible chain of events leading to his death, once that chain had begun to be wound around him. We find these two apparently contradictory tendencies converging in the gospel narrative. (pp. 49–50; emphasis added)

This passage is interesting for a number of reasons. First, it acknowledges that the work of salvation, when conceived according to the pattern of exchange, has to be regarded as in some sense the work of omnipotence. In other words, God is in some strong sense the ascriptive subject of what Jesus undertook and underwent. Second, the Christology of this passage is much more Chalcedonian than Antiochan in type. Not only is the savior depicted as the incarnate Word of God, but the logic of mystery is also upheld against an over-

simplified consistency, and the convergence of omnipotence and powerlessness in the person of Jesus is explicitly described as miraculous.
Clearly, Jesus is here conceived as at once fully divine and yet also
fully human. Finally, the method underlying these remarks would
seem to include a mix of dogmatic and literary considerations. Among
other things, the reference to heresy would indicate that for the
moment at least all suggestion of methodological neutrality has been
dropped, yet the congruence of power and powerlessness—here
defined much more boldly than in the book—is nonetheless described
as manifest in the gospel narratives themselves. From the standpoint
of displaying the internal consistency of Frei's argumentation, this
passage is simply much more satisfying than the corresponding material in the book, which is highly truncated by comparison.

If Frei's method is construed as operating within the bounds of
dogmatic theology, then it also becomes possible to shed some light
on what is probably the most tangled piece of argumentation in the
book, namely that concerning the presence of Jesus Christ to the
believer. Frei begins the book with what he calls the problem of
Christ's presence and worries about it for a while in the most bewil-
dering and disjointed of ways. He drops it almost entirely throughout
the middle sections of the book and then picks it up again at the end,
ostensibly no longer a problem but as a mystery. However, in light of
the polemic, the method, and the Christological content of Frei's proposal as I have attempted to explain them, perhaps his ruminations
on presence can be clarified as well.

The first thing to note is the context in which the problem of
presence arises. That context is essentially soteriological. Frei's narrative Christology, as focused on the pattern of exchange, commits him
to what might be called an objectivist soteriology.[23] Salvation, that is
to say, is defined primarily as what takes place vicariously in the life,
death and resurrection of Jesus Christ. The story in which Jesus enacts
his identity and the story of our salvation are not two different stories.
"The story of salvation is the story he enacts—the story of his obedience in redeeming guilty men by vicarious identification with their
guilt and literal identification with their helplessness" (IJC 102). "The
pattern of exchange," as it is enacted in the story, "becomes the means
of salvation" (IJC 104). "The story of salvation and the savior in the
New Testament is completely one and the same with the story of Jesus'
singular obedience in passion and death" (IJC 60). Yet if the story of
salvation is so completely the story of Jesus, then how does salvation
effectively connect with the life of the believer here and now? If salvation is what took place apart from us (*extra nos*) in the story of Jesus,
then how does it occur in and among us (*in nobis*) concretely in the
present? Are we to think of salvation as some kind of objective fact
which simply takes place over our heads? Does it come to us, in Paul
Tillich's arresting phrase, like a stone thrown down from heaven?

The problem confronting Frei at this point is the reverse of the problem he attributes to liberal theology. Liberalism, it will be recalled, is charged with so starting from a preconceived notion of presence as the basis for identifying Jesus Christ that in the end both the identity and the presence dissolve. (That was the internal critique.) At the same time, liberalism is also charged with so importing a prior determination of contemporary meaningfulness to the gospel narratives that it directly contradicts the sense of the narratives when they are taken on their own terms. (That was the external critique.) Despite what he sometimes seems to be saying, however, Frei cannot dispense with such questions. Given the result of a soteriology that is essentially objectivist, he cannot dispense with the question of how salvation is present here and now, nor can he avoid the question of how the gospel narratives are meaningful for the contemporary believer. Although in polemical settings the sense of a realistic narrative is sharply contrasted to its putative meaningfulness, Frei does not finally treat sense and meaningfulness as mutually exclusive. He simply orders them in a particular way. Rather than making sense a function of meaningfulness, he makes meaningfulness a function of sense. That is his hermeneutical counterpart to making soteriology a function of Christology rather than the reverse. What he rejects is the attempt to identify Jesus on the basis of some prior determination of his contemporary meaningfulness or presence, one that is independent of the gospel narratives. What he has to demonstrate, therefore, is how the sense of the gospel narratives, when taken on their own terms, generate a conception of Jesus' contemporary meaningfulness and presence. But can this demonstration really succeed? If one starts with the depicted identity of Jesus, as Frei does, can one ever really get to his contemporary meaningfulness and presence? If liberalism could not establish the identity of Jesus Christ, can Frei really establish his present religious significance?

As Frei himself is aware, his method at this point consists almost entirely of conceptual analysis. Regardless of what he sometimes says, I can see no good reason not to locate this analysis within rather than outside the bounds of dogmatic theology, and as already indicated I think this location has some considerable advantages for understanding what Frei is up to. In any case, the analysis goes something like this. Since the story of salvation in the New Testament is one and the same with that of Jesus as the savior, it follows that salvation cannot be conceived as independent of or detachable from the savior himself (IJC 60). What, then, is salvation? When death is conceived as the dissolution of identity which befalls sinners who are guilty before God, salvation means that death itself has been borne, overcome and destroyed by the savior, Jesus Christ. He himself submitted to death voluntarily and vicariously in order to enact God's saving intention for the good of all others. It is therefore impossible to conceive of

Jesus—as depicted by the narratives and confessed by faith—as not having been raised from the dead (IJC 145). It is impossible to conceive of him as being bound by death, for it was precisely death which it was his office as savior to overcome. As the one who conquered death, he is present to the believer; and precisely as the one who is so present, he is identified by the narrative which depicts him. He is therefore present to the believer as the singular and self-focused person that he is, and his presence is the presence of salvation. Because he has identity as the one who bore the dissolution of all identities and bore it away, others will have identities also (IJC 138; cf. 133).

With this conceptual analysis I think Frei has successfully displayed the logic he needs to demonstrate. He has shown that although there is no viable way from Jesus' presence to his identity, there is a way from his identity to his presence. He has shown that while the way from presence to identity ends in dissolution, the way from identity to presence is at once both necessary and possible. It is necessary, because otherwise Jesus' presence is not really his own; it is not self-focused, singular, and personal. This way is also possible, because an analysis of who Jesus is as the savior leads inexorably to the conclusion of his presence. As the one who conquered death by death, Jesus cannot be conceived, within the web of Christian belief, as not having been raised from the dead and as not being present to faith. A narrative-based understanding of Jesus' identity, far from undermining a conception of his personal presence, is actually its tacit and indispensable presupposition. The risen Jesus Christ who is present to faith identifies himself by means of just that narrative which depicts him, and none other, as the savior.

There is yet a further point which Frei needs to establish. He needs to demonstrate a connection between sense and meaningfulness. He needs to show that the sense of the Gospels, when read as realistic narratives, is not incompatible with contemporary meaningfulness or religious significance. As already indicated, this question arises in a special way within the context of an objectivist soteriology. If salvation is what takes place in the story of Jesus, then how does that salvation become significant here and now? Although Frei does not dwell on this question, at the very end of the book he does address it sufficiently, I think, to establish his essential point—namely, the logic of how a conception of contemporary meaningfulness can be compatible with a conception of realistic narrative sense.

The contemporary meaningfulness for faith which Frei sets forth as a function of the Gospels' narrative sense can be summarized in three points. First, it must be recognized that the meaning of "contemporary" and, therefore, also of "presence" is essentially eschatological. The presence of Jesus Christ to faith is as unique and inconceivable as the resurrection from which it arises and the future summing up of all history to which it points. The contemporary mode of Christ's presence is indirect. It is not direct in the way that it was during his earthly career, nor in the way that it will be again at the end of all things (cf. IJC 2–3). Yet even in this indirect and penultimate mode, his presence is nothing less than the mysterious and self-focused presence of God (IJC 154–55, 160–61, 163–64).

Second, the unique mode of Jesus Christ's presence elicits a unique response. The response consists essentially in worship and discipleship. As the mystery of the presence of God, Jesus Christ is properly the object of adoration and praise as well as the object of commitment and imitation. Because his enactment of salvation is singular and unrepeatable (IJC 65, 82, 84), believers can only follow him in discipleship at a distance. Yet at the appropriate distance they will seek to enact in their own lives parables of the pattern of exchange. That is, they will seek to serve rather than to be served, and to accept the enrichment given to them by their neighbors (IJC 160). (Note that the pattern is here described in two-directional terms.) Through works of love, risks of nonconformity, and identifications with the rejected of this world, they will honor and attest the One who is present to them (IJC 156–57, 160).

Finally, the mystery of Christ's presence will be meaningful to faith through Word and Sacrament in the church. The Word is conceived as the temporal, and the Sacrament as the spatial, basis for knowing Jesus Christ here and now. Just as the Word bears witness to the presence of God in Jesus Christ, so does the presence of God in Jesus Christ bear witness to the Word. And just as Jesus Christ gives himself to sinners in physical form through his death, so he also gives himself to them as forgiven sinners in physical form here and now through the Sacrament (IJC 158–59, 164–65).

In short, in these three ways Frei demonstrates the contemporary meaningfulness of an objectivist soteriology grounded in the narrative sense of the Gospels. He thereby successfully shows that such a soteriological conception does not entail the kind of reified presence suggested by the metaphor of a stone thrown down from heaven. It rather entails the mutual self-presence of Christ to the believer and of the believer to Christ. They exist together here and now in a fellowship of reciprocal commitment, self-giving, and mission, under the sign of universal hope.

Part IV. Conclusion

Frei's theological proposal has now been surveyed with a special eye toward its polemic, its method, and its content. Based on a sophisticated analogy between myth and modernity his polemic is conducted through both an internal and an external critique. According to the internal critique, the logic of theological liberalism recapitulates the logical flaws endemic to myth. As in myth so also in liberalism, conceptions of identity and presence are based on premises which end in dissolution. According to the external critique, liberalism is useless or misleading in its interpretation of the Gospels, because its apologetic concerns are in conflict with the requirements of realistic narrative interpretation. Untenable as it stands, liberalism is forced to yield either to realistic narrative interpretation or to the dead end of religiously useless hyperfiction. I have suggested, however, that liberalism may turn out to be more conceptually resourceful than Frei's forced option would imply.

The method by which Frei constructs his counter-proposal consists in a mixture of literary and conceptual analysis. Although Frei considers this analysis to fall somewhere between or beyond apologetics and dogmatics, I have suggested that it would perhaps be better to regard his proposal as an exercise in ad hoc apologetics within the bounds of dogmatic theology.

Finally, I have suggested that the content of Frei's proposal consists in an imperfectly realized high Christology and a well realized outline of soteriology. In the book Frei seems to leave us with the incongruity of a relatively low depiction of Christ's person in conjunction with a relatively high depiction of his work. Material drawn from outside the book indicates that Frei intends to offer a higher view of Christ's person—one which sees omnipotence and powerlessness converging in the narrative of a singular, unsubstitutable individual—than the book itself quite sets forth. This higher view of Christ's person would seem to be necessary if Frei's view of the work of Christ is to be sustained.

Frei's narrative Christology yields an objectivist soteriology which in turn raises questions about the order of knowledge and the order of meaning relative to faith in Jesus Christ. Judged on internal grounds, Frei successfully shows, it seems to me, that in the order of knowledge believers must (logically must) understand that their knowledge of Christ as present to faith is grounded in their prior knowledge of his identity as depicted in the Gospel narratives. Similarly, Frei would also seem to be successful with respect to his conception of the order of meaning. For he demonstrates how a conception of contemporary meaningfulness for faith can cohere with an analysis of the sense intrinsic to the Gospels when they are read on their own terms as realistic narratives.

One last word. In the year before he died Frei published a brief article in which he suggested something which I think captures his theological work as a whole. "We need," he remarked, "a kind of generous orthodoxy which would have in it an element of liberalism . . . and an element of evangelicalism."[24] Both elements are present in *The Identity of Jesus Christ*. In the wide range of learning brought to bear upon the argument, in the carefully formulated and nuanced judgments, and in the reticence to say more than one could really support, an element of liberalism is in evidence.[25] Yet in the respect accorded to the Gospels for their own sakes and on their own terms, in the espousal of the historic faith of the ecumenical church as represented by Nicea and Chalcedon, and in the struggle to understand the dilemmas of modernity squarely from the standpoint of that faith, an element of evangelicalism is also in evidence. It is as though Frei sensed in his theological bones that generosity without orthodoxy was empty but that orthodoxy without generosity was blind. He therefore strove to incorporate a generosity of mind and spirit akin to Schleiermacher's and yet an orthodoxy of belief and conviction akin to Barth's. Frei's entire theological project can be seen as the enactment of this intention. His identity as a theologian thus emerges. In the quest for a generous orthodoxy, Hans Frei so distinctively manifested himself in his writings that at last we may fairly say, "This is who he really was. Here he was most fully himself."

Epilogue

These reflections have been based on the premise that Hans Frei's central statement as a theologian appears in *The Identity of Jesus Christ*. Frei himself took steps to have that volume issued concurrently with what would turn out to be his magnum opus, *The Eclipse of Biblical Narrative*, because he believed that the theological viewpoint informing the latter was made more explicit in the former. (A correlation between *The Identity* and the theological portions of *The Eclipse* can be found by consulting the notes to this essay.) With respect to his theological viewpoint (as opposed to his views on matters of hermeneutics or history per se), it seems fair to say that *The Identity* remained definitive. Now that Frei's posthumous *Types of Christian Theology* has become available, however, it may be of use to extend the previous analysis further so as to encompass his thinking as expressed in that work.[26] At the same time it might also be useful if something were said about the relationship between *The Identity* and the stance evident in Frei's late essay on the "literal reading" of scripture (Chapter 4 in this volume). (In the development of Frei's thought, the "literal reading" essay represents a kind of watershed between his earlier and later work.) Although these later writings show Frei's ideas in ferment on a number of points, it is worth noting that his theological outlook nonetheless remained consistent with that of *The Identity*.

The "Literal Reading" Essay

For roughly the last ten years of his life, Frei's hermeneutical interests shifted from a focus on "realistic narrative" in the synoptic gospels to a concentration on their "literal sense." No account of his work as a theologian would be complete unless at least something were said about how this later interest relates to his earlier concerns, even though it was never as fully developed in writing as they. In Frei's most important essay from the later period—"The 'Literal Reading' of Biblical Narrative in the Christian Tradition: Does It Stretch or Will It Break?"—strong continuities can be discerned with his earlier work as well as some interesting and uncertain developments. Frei's immensely difficult, learned, and sophisticated essay can be analyzed, though only briefly, along the same lines as the earlier writings.

Polemic

The literal-reading essay seems to present many of the same roles as before but with a new cast of characters. The role of the Misguided Opponent who approaches biblical narrative interpretation with a cache of prior determinations about "meaningfulness," once played by modern liberal theology, is now taken over by the "phenomenological hermeneutics" of Paul Ricoeur in league with its "regional application" by David Tracy. (This association is made explicit; see p. 138.) The role of the Worthy Skeptic, who makes no more than an anonymous cameo appearance in *The Identity* (yet who is represented by Reimarus and Strauss in *The Eclipse*), is now assigned to "Deconstructionism," though this time the role is more integral since the deconstructionist is brought on stage to deliver the "internal critique," which is accomplished with great subtlety and nuance (pp. 130–36). An "external critique" is also developed, very much along the same general lines as before, yet with an almost crushing wealth of complexity and detail (pp. 124–30; for a summary of the two critiques, see p. 137). This time the Worthy Skeptic is also subjected to some searching criticism (pp. 136–37) as is the Dubious Friend or False Twin, a role previously played by "literary Christ figures" in the modern novel but now assigned to the "New Criticism" (pp. 140–43).

Method

The new and in some ways perplexing developments in Frei's thought are almost entirely methodological. The plea that readers should keep their interpretive schemes as unencumbered by general theories as possible, which runs throughout Frei's career, is strongly reiterated here (e.g., pp. 119, 124, 139–41). Indeed, that plea is, if anything, intensified insofar as Frei is even prepared to question whether the cate-gory of "realistic narrative" might not itself perhaps be a piece of misleading theoretical construction (p. 142). Cognizance of the gospels' formal narrative structure in itself—though still significant—is clearly no longer quite as decisive to Frei's argument as it once was. He is now prepared to contend only that this structure has in fact governed the Christian tradition's *sensus literalis,* that outside that tradition any single interpretive key for uncovering the meaning of the gospel narratives would be hard to come by (in other words, taken abstractly the narratives are perhaps of fairly indeterminate meaning), and that within the Christian tradition a multiplicity of interpretations is possible and legitimate just as long as they do not conflict with the primacy of the realistic or literal sense. What is important to note is that the *primary* warrant for seeing Jesus as the unsubstitutable ascriptive subject of the gospel narratives is now said to be a matter of "traditional consensus" among Christians regarding the "literal sense" rather than, as before, a matter of formal literary structure (pp. 118–24, 143–46). What remains perplexing, however, is just how Frei thinks text and tradition, formal narrative structure and communal *sensus literalis,* are finally related in the justification of how the church reads scripture. (In other words, why does Frei suppose that the traditional *sensus literalis*—its ascription of certain predicates to Jesus alone—is still really justified, and to what extent is this justifiability thought to depend on a description of the gospels' formal narrative structure?) What is clear is that a "cultural-linguistic" turn, under the influence of George Lindbeck, has been effected in Frei's thought (pp. 147–48). In conjunction with the eschewal of high-powered theoretical explanatory schemes, this turn leads to a new interest in describing how and in what social context the literal reading of the gospel narratives functions within the Christian community (pp. 144–49).

Content

Little or no change seems to take place on this score, unless it should be that by enriching his methodological interest in descriptive formalism with the conceptuality of the *sensus literalis* (and cognate matters) Frei seems to feel much freer about openly discussing a full-bodied "high Christology" (pp. 141–42; cf. pp. 49–50). Although located in a much wider and more abundant context than before, Frei's previous work on the Christological meaning of the biblical narratives is simply reiterated and endorsed (pp. 120–23, 126, 139–40). In short, the church's high Christology is now regarded as resulting from its *sensus literalis,* which in turn is thought to be strongly if not exclusively based on the gospels' realistic narrative structure.

Types of Christian Theology

At least four interrelated themes criss-cross through the complex and rough-hewn argument of Frei's *Types of Christian Theology* (which, it must be remembered, is little more than a pastiche of posthumous fragments put together by his editors). (1) What criteria of meaning, intelligibility, and truth are pertinent in Christian theology? Are they (to use Frei's terms) "general" or "specific," field-encompassing or singular? (2) What modes of descriptive analysis are theologically pertinent for Christianity as a religion? Are they "external" or "internal," logically independent of Christian beliefs or logically dependent upon them? (3) What use of language predominates in Christian discourse? Is the language of faith primarily descriptive, objective, and cognitive (*fides quae creditur*); or confessional, self-involving, and performative (*fides qua creditur*)? (4) Finally—and here is what Frei calls his "central topic" (p. 5)—what mode of interpretation or reading is theologically pertinent in the case of biblical texts, especially the New Testament narratives about Jesus? Is the sense of those narratives to be taken as "literal" or "symbolic," as ascribing certain predicates exclusively to Jesus as an unsubstitutable person, regardless of the status of that ascription in reality, or else as ascribing certain predicates to some other subject (such as human nature in general) by way of "Jesus" as an essentially symbolic figure? (This latter question, of course, had preoccupied Frei since the days of *The Identity of Jesus Christ*.)

If the argument of *Types of Christian Theology* were constructed more tightly, these themes would all be discussed systematically with respect to each of the "types" that Frei distinguishes. As matters stand, however, the four major themes are not always fully developed for each of the five types. Nevertheless, at the risk of oversimplification, the following summary may be ventured.

Type I, exemplified by Immanuel Kant and Gordon Kaufman, regards theology as a philosophical discipline, or rather it subsumes theology critically into philosophy so that what cannot be philosophically validated is not legitimate. (1) The pertinent criteria are thus regarded as "general" or field-encompassing. (2) The Christian religion is analyzed and described from an "external" standpoint that is logically independent of Christian beliefs. (3) The language of faith is essentially self-involving rather than cognitive in significance. (4) The gospel narratives are read in such a way that "Jesus" is a symbolic figure who stands for the content of rational morality and who motivates people to practice it.

In Type II themes 1, 2, and 4 are handled in essentially the same way as in Type I. The criteria are field-encompassing rather than singular, the language of faith is essentially non-cognitive in significance, and the narratives about Jesus are read symbolically rather than literally. What distinguishes Type II from Type I is its treatment of theme 2. Whereas Type I simply subsumes theology critically into the external discipline of philosophy, Type II correlates them instead. That is, an "internal" description based on norms that are logically dependent on Christian beliefs is correlated with an "external" description based on universally applicable criteria. This type is associated with Paul Ricoeur, David Tracy, and, on themes 1 and 2 at least, Carl F. H. Henry.

Type III agrees with Type II at two places where Type II agreed with Type I, namely, on themes 1 and 3. The distinguishing characteristics of Type III thus pertain to the treatment of themes 2 and 4. Type III parallels Type II by correlating "internal" and "external" descriptions of Christianity (as opposed to merging the former into the latter, as in Type I), but Type III differs from Type II in that the correlation occurs on different terms. For unlike Type II, Type III has no overarching philosophical system of meaning which determines and subsumes the correlation. In Type III any correlations are carried out in an ad hoc fashion without any integrating theory. This difference on theme 2 reflects a basic difference on theme 4. In Types I and II Jesus, though symbolically valuable, is neither materially decisive nor logically indispensable to theology.[27] In Type III, however, Jesus is not only symbolically valuable, but also materially decisive as the source of the Christian community's faith. (Whether for Type III Jesus is also logically indispensable is a matter Frei does not really address.) To the extent that Jesus himself is materially decisive for faith, the gospel narratives about him are read literally, not merely symbolically. (However, they are also read symbolically insofar as Jesus remains a representative figure over and above his historical status as the uniquely germinal source of faith.) Schleiermacher and perhaps Tillich are instances of Type III.

Type IV differs substantially from the previous three on all four major questions. (1) Field-encompassing criteria of meaning, intelligibility, and truth are regarded as limited in their applicability to Christian theology by virtue of the singularity of Christian beliefs. (2) Internal description of Christianity thus takes precedence over external description; and cultural anthropology becomes not only a more pertinent form of external description than philosophy, but also a more promising discipline for correlation. (3) The language of faith is at least as cognitive as it is self-involving (and thus is not essentially non-cognitive). (4) Jesus is not only materially decisive but also logically indispensable to theology and faith. As God incarnate he is more than merely faith's contingent or historical source; he is the unique and unsubstitutable Savior. The gospel stories about him are thus to be read literally in the sense that he himself and no one else is the ascriptive subject of what he undertakes and undergoes for the world's salvation. This type is exemplified by Karl Barth (except for the point about cultural anthropology, which is Frei's own special contribution).

Type V looks like Type IV in some ways, yet in others also like Type I. (1) Field-encompassing criteria are applicable to theology, but these are necessarily very minimal. (2) The distinction between "internal" and "external" description disappears, because external, philosophical analysis of Christianity as a religion is necessarily dependent on the logic of Christian beliefs; philosophy, properly conceived as linguistic analysis, is not in the business of providing overarching integrative theories. (3) The language of faith is essentially performative rather than cognitive in significance. (4) Whether the gospel narratives are read literally or symbolically with respect to Jesus remains indeterminate; Type V seems to allow for either possibility. In any case Frei says almost nothing about the bearing of this type on the hermeneutical question, except to note that even when opting for the "literal sense," the type tends to substitute repetition for interpretation in its use of biblical texts. As representatives D. Z. Phillips and Fergus Kerr are mentioned.

With this sketch as a background, the point of view in *Types of Christian Theology* can now be analyzed more directly. Once again, it will be worthwhile to conduct the analysis by asking about the polemic, method, and theological content of Frei's argument.

Polemic

It is evident that Frei has refined his polemic considerably. Whereas he had initially criticized "modern liberal theology" as a whole for replacing christology with anthropology and for thereby disregarding the hermeneutical significance of the gospel narratives, he now differentiates between those variants of modern liberal theology which can do justice to the narratives' "literal sense" and those which cannot. His abiding concern has been to reject any independent conceptual scheme which purports to be the necessary precondition for making Christian discourse meaningful. "There can be no systematic 'pre-understanding,' no single, specific, consistently used conceptual scheme, no independent anthropology, hermeneutics, ontology or whatever, in terms of which Christian language claims must be cast in order to be meaningful" (*Types*, p. 156). Such schemes are the fatal premise of Types I and II, but, as Frei now discerns, not necessarily of Type III.

Where independent theories or schemes hold sway in theology, the literal sense of the gospel narratives must inevitably be discounted. The figure of Jesus cannot possibly be materially decisive as a specific person (to say nothing of his being logically indispensable). He can be no more than a symbol for an independently grounded form of meaning. By contrast, where the figure of Jesus is conceived as the materially decisive source of faith, no such overarching scheme is necessary even if the content of specifically Christian beliefs is correlated with independent conceptions. In such cases the correlations are ad hoc rather than systematic, and Jesus is not merely a religious symbol but an ascriptive subject in his own right. In Frei's polemic, Types I and II thus continue in the role of the Misguided Opponent, whereas Type III, now recast in a new and surprising script, becomes a Strategic Ally in common cause with Type IV against the foes of the literal sense.[28]

Method

In *Types* of *Christian Theology* Frei presupposes and extends the method he adopted in the "literal reading" essay. That is, he again stresses the *sensus literalis* as a communal consensus rather than as a literary structure, allowing the relation between the two to remain implicit though vague. In any case, the *sensus literalis* becomes the measuring rod against which the various types are assessed. "What kind of theology," Frei asks, "is most nearly hospitable to the literal sense of Scripture?" *(Types,* p. 18). The answer is found in Type IV, the theology of Karl Barth. "Barth goes as far, I believe, as one can in articulating the largely implicit logic governing the *sensus literalis*. . . . If one is interested in the *sensus literalis*, his theology represents the type with which it is most nearly congruent" *(Types,* p. 44). By the same standard—an appeal to the historic consensus of the Christian community about how to read the gospel narratives—Types I, II, and V are ruled out as inhospitable, whereas Type III is affirmed as a genuine if ambiguous counterpart.

Content

Although it may seem strange for the *sensus literalis* to take precedence over Christology in evaluating the various types (as though Christology developed for the sake of the *sensus literalis* rather than the reverse!), that is perhaps precisely Frei's point. The *sensus literalis* as a standard of assessment is broad enough to make significant distinctions and yet also to allow for actually existing diversity in the history of Christology. It seems fair to say, however, that by increasingly focusing on the *sensus literalis*, Frei effectively arrested any further development in his own proposal about the person and work of Jesus Christ. Nevertheless, an implicit Christology emerges between the lines.

Where the literal sense of the gospel narratives is taken seriously, Frei avers, "an irreducibly unique and unsurpassable place" is assigned to Jesus "in relation to salvation" *(Types,* p. 63). "Salvation here and now" is thus "dependent on one person then and there" (p. 62). Our being redemptively incorporated into Jesus Christ, into "the reality he shares with God," occurs in such a way that "this incorporation is not only a *possibility* but is *actualized* in what he did for us," so that "his very being or essence was a being-for-us" (p. 88). The singularity or uniqueness of this redemptive occurrence is the deepest reason why Jesus himself as an unsubstitutable person sets the terms for meaning and truth in Christian theology. "It is the particularity of Jesus, enacted in and inseparable from history, that makes him significant for salvation" and that also provides the criteria for his significance (p. 88). As the agent of our salvation, Jesus Christ is "at once human and divine"; therefore, "even the meaningfulness, to say nothing of the truth of Christian statements, is a matter of faith seeking understanding rather than faith arising from the statement of general meaning" (pp. 80–81). In short, attested by the historic consensus of literal reading, the reason why "Jesus has the primacy in these stories" (p. 140) is basically that they wish to affirm him "in his uniqueness and finality for Christian faith" (p. 72). Frei's views as so interpreted would seem to be entirely of a piece with what he stated in his earlier work.

Notes

An earlier version of this essay appeared as "Hans Frei as Theologian: The Quest for a Generous Orthodoxy" in *Modern Theology*, vol. 8, no. 2 (April 1992), pp. 103–28.

*I would like to thank the following persons for helpful comments on an earlier draft of this essay: David Ford, David Kelsey, William Placher, Ronald Thiemann, Thomas Tracy, John Webster, Nicholas Wolterstorff, and John Woolverton.

1. See chap. 2. References to this work will be cited in the text.

2. Frei, "The Mystery of the Presence of Jesus Christ," *Crossroads* 17, no. 2 (January–March 1967), pp. 69–96 and no. 3 (April–June 1967), pp. 69–96.

3. Frei, *The Identity of Jesus Christ: The Hermeneutical Bases of Dogmatic Theology* (Philadelphia: Fortress Press, 1975). References to this work will be cited in the text as IJC.

4. Frei, *The Eclipse of Biblical Narrative: A Study of Eighteenth and Nineteeth Century Hermeneutics* (New Haven: Yale University Press, 1974).

5. Cf. Frei, *The Eclipse*, p. 117.

6. For a very similar passage, see *The Eclipse*, p. 128.

7. Although Frei distinguishes between myth as an aspect of "mystery religion" and myth in gnosticism, his emphasis falls on the latter. Frei defines Gnostic myth in terms of the figure of a dying-and-rising savior who has no personal specificity of his own, but who functions instead to symbolize a universal or at least general experience of spiritual alienation and deliverance (IJC 54–62). Frei later came to have reservations about the term "Gnostic," but not about what he meant to signify by it (IJC ix–x). The parallel Frei draws between mythic and modernist Christ figures is sometimes merely formal and sometimes quite substantive. Insofar as both Christ figures do no

more than provide symbolic form for some kind of independently derived anthropological content, the parallel is merely formal. Yet insofar as an alienation-and-deliverance syndrome is found to be symbolized by modern Christ figures, more substantive parallels are suggested. Either way, however—and this is the key hermeneutical point which interested Frei—there is a disjunction between form and content, sense and subject matter, or meaning and meaningfulness. It is this kind of disjunction which, as Frei argues, distinguishes the genre of myth from that of realistic narrative.

8. Frei's point about the ultimate disappearance and dissolution of our own identities is not entirely clear to me. I have tried to interpret it in a soteriological sense; see pp. 251–52.

9. Frei regarded Immanuel Kant's *Religion Within the Limits of Reason Alone* as paradigmatic in this regard. "One of the most interesting features of this fascinating book is the fact that it renders an account of the process of conversion which has been such a preoccupation of liberal Protestant theologians. . . . They have always wanted to find the coherence between a descriptively universal human situation (such as that of sin) and the contingent free historic act (and/or miracle) of faith" (*The Eclipse*, p. 263).

10. Note in this regard what Frei says in *The Eclipse* about J. A. Ernesti, the eighteenth-century German Lutheran theologian, whom Frei considers to have been a lonely but essentially correct theorist of interpretation. Frei sees his own hermeneutical proposals as standing in continuity with Ernesti. Frei suggests that if Ernesti had really been understood, biblical narrative would not have fallen into such serious eclipse in the modern period. Further, in light of the critique which I later go on to develop, it is interesting that Frei describes Ernesti's hermeneutics as "theologically neutral" (*The Eclipse*, p. 251).

11. More precisely, what Frei rejects in this regard are interpretations which disjoin the author's intention from the formal structure or the literal sense of the narrative. As long as the author's intention is conceived as consonant with meaning-as-formal-narrative-structure, Frei has no quarrel with seeking to identify the "author's intention." On this matter Frei sides with Ernesti over against someone like Schleiermacher. (Cf. *The Eclipse*, pp. 252–53, 257, 261, 271, 301–2, 308–9; IJC 48.)

12. In his excellent interpretation and extension of Frei's hermeneutics, Garrett Green does not always bring out clearly enough the point that for Frei the category "fiction-like" is strictly a *formal* category which as such remains non-committal about the narrative's truth or fiction. To say "fiction-like" is thus not quite the same as saying "fictional yet true," especially if the latter could be construed as meaning "historically fictional, yet theologically true." See Green, " 'The Bible As . . .': Fictional Narrative and Scriptural Truth," in Garrett Green, ed., *Scriptural Authority and Narrative Interpretation* (Philadelphia: Fortress Press, 1987), pp. 79–96, esp. pp. 84 and 94.

13. Frei's position on the relation of meaning and truth in the gospel narratives is very subtle and complex. His position has often been misunderstood, especially when what he rejects is not seen in relation to what he actually affirms. Perhaps one way to bring out what Frei actually affirms would be to put the question like this: If the gospel narratives mean what

Frei thinks they mean, then what grounds would be logically appropriate on which to affirm their truth? The meaning of the narratives, according to Frei, is their depiction of the identity of Jesus Christ. Jesus is depicted as the savior. He is depicted as the one who so obeyed God and who so loved the guilty in their distress that he voluntarily and vicariously enacted their salvation at untold cost to himself. He did this by sharing their burdens and so dying their death that the power of those burdens and that death was broken. But to say that on behalf of others Jesus conquered death by death is tantamount to saying that he was raised by God from the dead and that he is present here and now to faith. Something like this is what Frei takes to be the "fact claim" or meaning of the gospel narratives. This fact claim is neither simple nor simply "historical." It follows that the grounds on which it would be appropriate to affirm the truth of this claim will be as unique and mysterious as the claim itself. If the claim is true, the narratives are pointing to a "self-warranting fact" (IJC 143) to which we have no direct epistemic access apart from the narratives themselves. Why some accept this "self-warranting fact" (i.e., the self-attestation of the risen Christ by means of the narratives which disclose who he is) and others do not "is impossible for the Christian to explain" (IJC 152; cf. IJC xii). But if Jesus really is who he is depicted as being by the narratives, then his non-resurrection is "inconceivable" (IJC 145) and disbelief in his resurrection is "rationally impossible" (IJC 151). In any case, "actual belief in the resurrection is a matter of faith and not of arguments from possibility or evidence" (IJC 152). In other words, the mode of affirmation (faith) is conceived as logically appropriate to the nature of the claim (Jesus is the risen savior whose mysterious presence here and now points toward his ultimate and universal manifestation at the end of all things) (IJC 160–61). "Concerning Jesus Christ and him alone, factual affirmation is completely one with faith and trust of the heart, with love of him, and love of the neighbors for whom he gave himself completely" (IJC 157; cf. 147). The meaning of the narratives is such that there can (logically) be no factual affirmation without faith, and no faith without factual affirmation. In this case, how could it be otherwise than that the two should coincide?

In this light it becomes clear that Frei is not claiming that the gospel narratives make no ostensive reference. He is rather claiming that they make no ostensive reference to an object to which we have independent epistemic access and whose factuality can be affirmed on any grounds other than faith. In other words, he is claiming that they make ostensive reference to the mystery of the presence of Jesus Christ, the risen savior, whose identity as such they depict. The narratives are said to have no meaning other than themselves, because formally their meaning is their realistic narrative shape, and substantively it is their depiction of Jesus as the savior, who as such cannot be conceived as not risen and present. But none of this means that the gospel narratives refer to nothing other than themselves, only that their meaning is not detachable from the realistic formal structure which constitutes them for what they are. In the case of the gospel narratives, meaning-as-ostensive-reference is conceptually dependent on and subsequent to meaning-as-realistic-narrative-identity-depiction.

The relationship between faith and history, as Frei understands it, can be explained in this context.

(a) The nature of the truth-claim about Jesus (that he is the risen savior) is such that in principle it could not possibly be validated or confirmed by historical-critical method, although it might be disconfirmed by that method. In fact, however, what little evidence there is one way or the other is not sufficient to disconfirm resurrection faith (IJC 151; cf. 103).

(b) Aptness is one thing, factuality quite another. Everything depends on a proper determination of what genre the gospel narratives really exemplify. If they belong primarily or at least decisively to the genre of "historical report," then in principle their truth-claim will to that extent be open to historical-critical methods of assessment, and factuality (understood as a strong correspondence between literary depiction and actual historical occurrence) will be a relevant criterion of truth. However, if the narratives belong to the genre of "realistic identity depiction" (when regarded from a *literary* standpoint) and of "witness" (when regarded from a *theological* standpoint), then *to that extent* historical-critical method is categorically irrelevant or at least insufficient. Certain aspects of the gospel narratives may indeed be historically factual and yet contribute little besides bafflement to our understanding of what the Gospels want to tell us about Jesus' identity. Other aspects may actually be depictions of the risen savior in the lineaments of the earthly Jesus much more than historically accurate reports about the earthly Jesus, and yet they may function quite aptly to depict his identity as the Gospels intend to convey it. Therefore, factuality does not necessarily contribute to aptness, and aptness does not necessarily depend on factuality as narrowly conceived (IJC 140–141).

(c) The lack of consensus among reputable biblical scholars and the wide range of opinion among them on questions of historical factuality (ranging from measured credence to near total skepticism) would seem to suggest something about the actual state of the evidence. It would seem to suggest that the evidence is insufficient for firm historical judgments and that no such judgment about the gospel narratives can escape a large measure of speculation. Until the experts can come to a greater agreement among themselves, the rest of us are entitled to a stance of relative agnosticism. But since the significance of the Gospel narratives, understood as realistic identity depictions and as witnesses to the presence of Jesus as the risen savior, does not heavily depend on their strict historical factuality—except at certain points, most especially concerning his resurrection—the church ought not to stray too far from the received narrative text, which as such functions as a good-enough depiction of what the Gospels want to say about his identity (IJC 48, 132, 141).

(d) Although there are many points where the gospel narratives themselves inevitably raise questions in our minds about historical factuality, the state of the evidence does not allow historical-critical methods to answer them with any great certainty. Yet little more is required by faith when it comes to historically verifiable knowledge than what most commentators can agree upon: "That a man, Jesus of Nazareth, who proclaimed the Kingdom of God's nearness, did exist and was finally executed" (IJC 51). Little more than this is required, because aptness in the realistic narrative depiction of Jesus as the risen savior does not heavily depend on historical factuality as narrowly conceived. Aptness depends, rather, on the narrative's overall suitability as an identity-depiction-cum-witness regarding Jesus as the risen savior.

14. The figure whom Frei regards as paradigmatic of the latter option (and thus of a certain integrity which eschews dubious reinterpretations and apologetics) is Reimarus. See *The Eclipse*, pp. 119, 122–23, 132–33.

15. Frei's possible rejoinder to the retort I have ascribed to his liberal opponent may be found in *The Eclipse*, pp. 62–63.

16. This type of apologetics is nicely summarized in *The Eclipse*, pp. 117 and 128.

17. For Frei's endorsement of ad hoc apologetics, though in somewhat more general terms than I have focused upon here, see IJC xii–xiii. The upshot of Frei's ad hoc conceptual clarifications would seem to be that he regards the real alternative to arise essentially between orthodoxy (a high Christology) and skepticism (à la Reimarus), a choice which effectively excludes liberalism (symbolic Christology) as a viable possibility. It would seem that Frei is more concerned to refute liberalism (à la Schleiermacher) than skepticism (à la Reimarus).

18. Frei seems to approach the coherentist position I am ascribing to him when he remarks: "Essentially, what I shall write about constitutes a reflection within belief" (IJC 4). As the term is here being used, "coherentism" is that epistemic procedure which would justify an assertion by demonstrating that it is a member of a coherent set of assertions. The coherentism which would seem to be pertinent is of the "weak" rather than the "pure" variety. Weak coherentism combines aspects of the coherence theory of justification with aspects of the correspondence theory of truth. It thus seems to comport well with a mode by which Frei could justify his conceptual analysis of gospel narrative while still allowing for the kind of ostensive reference to the risen and present Christ which that analysis entails. For excellent discussions of these matters, see Jonathan Dancy, *Introduction to Contemporary Epistemology* (Oxford: Basil Blackwell, 1985) and Keith Lehrer, *Theory of Knowledge* (Boulder and San Francisco: Westview Press, 1990). For a relevant survey with the non-expert in mind and with an eye toward theology, see William Placher, *Unapologetic Theology: A Christian Voice in a Pluralistic Conversation* (Louisville: Westminster/John Knox, 1989), pp. 24–38.

19. For a discussion of the way in which Frei's position here finds its background in Barth's Christocentric anthropology, see Gene Outka, "Following at a Distance: Ethics and the Identity of Jesus," in *Scriptural Authority and Narrative Interpretation* (see n. 12), pp. 152–53. It is noteworthy, however, that "the pattern of exchange" is a soteriological rather than an anthropological term. Outka's key point seems to be that this soteriological pattern has anthropological and ethical consequences; namely, an essential asymmetry exists within the pattern so that we do not give to Jesus in the way that he gives to us, nor does he receive from us in the way that we receive from him. Outka's discussion throws light on why Frei may have presented the pattern of exchange in unidirectional terms. Nevertheless, in Frei's own usage the term "pattern of exchange" is employed in its tradi-

tional and thus *soteriological* sense. Therefore, the exchange is not sufficiently analyzed if it is explained only in unidirectional rather than two-directional terms, that is, if Jesus' saving movement into our guilt and misery is not finally counterbalanced in the account by our entry into his righteousness and communion with God.

20. I do not mean to imply that Frei's presentation of Jesus as fully human is anything more than incidental to the focus of Frei's analysis. The emphasis in that analysis is that the identity of Jesus in his death and resurrection, as depicted in the gospel narratives, is consistent with the intention he is portrayed as enacting.

21. Note the following remark from *The Eclipse:* "Whatever the resurrection as a historical or fictional claim, its status *in the story* is then not that of reference to an occurrence but simply the affirmation that the whole of Jesus' self-manifestation is in fact the self-manifestation of God, a disclosure that cannot be seen until the end of the story *and thence covers all of it in retrospect"* (p. 315; second emphasis added). This latter point—the retrospective force (within the narrative) of the resurrection account for identifying the *whole* career of Jesus as the self-manifestation of God—is never clearly made in the argument of IJC.

22. In other words, Frei needs to explain the sense in which he thinks that his formal method of narrative analysis yields a high Christology as well as the sense in which he thinks that the full divinity of Jesus is more nearly a dogmatic than a hermeneutical conclusion with respect to such analysis. It would be foolish to attribute either to Frei or to my internal critique of his argument the implausible belief that a full-blown high Christology (and corresponding soteriology) can be found on the surface of the synoptic narratives. Although he never quite makes this clear, Frei's argument, it seems to me, needs no more at this point than the claim that the synoptic narratives (not excluding Mark) contain a number of direct and indirect indicators which can be read as pointing in the direction of such a Christology. It is on some such basis that C.F.D. Moule, for example, can speak of "a high Christology being unobtrusively embedded in the [gospel] traditions about Jesus' and about "evidence of a consistently 'high' Christology from the very earliest datable periods of the Church's life" (*The Origin of Christology* [Cambridge: Cambridge University Press, 1977], pp. 30, 96).

23. For some remarks on how Jesus as "an objective savior" can pertain to the pilgrimage of the Christian life see *The Eclipse,* pp. 153–54.

24. Frei, "Response to 'Narrative Theology: An Evangelical Appraisal,'" chap. 9 above, p. 208.

25. Are there perhaps certain more substantive senses in which an element of liberalism might be seen in Frei's thought? He certainly believed that theology and historical criticism at least should not be in conflict, even if criticism could not furnish the foundation for theological interpretation (*The Eclipse,* p. 163). Moreover, he certainly doubted that "realistic depiction, especially simplicity" could be taken as "evidence in favor of historical factuality" (*The Eclipse,* p. 169). Finally, if one substitutes the word "perspective" for the word "synthesis," what Frei once wrote of Troeltsch would apply equally well to himself: "All his life Troeltsch looked toward a synthesis in

which formal philosophy, the interpretation of culture and history, and theology would all cohere without undercutting one another's autonomy" ("Niebuhr's Theological Background," in Paul Ramsey, ed., *Faith and Ethics* [New York: Harper & Row, 1957], pp. 53–54).

26. Frei, *Types of Christian Theology*, ed. George Hunsinger and William C. Placher (New Haven: Yale University Press, 1992).

27. I have taken the terms "materially decisive" and "logically indispensable" from Bruce Marshall, *Christology in Conflict* (Oxford: Basil Blackwell, 1987), although I do not necessarily use them exactly in Marshall's sense. My remarks here assume that it is possible for Jesus to be conceived as "materially decisive" in such a way that he is not also "logically indispensable." There seems to be no reason why Jesus could not be so conceived as to be "materially decisive" in fact, but "logically dispensable" in principle. For example, if some other (perhaps less remote) figure were to become equally decisive as a generative source of faith, there seems to be no reason (within the logic of Type III) why Jesus might not be relativized or even eventually dispensed with.

28. It might also be noted that in *Types of Christian Theology* Frei takes pains at various points not only to align himself but also to differentiate himself from his colleague George Lindbeck (though without mentioning him by name). Frei not only leans heavily on Lindbeck's view of the Christian religion as a cultural-linguistic system, but also endorses Lindbeck's more specific understanding of the relationship between language and experience: "The language we use is what enables us to experience in the first place. There is no such thing as a non-interpreted, nonlinguistic experience: language is a social, not an individual structure or system" (*Types*, p. 74). On the other hand, Frei seems to distance himself from some of Lindbeck's other well-known positions. In particular he refrains from relegating doctrines as such merely to the status of rules. Although doctrines do function as rules, Frei also regards them as having constitutive or cognitive status (pp. 42 and 124). He also affirms (if, as seems likely, what he says of Barth would also hold for himself) that a doctrinal utterance in some sense remains true "regardless of the attitude of the person or persons articulating it" (p. 42).

Index